THE THEORY OF
GRAMMATICAL
RELATIONS

THE THEORY OF GRAMMATICAL RELATIONS

John S. Bowers

Cornell University Press

ITHACA AND LONDON

First published 1981 by Cornell University Press.
Published in the United Kingdom by Cornell University Press Ltd., 2–4 Brook Street, London W1Y 1AA.

International Standard Book Number 0-8014-1079-7
Library of Congress Catalog Card Number
Printed in the United States of America 80-21018

Library of Congress Cataloging in Publication Data

Bowers, John S
  The theory of grammatical relations

  Bibliography: p.
  Includes index.
  1. Generative grammar. I. Title.
P158.B68   415   80-21018
ISBN 0-8014-1079-7

To the memory of
JACK CATLIN

Contents

Contents

Preface

The idea for this book was born about five years ago, when it struck me that though every imaginable aspect of the classical theory of transformational grammar had been subjected to critical scrutiny since Noam Chomsky's works began to appear in the mid-1950s, the one part of the theory that had managed to elude systematic investigation was the theory of transformations itself. This realization turned out to be the key to an understanding of a number of fundamental syntactic problems with which I, along with many other linguists, had been struggling for some time. Up to that point I had been groping in the dark. After that a wide range of problems suddenly fell into place.

The classical theory of transformations, as formulated in Chomsky's earliest writings, is simultaneously too weak and too strong. It is too weak in that it does not permit fundamental grammatical processes to be stated in terms of grammatical relations, contrary to what traditional grammarians of every variety assume, albeit in an inexplicit and informal fashion. At the same time it is too strong in that it permits sentences to be derived from underlying structures by means of derivations of unbounded length and complexity, rather than grounding the formal statement of grammatical processes firmly in observable reality.

Strangely enough, certain fundamental problems, such as the difficulty of assigning the correct derived constituent structure to the passive *by* phrase, showed up very early in the literature, as I point out in Chapter 1. When a new theory is first being expounded and developed, however, the enthusiasm of its adherents often exceeds their critical detachment, and certain crucial assumptions come to be regarded as fixed verities rather than as empirical hypotheses which, like any other part of the theory, are subject to empirical confirmation or disconfirmation. As time goes on and the problems begin to accumulate, the sheer mass of them will eventually force a reevaluation of those most fundamental assumptions. Otherwise, the theory will become increasingly artificial and ad hoc in its treatment of new phenomena.

It is my contention that the theory of transformational grammar is at such a stage in its development right now and that further progress is impossible unless the theory of transformations in its classical form is abandoned completely and replaced with a more adequate one. Accordingly, I have proposed in Chapter 2 an alternative theory in which transformational relationships are stated in terms of *surface grammatical relations*. I then try to demonstrate not only that such an approach is able to resolve the many problems that plague the classical theory, but that it also reveals the existence of new grammatical phenomena, previously unnoticed or passed over in silence.

My approach in this book is primarily empirical. I discuss a wide range of syntactic problems, showing that in each case the new theory requires descriptions that are superior to any that are possible in the classical theory. Chapters 2 and 3 are devoted to so-called voice phenomena—that is, to the relationship between simple sentences that differ in propositional form but at least some of whose arguments bear the same relationship to the head of the phrase type in question. In Chapters 4 and 5 I examine infinitive complements in some detail and show that any theory that incorporates a level of deep structure of the kind presupposed in the classical theory necessarily fails to describe adequately a number of fundamental syntactic processes. Finally, in Chapter 6 I examine topicalized sentences of various kinds and show that only a theory in which transformations are stated over surface grammatical relations is capable of explaining a wide range of otherwise incomprehensible co-occurrence restrictions governing the form of such sentences in English.

Certain general consequences flow from a theory of the form proposed here. The most fundamental is that the grammatical processes themselves determine the semantic interpretation of sentences. Hence I reject the claim of the classical theory that syntax is autonomous. On the contrary, examination of the facts shows over and over again that in natural languages, form and meaning are inseparable. It follows that no single "level" of structure (either deep *or* surface) can alone determine the meaning of sentences. Rather, the syntactic processes that enter into the formation of syntactic structures contribute to the meaning of sentences. A full justification of this hypothesis depends, of course, on the explicit formulation of the semantic rules associated with grammatical processes—a task that goes beyond the bounds of the present work, though some progress has been made in recent research.

A second consequence of the theory advocated here is that any separation between "syntactic" processes and "lexical" processes is quite arbitrary. It is a matter of fact that the central grammatical processes in natural languages are characteristically both syntactic and lexical. Some processes are "more lexical" and others are "more syntactic." Languages vary widely, however, in the ways in which they can encode fundamental semantic relations into grammatical form, so that it is neither theoretically nor practically possible to maintain a strict separation between lexicon and syntax.

Finally, the evidence gathered here strongly suggests (though it does not prove) that much more grammar is learned than many transformational theorists are willing to admit. In contrast to Chomsky's recent writing, in which all syntactic processes are reduced to a single rule of the form "move NP," leaving all of the real complexity of natural languages to be accounted for by the (presumably innate) principles of human grammar, the theory proposed here suggests that language is a complex cognitive system whose rules are learned through a gradual process of hypothesis formation and testing. This is not to say that it is useless to search for general principles of universal grammar that impose restrictions on the sorts of linguistic systems that are in principle learnable. I do not think, however, that the theory proposed here is compatible with an extreme rationalist view of the language-acquisition process. Furthermore, the data that are currently available accord better, in my opinion, with a theory in which syntactic relationships are transparent on the surface and directly related to their corresponding semantic relationships than with a theory in which syntactic relationships are encoded into a single level of representation (whether ''deep'' or ''surface'') whose relationship to the 'semantic component' is determined completely by innate principles of universal grammar.

I am grateful to the many colleagues and students whose comments on this book have influenced me. I am particularly indebted to Leonard Babby, Richard Brecht, Jack Catlin, Bernard Comrie, Sally McConnell-Ginet, Margarita Suñer, Uwe Reichenbach, and Roger Epée.

I acknowledge with gratitude the help of the National Endowment for the Humanities, whose support during the academic year 1976–77 enabled me to write the first draft of this book. I also thank the Cornell Research Grants Committee for providing financial assistance in getting the final version typed; Bernhard Kendler of Cornell University Press for his patient support and goodwill; and Celia.

J. S. B

Ithaca, New York

THE THEORY OF
GRAMMATICAL
RELATIONS

1 The Classical Theory of Transformations

1.1 Introduction

There are two senses in which a theory of grammar may be said to be 'transformational' or to incorporate transformational rules. In the broad sense, any theory that contains rules that are essentially more powerful than phrase-structure rules (whether context-free or context-sensitive) can be said to be a transformational grammar. In particular, any theory that claims to relate classes of P-markers to one another, or to exhibit systematic relationships between classes of sentences, is in some sense a transformational grammar. On the other hand, the term 'transformational grammar' may be used to refer to some particular formal theory that incorporates a specific definition of the notion 'transformational rule.' As John Lyons (1968) has noted, failure to distinguish between the broad and the narrow senses of the term 'transformational' has "engendered a good deal of unnecessary controversy and confusion in the recent literature of linguistics." This confusion arises primarily from the fact that the best known and most fully developed theory of transformational grammar is the one proposed by Chomsky (1955, 1957, and many subsequent publications). Hence the term 'transformational grammar' has come to refer, somewhat by default, to one particular proposal for the incorporation of transformational rules into the theory of grammar.

One unfortunate consequence of this terminological confusion is that arguments concerning the merit of transformational grammar (whether pro or con) rarely take care to distinguish those features that are peculiar to Chomsky's conception of grammar from those that can reasonably be taken to characterize any theory that is transformational in the broad sense. The roots of this confusion stem from the earliest work on formal generative grammars. In Chomsky's early writings (for example, in *Syntactic Structures,* 1957), two rather different sorts of arguments are frequently presented as though they were essentially the same. On the one hand, Chomsky is concerned with demonstrating the inadequacies of phrase-structure grammars as characterizations of natural languages. These are arguments for transformational grammar in the broad sense. At the same time, he is concerned with proposing and justifying a particular definition of the notion 'transformational rule.' It is a startling fact that though the early literature of transformational grammar contains many novel and interesting empirical arguments in support of the view that grammars must be transformational in the broad sense, very few explicit arguments (aside from those that are implicit in particular analyses) support the particular definition of the notion 'transformational rule' first put forward by Chomsky in 1955, and thereafter adopted in the vast majority of works within the general framework of transformational grammar without discussion or critical examination. In fact it is only relatively recently that linguists have begun to explore alternative formal realizations of the notion 'transformational rule' in any systematic way. Tentative suggestions have appeared from time to time, but they typically have been by-products of investigations concerned with issues of quite another sort. Hence there has as yet appeared no full-scale critical examination of the foundations of transformational-generative grammar as it was set forth by Chomsky in 1955.

The present study is motivated by the conviction that many unsolved problems in the theory of syntax are a direct consequence of Chomsky's original definition of the notion 'transformation rule,' and, more important, that a significant proportion of these problems can be satisfactorily resolved if the notion 'transformational rule' is redefined in a particular way. Furthermore, I believe that it can be shown that a redefinition of the appropriate sort necessarily leads to a conception of syntax that differs in fundamental ways from that which is currently accepted by the majority of linguists. Consequently I shall begin by examining in some detail the definition of 'transformation' proposed in the early literature of transformational-generative grammar.

1.2   Chomsky's Definition of 'Transformation'

The fundamental idea underlying Chomsky's definition of 'transformation' is, as Chomsky himself has stated on numerous occasions, the notion of *analyzability*. In order to establish just what is meant by this term, I shall quote the following passage (from Chomsky 1961:19) in which this term is introduced in a straightforward and reasonably nontechnical way:

> Suppose that Q is a P-marker of the terminal string t and that t can be subdivided into successive segments $t_1, \ldots, t_n$ in such a way that each t_i is traceable, in Q, to a node labelled A_i. We say, in such a case, that
>
> t is *analyzable* as $(t_1, \ldots, t_n; A_1, \ldots, A_n)$ with respect to Q.   (11)
>
>   In the simplest case, a transformation T will be specified in part by a sequence of symbols $(A_1, \ldots, A_n)$ that defines its domain by the following rule:
>
> a string t with P-marker Q is in the domain of T if t is analyzable as $(t_1, \ldots, t_n; A_1, \ldots, A_n)$ with respect fo Q.   (12)
>
>   In this case, we will call $(t_1, \ldots, t_n)$ a *proper analysis* of t with respect to Q, T, and we will call $(A_1, \ldots, A_n)$ the *structure index* of T.

Put slightly differently, a string t is analyzable into a sequence of nodes $A_1, \ldots, A_n$, just in case t can be divided into a sequence of n substrings such that each t_i is dominated by A_i. If we take the structure index of a transformation T to be a sequence of nodes $A_1, \ldots, A_n$, then a string t will be in the domain of T just in case it can be divided into a sequence of substrings $t_1, \ldots, t_n$ such that each t_i is dominated by A_i, in other words, just in case it is analyzable as $(t_1, \ldots, t_n; A_1, \ldots, A_n)$.

Given these definitions, Chomsky then goes on to define the *struc-*

tural change of a transformation in terms of its effect on the terms of the proper analysis of the string to which it applies:

> Thus, T may have the effect of deleting or permuting certain terms, of substituting one for another, of adding a constant string in a fixed place, and so on. Suppose that we associate with a transformation T an underlying *elementary transformation* T_{el} which is a formal operation of some sort on n terms, where the structure index of T is of length n. Let

$$T_{el}\ (i; t_1, \ldots, t_n) = \sigma_i \tag{13}$$

> where $(t_1, \ldots, t_n)$ is the proper analysis of t with respect to Q, T, and T_{el} underlies T. Then the string resulting from the application of the transformation T to the string t with P-marker Q is

$$T(t, Q) = \sigma_1 \ldots \sigma_n \tag{14}$$

Thus, for example, the elementary transformation that converts an arbitrary string $x_1 - x_2 - x_3$ to $x_2 - x_1 - x_3$ Chomsky defines as follows:

$$\begin{aligned} T_{el}\ (1; x_1, x_2, x_3) &= x_2; T_{el}(2; x_1, x_2, x_3) \\ &= x_1; T_{el}(3; x_1, x_2, x_3) = x_3 \end{aligned} \tag{19}$$

In particular, given the string *John will try*, an elementary transformation of just this sort (defined over the appropriate structure index) will convert it into the question form *will John try?* In order to prevent transformations from applying to strings of actually occurring words, Chomsky states a condition (his 16), which I shall not repeat here, whose effect is to make the structural change brought about by an elementary transformation ''independent of the particular choice of strings to which it applies.'' Further elaborations of the basic definition include an extension allowing transformation to apply to pairs of P-markers (*generalized* transformations); an extension of the specification of the domain of a transformation to allow the terms of a structure index to contain more than one symbol; an extension permitting the domain of a transformation to be given by a finite set of structure indices; an extension allowing the terms of the structure index to be unspecified; and so on. These extensions will not be elaborated here, since they do not affect the basic definition of the notion 'elementary transformation' given above.

Without belaboring the details of the definitions just quoted or entering into further discussion of the formal problems associated with a definition of this sort, we may note immediately a number of striking properties of transformational rules, as thus conceived. First of all, the structural change of a transformation is an operation that affects only the terminal string of a P-marker. Thus an elementary transformation T_{el} performs a formal operation of some sort *on the proper analysis* of the terminal string t of some P-marker Q; that is, it applies to the substrings $t_1, \ldots, t_n$ into which t is divided by virtue of the conditions on analyzability that are imposed by the structure index of T_{el}. The only effect of a transformation, therefore, is to rearrange the terminal string of a P-marker. In particular, no constituent structure is assigned *by the transformational rule itself* to the terminal string that it produces. Since the result of applying a transformation to a P-marker must be a derived P-marker, however, there must be some method of assigning constituent structure to the terminal string produced by a transformation. The general outlines of Chomsky's solution to this problem are revealed in the following quotation (Chomsky 1961:21–22):

> It seems that the best way to do this is by a set of rules that form part of general linguistic theory, *rather than by an additional clause appended to the specification of each individual transformation*. Precise statement of these rules would require an analysis of fundamental notions going well beyond the informal account sketched above, or for that matter, the more precise versions of it that have appeared previously. Nevertheless, certain features of a general solution to this problem seem fairly clear. We can, first of all, assign each transformation to one of a small number of classes, depending on the underlying elementary transformation on which it is based. For each such class we can state a general rule that assigns to the transform a derived P-marker, the form of which depends, in a fixed way, on the Phrase-markers of the underlying terminal strings.

The key passage is contained in the first sentence. Why should derived constituent structure be assigned by means of a set of rules that are separate from the statement of the transformations themselves? The answer to this question is contained in the italicized clause. If no "set of rules that form part of general linguistic theory" governs derived constituent structure, then derived constituent structure will have to be provided "by an additional clause appended to the specification of each individual transformation." In other words, derived constituent structure will have to be specified ad hoc for each particular rule, rather than being predictable on the basis of general principles.

The need for rules of derived constituent structure, however, is dictated solely by the nature of Chomsky's definition of the notion 'transformation': the structural change of a transformational rule applies *only* to the proper analysis of the terminal string. The transformation itself, in other words, says nothing about what happens to the nodes that *dominate* the substrings affected by the structural change. To take a concrete example, the rule for forming questions in English will take a terminal string of the form *John will try* and convert it into a string of the form *will John try?* Unless auxiliary principles of derived constituent structure are available, however, the result of this operation will not be a well-formed P-marker. In particular, the element *will* will not be assigned to any category, it will not be dominated by any higher node in the tree, and so on.

In the case of permutation rules of this sort, the rule of derived constituent structure that Chomsky offers is in fact extremely vague. Referring to the rule that converts a string of the form *turn out some of the lights* into one of the form *turn some of the lights out,* Chomsky (1961:23) states without further elaboration, "The general principle of derived constituent structure in this case is simply that the minimal change is made in the P-marker of the underlying string, consistent with the requirement that the resulting P-marker again be representable in tree form." It is far from clear, however, what counts as a "minimal change" in the P-marker of the underlying string. In the case at hand, there would seem to be a number of possible derived constituent structures, all "consistent with the requirement that the resulting P-marker again be representable in tree form.'' The particle *out*, for example, might be immediately dominated in the derived P-marker by the NP *some of the lights*, by the VP-node dominating the whole phrase (this is the structure that Chomsky indicates is the correct one, but on what grounds he does not state), or by the highest S node. The change made in the P-marker of the underlying string seems equally ''minimal'' in all three cases, especially in view of the fact that the particle *out*, in Chomsky's underlying string, is immediately dominated by the node 'Verb,' which also immediately dominates the 'V' *turn*. Likewise, in the example discussed previously, it is unclear whether the modal element *will* should be dominated in derived constituent structure by VP, Aux, or S. Similar problems occur in a mass of other cases as well. Furthermore, even if some justification can be found in each particular case for choosing one derived constituent structure over another, it is certainly far from obvious that all of these cases can be explained in terms of the notion 'minimal change in the P-marker of the underlying string.'

In the case of substitution transformations and ''attachment'' transformations, the principles governing the assignment of derived constituent structure are somewhat clearer, though rarely made entirely explicit. For example, in the case of a generalized transformation that substitutes a transformed version of the second of a pair of underlying terminal strings for some term of the proper analysis of the first of this pair, the general principle is as follows (Chomsky 1961:22):

> Suppose that the transformation replaces the symbol a of σ_1 (the matrix sentence) by σ_2 (the constituent sentence). The P-marker of the result is simply the former P-marker of σ_1 with a replaced by the P-marker of σ_2.

The same basic idea can (as Chomsky indicates in a footnote) be extended to cover singulary substitution transformations, except that it is not entirely clear what dominating nodes are to be carried along with the substituted segment of the terminal string. One might guess that it is the term of the structure index that most remotely dominates the substring in question that is actually substituted, along with any intermediate parts of the P-marker. This guess is based on the fact that a similar principle is explicitly stated to govern the derived constituent structure of attachment transformations (Chomsky 1961:22):

> It appears that all other generalized transformations are *attachment transformations* that take a term α of the proper analysis, with the term β of the structure index that most remotely dominates it (and all intermediate parts of the P-marker that are dominated by β and that dominate α), and attaches it (with, perhaps, a constant string) to some other term of the proper analysis.

Even so, it is still far from clear, in the case of attachment transformations, what node the relevant term of the proper analysis (along with its dominating nodes) is to be dominated by in derived constituent structure. Exactly the same problem arises also in the case of attachment transformations that introduce some constant string at a designated place in the proper analysis.

It is evident from the definitions quoted above that the need for special rules of derived constituent structure is simply a consequence of the way in which Chomsky chose to formalize the notion 'transformational rule.' Transformational rules, by definition, affect only the proper analysis of the terminal string, and are therefore incapable of specifying the derived constituent structure to be assigned to the resulting P-marker. Now it is a striking fact that in every known case the substring of the proper analysis that is affected by the structural change of a transformation must be assigned just the constituent structure that is imposed on it by the structure index of the transformation, in accordance with the principle of analyzability. This is true whether the substring in question is permuted with some other term of the proper analysis, substituted for some other term in the proper analysis, or attached to some other term. This observation suggests that it would simplify matters considerably if the notion 'transformation' were redefined in such a way that it applied to trees rather than to terminal strings. There would then be no need for special rules ensuring that the affected term of the proper analysis retains its constituent structure; this perfectly general property of transformational rules would simply be built directly into the definition of the notion 'transformational rule.'

It might be argued that redefining the notion 'transformation' along these lines would be ill advised on the grounds that it would increase the power of transformations, in the sense that the class of possible rules would be less restricted. At the same time, it might be argued, such a redefinition would entail a complication in the statement of particular rules. The theory proposed by Chomsky, in contrast, attempts to restrict the statement of particular rules very narrowly and at the same time simplifies the statement of particular rules, leaving the rules of derived constituent structure to be a part of general linguistic theory. Both of these arguments are invalid, however. First of all, the rules of derived constituent structure are no less general if they are incorporated into the notion 'transformational rule' than if they are relegated to a special part of general linguistic theory having to do with the assignment of derived constituent structure, since the definition of such notions as 'transformation' is itself provided by linguistic theory. Second, the appearance of greater simplicity in the statement of rules of particular grammar that is provided by Chomsky's theory is simply an illusion, since simplicity can be determined only by reference to a particular evaluation measure. Implicit in Chomsky's definition of 'transformation' is an evaluation measure that values rules that alter only terminal strings more highly than rules that alter trees. The point of the arguments presented here, however, is that such an evaluation measure is incorrect, as is shown by the fact that Chomsky's definition of 'transformation' must, in any case, be supplemented by a set of rules that assign derived constituent structure to the output of transformational rules. There is a sense, of course, in which the redefinition of 'transformation' suggested above is more powerful than Chomsky's (i.e., it permits a larger class of possible transformational rules). I shall show later on, however, that redefining 'transformation' in this way leads ultimately to a more restrictive theory of syntax, since it permits very strong constraints to be imposed on the class of possible transformational derivations.

Up to this point I have been primarily concerned with the part of Chomsky's definition of transformation that is concerned with the structural change, and I have tentatively suggested that a theory of transformations that permits only the terminal string to be affected by elementary operations is inadequate for the description of natural languages. We must now consider in more detail the part of Chomsky's definition that concerns the structure index. It is quite striking that just as the structural change can affect only a *linear string* of terminal elements in a P-marker, so the structure index is permitted to specify only a linear string of nodes that occur in a P-marker. Specifically, each term of the proper analysis of the terminal string must be matched by a dominating node in the structure index. It is extremely important to note that this is the only structural information that can, by definition, be specified in the structure index of a transformation. In particular, it is impossible to incorporate into the structure index the information that some term dominates or is dominated by another node in the tree. If, as has generally been assumed, grammatical relations are defined in terms of the structural relationships between nodes in a P-marker, one specific consequence of this restriction is that it is impossible, under Chomsky's definition, to refer to grammatical relations in specifying the domain of a transformational rule.

Let us illustrate this point with reference to a concrete example. Suppose that we have a tree of the form shown in diagram 1. There are various ways in which the terminal string *the man Past give the book to the girl* can be subdivided so as to meet the conditions on analyzability,

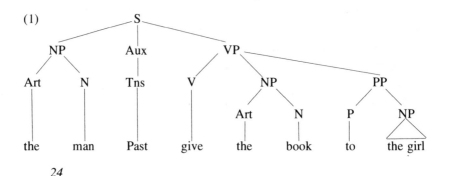

(1)

and corresponding to each will be a structure index consisting of a linear string of nonterminal symbols. Thus we may analyze the terminal string into the three substrings *the man –Past –give the book to the girl,* in which case the correct structure index will have the three terms NP-Aux-VP. The conditions on analyzability are met, since each substring is dominated by some nonterminal node in the P-marker. Alternatively, we could divide the terminal string into five substrings in the following manner:

(2)   the man–Past–give–the book–to the girl

in which case the corresponding structure index will have the following form:

(3)   NP-Aux-V-NP-PP

Once again, the conditions on analyzability are met, since each substring can be traced back to a single node in the structure index. Similarly, we could break any or all of the substrings *the man, the book, to the girl,* and *the girl* into their constituent parts, in which case we would have structure indices such as the following:

(4)   *a.* Art-N-Aux-VP
      b. Art-N-Aux-V-NP-P-NP
      c. Art-N-Aux-V-Art-N-P-Art-N
      d. NP-Aux-V-Art-N-PP

Obviously there are other possibilities as well. The important point is that in no case is it possible to specify that a given term of the structure index, or a given substring of terms, dominates or is dominated by some other node in the tree. It is impossible, for example, to indicate that the third, fourth, and fifth terms of structure index 3 are immediately dominated by the node VP. Likewise, it is impossible to refer to the fact that the first and second items in 4*a*, 4*b*, or 4*c* are dominated by NP. Chomsky's definition permits one to refer to any level of structure in a P-marker, but does not permit one to refer to more than one level of structure for any given term of the proper analysis of the terminal string. It follows that the grammatical relation of a given constituent in a sentence—for example, the grammatical relation of subject-of—cannot be referred to directly in the structure index of a transformation. It may happen, of course, that the P-markers generated by the base rules are such that one can specify *indirectly* the grammatical relation of a constituent mentioned in the structure index. If, for example, the rules of the base generate only a single NP constituent to the left of VP, then a structural description for the passive rule that specifies the four terms NP, Aux, V, NP, in that order, will ipso facto apply to subject NPs.

Obviously it is an empirical question whether a definition of the notion 'transformation' which restricts the structure index of transformational rules in this way is adequate for the description of natural languages. It is therefore somewhat surprising that until very recently almost no justification, or even discussion, of this point has appeared in the linguistic literature. In fact, there is strong evidence that Chomsky's definition is too restrictive, and that transformations must be allowed to refer to the grammatical relations. The problem is to find clear cases in which the two competing definitions 'transformation' make different predictions, so that empirical evidence can be brought to bear on the problem. I shall discuss a number of such cases directly.

But before doing so, I must discuss a number of related points. One of the persistent problems with Chomsky's definition of 'transformation' is that it is difficult to find general principles for determining the derived constituent structure of the strings that are the output of the transformational rules. In particular, it is difficult to determine just what the dominance relations should be in the derived P-marker. Now it is apparent that in many cases, this problem is directly related to the fact that the structure index of a transformation may not refer to any dominance relations other than those that are required by the conditions on analyzability. Consider the rule of particle movement, mentioned earlier, which relates such sentences as *John turned out some of the lights* and *John turned some of the lights out*. This transformation presumably must have a three-termed structure index of roughly the following form:

(5)   V, Prt, NP

The problem is to determine which node the element Prt is immediately dominated by in the derived P-marker. If the structure index is simply a linear string of elements, there is no way of specifying directly in the rule the dominance relationships in the derived P-marker. Suppose, however, that we are permitted to indicate in the structural description of particle movement the fact that the three terms, V, Prt, and NP, are themselves immediately dominated by VP:

(6) [$_{VP}$ V-Prt-NP]

Suppose further that we are permitted to indicate in the structural change of a rule whether or not a "moved" element (in this case, the element Prt) occurs within the scope of the dominating node VP. In that case, the rule of particle movement would have two possible outputs:

(7)   *a.* [$_{VP}$ V-NP-Prt]
      b. [$_{VP}$ V-NP] Prt

and depending on which derived constituent structure is correct, we can state the rule directly in one way or the other.

It is clear, then, that the problem of assigning derived constituent structure is directly related to the way in which one chooses to define 'transformational rule.' By defining transformations in the way he does, Chomsky appears to be claiming that grammatical rules "don't care" about any of the dominance relations in a P-marker other than the rather restricted set determined by the conditions on analyzability. The fact that transformations, defined in this fashion, must then be supplemented by a set of rules for the assignment of derived constituent structure is highly suspicious, since we can eliminate the need for such rules by widening the domain of application of the transformational rules.

Finally, notice that both of these problems—the problem of determining the domain of application of transformational rules and the problem of determining derived constituent structure—are related to the fact (pointed out earlier) that in all known cases transformations act as though they apply to constituents, despite the fact that under Chomsky's definition transformations are explicitly restricted in such a way that they apply only to terminal strings. There is something curiously self-defeating about the procedure that Chomsky adopts. Transformations, according to his conception, affect no part of a P-marker except the terminal string. At the same time the structural conditions that may be imposed on the terminal string are explicitly restricted to a very limited number of the possible relations that can be defined in terms of P-markers. As a consequence, the output of any given transformation is something that is not itself a P-marker and is therefore not appropriate as the input to further transformational operations. In other words, the transformational rules themselves do nothing but destroy structure. At this point a special set of rules is set up solely for the purposes of replacing the very structure that was destroyed by the transformational rules and determining the derived constituent structure that is to be assigned to their output in those cases in which the structural information specified in the structure index of the transformation was insufficient to state the precise effect of the rule. It is as though one were to attempt to simplify the game of tennis by removing the net and replacing it with a complex procedure that involved photographing the position of the ball during each volley in order to determine later, through complex calculations, whether or not the ball would have hit the net in each case if one had been there. The obvious solution is simply to replace the net, or, in the case at hand, to "complicate" the grammar by defining transformations directly in terms of P-markers, rather than in terms of string operations.

1.3   Arguments against Chomsky's Definition of 'Transformation'

We have seen in Section 1.2 that a close examination of the notion 'transformational rule' presupposed in virtually all work on transformational-generative grammar since 1955 raises three separate but related issues: (1) How is the domain of a grammatical transformation to be specified, that is, to what entities do transformations apply? (2) What sorts of structural conditions are permitted in the structural description of a transformation, that is, what properties of P-markers can be taken into account in defining the domain of a transformational rule? (3) How is derived constituent structure to be assigned to the output of a transformational rule? Chomsky attempts to provide a definition of 'transformation' that restricts as narrowly as possible the class of possible transformational rules. In particular, his definition provides the following answers to the above questions: (1) The domain of a transformational rule is the terminal string of a P-marker, that is, transformations apply to strings of terminal symbols, performing various elementary operations on these strings, such as permutation, substitution, adjunction, and deletion. (2) The structural conditions that can be imposed on the terminal string are just those that are permitted by a set of Boolean conditions on analyzability. The effect of this condition is to permit reference to a linear string of nonterminal nodes in a P-marker, each of which dominates some substring of the terminal string, or to some conjunction or disjunction of such conditions. Given such a set of conditions, no other dominance relationships in the P-marker can be specified, or at least an extra, ad hoc statement would be required to specify any additional conditions of this sort. (3) Derived constituent structure is assigned to the output of the transformations by special rules (which are a part of general linguistic theory) associated with each elementary operation that can be performed on the proper analysis of the terminal string. Thus there would be one set of rules for permutation operations, another for substitution operations, another for deletion operations, and so on.

The motivation for a definition of this sort is quite clear. Chomsky hopes to constrain as narrowly as possible the class of rules that are permitted in the grammars of particular languages and at the same time to assign as much complexity as possible to general principles of linguistic theory which are language-independent and which therefore do not have to be included in the grammars of particular languages. Given the general framework of assumptions within which Chomsky is operating, this is obviously a highly desirable goal. In fact, it is essential if his theory is to have any empirical content. The reason is that his initial conception of a transformational rule as an arbitrary mapping of P-markers onto P-markers is totally unconstrained. Since transformational operations can be concatenated to produce transformational derivations of arbitrary length and complexity, the class of possible transformational rules must be constrained as narrowly as possible, since otherwise virtually any conceivable underlying form could be mapped by some sequence of transformational rules onto the surface forms of a given language. It is not impossible, of course, that such a program can be carried out successfully, that is, that a set of constraints on the functioning of arbitrarily chosen transformational rules can be found which will be sufficient to constrain adequately the class of possible transformational derivations.

It may turn out, however, that even constraints of the severest sort on the functioning of transformational rules will be insufficient, in which case it will be necessary to look for general principles that constrain directly the class of possible underlying forms and transformational derivations. Furthermore, there are strong indications that this latter approach may be more fruitful in the long run. For one thing, notice that if the class of possible base forms can be limited severely enough, the power of transformational rules might actually be *increased* without significant effect on the class of languages generated by the grammar.

Finally, it is entirely possible that the excessive power of transformational grammar is an inescapable consequence of the way in which 'transformation' is defined in the classical theory. In particular, one might wonder whether a theory that assigns a class of P-markers to each surface syntactic form is not inherently too powerful to constrain adequately the grammars of natural languages. If that should turn out to be the case, it would obviously be necessary to reexamine the whole foundation of the classical theory of transformational-generative grammar. Many of the arguments that I shall present here are of necessity inextricably bound up with general considerations of this kind. I shall argue not only that the usual notion of transformational rule is too *weak,* in the sense that it makes it difficult and sometimes impossible to describe adequately the form and functioning of particular grammatical rules, but that it is also too *strong,* in the sense that it makes it impossible to constrain adequately the class of structural descriptions that can in principle be assigned to the sentences of natural languages. Hence I emphasize that my aim is not merely to show that the power of transformations should be increased. Such an argument would be of little theoretical interest, since it is easy enough to show that the power of transformational grammars is already much too great. The claim that transformational rules are not powerful enough is of significance only when it is coupled with a theory that effectively *reduces* the power of the grammar as a whole. Bearing these general considerations in mind, let us turn to some specific empirical arguments.

1.3.1   The Passive

One of the earliest difficulties that was encountered in applying the theory of transformational grammar to specific linguistic data was the problem of accounting correctly for the derived constituent structure of passive sentences in English. In the first descriptions of English syntax, the rule for the formation of passive sentences was conceived of as simultaneously performing three elementary operations: (1) permutation of the subject and object; (2) insertion of the discontinuous auxiliary element *be* + EN; (3) insertion of the element *by* to the left of the permuted subject. Thus it would apply to a terminal string of the following form:

(8) John-Past-kiss-Mary

and produce such a string as the following:

(9) Mary-Past-be + EN-kiss-by + John

Chomsky noted in *Syntactic Structures*, however, that under the usual conventions for assigning derived constituent structure, this rule would yield the incorrect structure for the passive *by* phrase, which should, of course, be a prepositional phrase in surface structure. This consequence follows directly from the facts that (*a*) transformations cannot create new nodes (in this case, the node PP) and (*b*) the element *by* is a transformationally inserted item. In order to rectify this situation, Chomsky proposed a special rule of derived constituent structure, which he stated as follows (Chomsky 1957:73–74):

> If X is a Z in the phrase structure grammar, and a string Y formed by a transformation is of the same structural form as X, then Y is also a Z.

Aside from the fact that this rule is entirely ad hoc (as Chomsky himself noted later on; see Chomsky 1965:104), since it is motivated solely by the passive transformation, it also begs the question at issue, which is whether the passive *by* phrase is in fact a PP (as it presumably would be if it were generated directly by the PS rules, an alternative that Chomsky does not consider) or whether it has the non-PP structure that is predicted by the existence of a passive transformation of the type proposed in *Syntactic Structures*. The reference to other phrases "of the same structural form" which are generated by the PS rules is thus completely gratuitous, since the issue is precisely whether the passive *by* phrase should be generated in the PS rules or by means of a transformational rule. Given Chomsky's definition of 'transformation,' it is clear that a transformational derivation in this case gives the wrong results. Hence if all of the syntactic tests for constituency show that the passive *by* phrase is a PP, and if there is no motivated way to ensure that this structure results from the application of the passive transformation, the only possible conclusion is that it is not in fact transformationally derived.

Chomsky makes a new attempt to solve this problem in *Aspects of the Theory of Syntax* (1965). Here Chomsky, following a suggestion in Jerrold Katz and Paul Postal's *Integrated Theory of Linguistic Descriptions* (1964), proposes to reformulate the passive transformation in the following way. The single permutation rule proposed earlier is now replaced by a sequence of two operations, the first of which substitutes the subject NP for the dummy element 'passive,' which is generated in the base along with the preposition *by* under the domination of a PP node that is itself dominated by the adverbial node 'Manner.' The second operation then adjoins the object NP to the left of the auxiliary element. Furthermore, passive is now an obligatory transformation, rather than an optional one, which is triggered by the presence of the dummy element 'passive.' Since verbs may be subcategorized for the presence or absence of this triggering element, this proposal in effect allows verbs to be classified in terms of whether they must, may, or may not undergo the passive transformation, thus providing a mechanism to describe (if not explain) the fact (noted earlier in Lees 1960) that certain verbs, though transitive in form, nevertheless resist passivization, as well as the fact that certain verbs in English occur only in passive form (e.g., *be born, be rumored to, be said to*).

This new proposal accounts for the derived constituent structure of the passive *by* phrase by, in effect, building the relevant part of the surface form of passive sentences into the underlying representation of passive sentences and then requiring that the passive transformation replace the dummy element 'passive' with the subject NP. The dummy element is thus a kind of "place holder" that has the function of marking the position that the subject NP is going to occupy in surface structure.

While this solution succeeds, on a purely technical level, in accounting correctly for the form and distribution of passive sentences, it raises serious problems of justification for the base forms that puta-tively underlie such surface constructions as the passive. In particular, just as it was clear that the rule of derived constituent structure pro-posed in *Syntactic Structures* was set up solely for the purpose of adjusting the output of the passive transformation, so it is clear that the only real motivation for setting up a PP in the base whose object is the dummy symbol 'Passive' is to ensure that the correct surface form is generated by the transformational component. The fact is that there is no independent syntactic motivation for the existence of a deep-structure element 'passive.' Chomsky does offer one argument that is intended to provide independent motivation for *by passive,* based on Lee's observation (Lees 1960) that certain impassivizable verbs, such as *resemble, cost, weigh, marry, fit,* also seem to lack manner adver-bials of the usual sort (e.g., **John resembles Mary happily, *the package weighed ten pounds eagerly*). It is for this reason that Chomsky assigns the *by passive* element to the adverbial node 'Man-ner,' the idea being that impassivizable verbs can be subcategorized with the feature $[- \_\_ \ldots \text{Manner} \ldots]$, thus accounting simultane-ously for the fact that they do not take manner adverbs and for the fact that they lack grammatical passive forms. However, aside from the fact that Chomsky gives no principled reason for excluding those *-ly* adverbs that *do* occur with the class of 'middle' verbs from the cate-gory 'Manner' (e.g., *John resembles Mary uncannily, the suit fits me perfectly, John married Suzy in a hurry*), it is difficult to see in what sense the element *by passive* can be considered a manner adverbial. For one thing, it does not contribute anything to the meaning of the sentence, whereas ''real'' manner adverbs obviously do contribute to the meaning of sentences. Furthermore, in all of the other cases where Katz and Postal proposed dummy triggering elements in base forms (i.e., 'Q,' 'Imp,' 'Neg,' and so on), there was at least some semantic justification for their existence (though I shall argue in a later chapter that the argument in these cases too is essentially circular). In this case, however, there is not even that minimal amount of semantic justifica-tion for the existence of a passive dummy element, since it is explicitly precluded from contributing to the meaning of the underlying active forms from which passives are meant to derive. (Katz and Postal proposed rather halfheartedly that such an element might somehow be used by the semantic component to account for differences in meaning between passive and active sentences containing quantifiers, for example, Chomsky's *few of the people in this room know many languages, many languages are known by few of the people in this room.* It is now universally acknowledged, however, that it is the surface order of quantifiers that correlates with the interpretation in such cases.)

In short, there is no independent syntactic (or semantic) evidence for the underlying *by passive* phrase that is needed to trigger the passive transformation, if any of the elementary operations permitted in the standard theory are to produce the correct derived constituent structure for the passive *by* phrase. Aside from the obviously ad hoc nature of the dummy element 'passive,' it is clear that the introduction of such abstract elements in underlying forms diminishes considerably the empirical content of the theory of transformational grammar. If dummy symbols of this sort can be set up in deep structure at will in order to account for recalcitrant syntactic data, the possibility of constraining and justifying base forms on empirical grounds vanishes to almost zero.

1.3.2   Emonds's Structure-Preserving Hypothesis

The fact that there is no syntactic motivation for a deep-structure element *by passive* strongly suggests that rather than looking for specific arguments in support of particular dummy elements such as 'passive,' we might more fruitfully look for some general theoretical motivation for the use of dummy symbols of this sort. The only serious attempt to explore this approach that I am aware of is Emonds' theory of structure-preserving rules. (See Joseph E. Emonds 1970, 1972a, 1972b, 1976.)

Emonds starts out with the observation that most of the transformations that have been proposed for English can be roughly divided into two types. The first type he calls *structure-preserving* rules and the second type he calls *root* transformations. (He also introduces a third class of rules, which he calls minor movement rules; I shall not be concerned with rules of this type here.) The paradigm example of a structure-preserving rule is the passive transformation (more precisely, the two components that make up the passive under the revised analysis of *Aspects,* discussed above), while a characteristic example of a root transformation is the rule inverting subjects and auxiliaries, which enters into the formation of questions in English and is involved in other constructions as well.

In what sense is the passive structure-preserving? The basic idea is that the output of the passive transformation has a structure that is needed in any case to characterize other nonpassive base forms of English. If we ignore for the moment the problem of the passive auxiliary, it is apparent that passives in English have roughly the following surface form:

(10) NP-Aux-V-PP

This is exactly the same structure that must be assigned to the base forms underlying such sentences as *John is in the living room, Bill looked at Mary,* and *John talked to us.* The passive transformation is therefore structure-preserving in the sense that the syntactic structures it produces are characterized by the independently motivated rules of the base.

The rule of subject-auxiliary inversion, in contrast, produces a surface form that is *not* generated by the base rules, since there is no apparent motivation for generating underlying verb-initial structures of the form V-NP-V . . . in English. Structures of this sort occur only as the result of applying transformational rules to base forms with the auxiliary verb in postsubject position.

Emonds's claim (the *structure-preserving hypothesis*) is that *all* syntactic rules except for the class of root transformations are structure-preserving. Furthermore, the root transformations are themselves restricted in the following ways: (1) they may apply only within the highest S node in a given sentence (a *root*), or in a conjunction thereof; (2) they are restricted to daughter-adjoining a constituent to the root S. The rules of English that Emonds claims are root transformations, in this sense, are thus topicalization and fronting rules of various kinds which have the effect of moving some constituent to the front of the main clause. There are a number of serious problems with Emonds's claim that root transformations cannot apply in embedded clauses, and consequently it is unclear whether the special status that Emonds assigns to these rules can be maintained. (See Langendoen 1973 and Bowers 1976 for some discussion of these problems.) Some of these rules I shall discuss later on; for the moment I shall concentrate on those rules, such as the passive, which are clearly structure-preserving.

So far, Emonds's hypothesis is little more than an empirical observation. The next question is whether this observation can be incorporated into the theory of grammar in such a way that it will effectively limit the class of possible transformational rules. The method that Emonds suggests is as follows. First, we permit such major phrase nodes as NP and VP, as well as such lexical categories as noun, verb, and adjective, to dominate the null terminal symbol ϕ. Following Emonds's terminology, I refer to a node that dominates ϕ as an *empty* node and a node that dominates a nonnull terminal string as a *filled* node. Second, we relax the requirement of the standard theory that all ϕs be replaced with lexical items before the application of any of the syntactic transformations, replacing it with a general condition that all ϕs be replaced at some point in a syntactic derivation. Finally, we restrict the transformational rules (or at least those that are structure-preserving) in such a way that they may substitute a filled node only for some empty node of the same category. If any empty nodes are left at the end of a derivation which have been neither filled in with lexical items nor replaced with a filled node by some transformational rule, then by the general condition mentioned above, the output of this derivation will be rejected as ill formed.

In the case of the passive, then, we shall have an underlying structure of roughly the form shown in diagram 11. Following Chomsky 1970, I refer to the first component of the passive transformation as agent postposing and to the second component as NP preposing. The

(11)

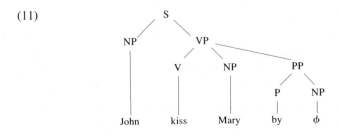

rule of agent postposing, reformulated as a structure-preserving rule, will then apply to diagram 11, producing an intermediate structure of the form shown in diagram 12. At this point, the second component of

(12)

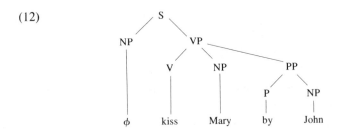

the passive, NP preposing, is applicable, and the empty NP node in the subject position will obligatorily be replaced with the object NP *Mary*, yielding the correct derived constituent structure shown in diagram 13.

(13)

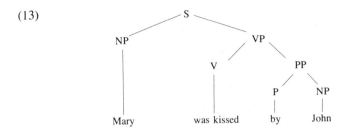

Note that if agent postposing had failed to apply to the deep structure in diagram 11, then the empty NP node in the *by* phrase would never have been filled in and the derivation would therefore have been rejected by the general condition governing the occurrence of empty nodes.

The case of the passive is of course not an isolated example. A number of standard syntactic transformations are discussed in detail in Emonds's *Transformational Approach to English Syntax* (1976), and it is shown in each case that the rule in question can advantageously be reformulated in the framework just described. (Further arguments in support of Emonds's theory can be found in Bowers 1973; see especially chaps. 2 and 3.) Thus it appears that there is considerable support for Emonds's claim that a significant number of well-studied syntactic transformations are structure-preserving. Nevertheless, there are some serious conceptual difficulties with Emonds's theory as it stands at present, which need to be clarified before any strong conclusions can be deduced from his observations.

1.3.3 Difficulties with the Structure-Preserving Hypothesis

It is apparent that Emonds's theory of structure-preserving transformations is a considerable improvement over the ad hoc analysis of the passive proposed in *Aspects*. If Emonds is even partially correct, the dummy element needed to trigger the application of the passive rules is not merely an isolated example. Instead of setting up the ad hoc dummy sumbol 'Passive,' we can set up an empty node in the *by* phrase, a device that is needed in any case to characterize the class of structure-preserving transformations. The passive, instead of being an exceptional type of rule requiring special treatment, is exactly the kind of rule we expect to find in natural languages.

Despite the virtues of Emonds's proposal, it fails to resolve a number of fundamental problems. In particular, it is necessary to ask under what circumstances empty nodes are to be permitted in underlying representations. In the absence of strong constraints on the occurrence of empty nodes in deep structure, it is not even clear whether Emonds's theory has empirical content, since any conceivable syntactic rule could trivially be made "structure-preserving" simply by the process of generating an obligatorily empty node of the right category in the position to which the constituent in question is to be moved.

Emonds is of course aware of this difficulty, and the answer he proposes is the following: an empty node of a given category is permitted in some position in deep structure only when there is *independent syntactic motivation* for setting up nodes of that category in the position in question. Unfortunately, it is still not clear what constitutes "independent syntactic motivation" for the existence of a node in deep structure. One reasonable interpretation might be that there must be at least one other construction that requires a *filled* node in the relevant position in deep structure. This interpretation would rule out, for example, the use of obligatorily empty nodes. Apparently, however, Emonds permits the use of obligatorily empty nodes in a number of cases (e.g., in his analysis of WH movement, which requires obligatorily empty nodes in the COMP position, and in his analysis of "true" *for-to* complements).

Or let us consider once again the case of the passive. What independent syntactic motivation is there for the *by* + ϕ phrase that triggers the passive rules? If it is only the PP node that requires independent motivation, presumably that is provided by the existence of any sentence with the base form NP-V-PP. The passive, however, requires more than just a PP node in the position to the right of the object NP. It is also necessary to assume that the head of the PP is the preposition *by*. Furthermore, it must be the specific *by* that occurs in passive sentences. It cannot, for example, be the locative *by* that occurs in such sentences as *the stool is by the table,* and *John drove by the house,* since that would give absurd semantic results. In fact, it is far from clear that there is any syntactic motivation, aside from the existence of the very passive sentences with which we are concerned, for an underlying "agentive" *by* + ϕ phrase. But if that is so, we are faced once again with the problem of circularity. If empty nodes can be set up in deep structure whenever they are needed in order to ensure the right derived constituent structure, what is to prevent us from setting them up in all cases, thus reducing the structure-preserving hypothesis to vacuity? It might be tempting to argue in the case of the passive that the existence of *get* passives and *have* passives (e.g., *Mary got kissed by John, I had a book stolen*) provides independent motivation for a deep-structure agent phrase. If we accept this argument, however, we then must derive normal *be* passives and *get* and *have* passives from different sources. But this conclusion seems wrong, since surely *John* in *Mary got kissed by John* is just as much the "deep" subject of the verb *kiss* as it is in the normal *be* passive *Mary was kissed by John.* Notice, incidentally, that if we were to retreat to the weaker position that it is only the PP node that requires independent motivation in deep structure, there would be no way of preventing such absurd analyses as the following. Consider the sentence *John rolled into the room.* Clearly, *John* is the deep object, as is shown by the existence of such sentences as *Harry rolled John into the room,* in which *John* shows up as the object in surface structure. At the same time, we know that such locative NPs as *the room* can occur in subject position, as in *the room is in the house.* It follows that the correct deep structure for *John rolled into the room* is of the form *the room–roll–John–into–ϕ.* We now extend the independently motivated rule of agent postposing, so that it now moves subject NPs into PPs whose head is *into* as well into PPs whose head is *by.* The application of this rule gives us the intermediate form *ϕ–roll–John–into the room,* at which point the independently motivated rule of NP preposing will automatically produce the correct surface form. Any number of equally absurd analyses of this sort could be justified in a similar manner, unless extremely strong constraints are imposed on the use of empty nodes in deep structure.

It seems, then, that Emonds's theory, appealing as it is in many respects, suffers from much the same defects as Chomsky's revised analysis of the passive. In the absence of specific criteria for determining when it is legitimate to set up empty nodes in deep structure, we can conclude only that the structure-preserving hypothesis is devoid of empirical content, a mere notational variant, in fact, of the standard theory. This is not quite correct, however, for notice that if no constraints at all are imposed on the use of empty nodes, then Emonds's proposals in fact amount to a decision to *increase* the power of transformational rules, for in Emonds's system (as in Chomsky's analysis of the passive) the derived constituent structure that is to be assigned to the P-marker resulting from the application of a particular transformation is incorporated into the statement of the rule itself. Thus the structure-preserving hypothesis not only fails to limit the power of transformations (as it was originally intended to do), but actually increases their power, since the constituent structure of the P-markers produced by transformational rules is now determined by the rules themselves, rather than by general principles of the sort originally envisaged by Chomsky.

The situation is therefore as follows: We can either give up the notion of structure-preserving rules and return to the standard theory, in which case we still do not have a non-ad hoc explanation for the derived constituent structure of the passive *by* phrase, or we can accept Emonds's proposals, which amounts to accepting a redefinition of 'transformational rule.' The first alternative is clearly unsatisfactory, since it leaves us with no adequate way of stating rules as basic as the passive. The second alternative is equally unsatisfactory, since it leads to an enormous increase in the power of transformational rules. Nevertheless, it seems inevitable that 'transformation' will have to be redefined along the lines suggested by Emonds's theory, since there is simply no non-ad hoc way that the theory of transformations as Chomsky originally conceived of it can be made to produce the correct derived constituent structure for passive sentences. In view of these considerations, it becomes imperative to find some way of constraining the form of grammars, in order to compensate for the increase in the power of transformational rules which is evidently necessary in order to state such rules as the passive.

1.4   A New Possibility

It should be apparent by now that there are difficulties inherent in the classical theory of transformational grammar which we cannot remove merely by patching up the theory in various ways. Transformational theory rests on the insight that certain relationships between sentences cannot be accounted for adequately within the limits imposed by phrase-structure description. Chomsky's theory of transformations, however, rests on the further assumption that certain *sentences* are more basic than others. Thus in "On the Notion of 'Rule of Grammar'" (1961) he criticizes immediate constituent analysis for "imposing too much structure on sentences." More specifically, he says (Chomsky 1961:15):

> Consider, for example, such a sentence as:
>
> Why had John always been such an easy fellow to please?   (6)
>
> The whole is a sentence; the last several words constitute a noun phrase; the words can be assigned to categories. But, there is little motivation for assigning phrase structure beyond this.

Later on in the same paper (p. 17) he says:

> The motivation for adding transformational rules to a grammar is quite clear. There are certain sentences (in fact, simple declarative sentences with no complex noun or verb phrases or, to be more precise, the terminal strings underlying these) that can be generated by a constituent structure grammar in quite a natural way. There are others (e.g., passives, questions, sentences with discontinuous phrases and complex phrases that embed sentence transforms) that cannot be generated in an economic and natural way by a constituent structure grammar, but that are systematically related to sentences of simpler structure. Transformations that are constructed to express this relation can thus materially simplify the grammar when used to generate more complex sentences and their structural descriptions from already generated simpler ones.

Chomsky's theory of transformations, then, was specifically designed to permit more complex sentences (such as passives and questions) to be derived from simpler sentences (such as actives and declaratives). In particular, his theory was designed in such a way that phrase structure would be explicitly assigned to simpler sentences but not to more complex ones. Thus in the case of the active and the passive, the simpler, more basic active sentences would be generated directly by the phrase-structure rules, whereas passive sentences could be characterized only indirectly, through the operation of a transformational rule.

The problem with this approach is that it fails to give the correct results in certain cases. Specifically, it fails to account for the derived constituent structure of passive sentences. Moreover, as Emonds's work shows, the passive is not an isolated example. In numerous cases, in fact, Chomsky's original theory of transformations fails to assign the correct derived constituent structure to the output of the transformational rules.

At this point it would have been reasonable to ask whether it was not the notion 'transformational rule' that was at fault. But that is not what happened. Instead, Chomsky attempted, as we have already seen, to build the derived constituent structure of passive sentences into the structures generated by the base rules. The difficulty with this approach is that there is clearly no motivation, in terms of Chomsky's original theory, for building aspects of derived constituent structure into the basic sentence structures generated by the PS rules. Such a move can be justified only if base forms are conceived of not as sentences, as they were in *Syntactic Structures,* but as *abstract structures* underlying the actual sentences (or surface structures) of the language.

This, then, was in part the motivation for the theory of deep structure proposed by Chomsky in 1965. In the new framework, the passive transformation is no longer thought of as a rule relating active and passive *sentences*. Rather, it is a rule that maps an underlying *deep structure* onto a more concrete, superficial representation, or *surface structure*. Since the structures to which transformational rules now apply are abstract representations, which need not be related in any obvious way to the surface syntactic forms of sentences, nothing prevents us from generating 'abstract' dummy elements such as *by passive* in the base forms of sentences, thus accounting correctly for the derived constituent structure of passive sentences and at the same time allowing the theory of transformations to be maintained in more or less its original form. (In fact, transformations can be restricted even further, Chomsky argues, since permutations can be eliminated altogether, leaving adjunction, substitution, and deletion as the only elementary operations permitted by general linguistic theory.) The appeal of this new way of looking at things was further reinforced by Katz and Postal's claim that optional singular transformations never changed the meanings of sentences, making it possible to argue that the abstract representations at the level of deep structure were the sole input to the semantic component.

Unfortunately, the syntactic advantages of the new theory are illusory in the case of the active-passive relationship, since there is no independent syntactic motivation for the underlying element *by passive*. Furthermore, in the absence of compelling evidence supporting the existence of such dummy elements in underlying representations, the theory of deep structure actually has the effect of increasing the power of transformations, since the derived constituent structure of passive sentences is now determined, in effect, by the passive transformation itself, rather than by general language-independent principles of derived constituent structure. In short, the theory proposed in *Aspects,* far from solving the problems raised by the active-passive relation, succeeds only in creating new problems of empirical justification and at the same time weakens considerably the theory of transformations proposed earlier.

How can these problems be resolved? It is obvious that we cannot simply return to the pre-*Aspects* theory of transformational grammar. At the same time, some increase in the power of transformations seem inevitable in the light of Emonds's work on structure-preserving rules. The only possibility, as was indicated in Section 1.3, is to find some independent constraint on the *form* of grammars that is sufficient to compensate for the extra power that must be allowed in the theory of transformations.

There is, however, one obvious and straightforward way of constraining grammars which will solve the problem of the passive *by* phrase, as well as numerous other syntactic problems that have arisen in the last ten years. The solution is simply to give up the notion that there is an abstract, underlying level of deep structure, which is mapped onto the level of surface structure by a linearly ordered sequence of transformational rules, and to return to the view implicit in the earliest work on transformational grammar (and explicit in Zellig Harris's theory of transformations) that the function of transformational rules is to state systematic syntactic relationships between the surface forms of sentences.

I shall present in Chapter 2 an explicit theory that embodies these assumptions. For the moment, let us consider in an informal way what the consequences of giving up deep structure would be in the case of the active-passive relation in English. First of all, if there is no level of deep structure, then active and passive sentences will obviously have to be assigned different syntactic structures. Second, suppose that we redefine the notion 'transformation' in such a way that transformations simply state systematic relationships between surface constituents that belong to the same syntactic category, but which have different grammatical relations within a clause. Suppose, in particular, that we think of the "structure-preserving" transformations discussed earlier in connection with Emonds's work not as transformations of the usual sort, which map "underlying" P-markers onto "surface" P-markers, but simply as rules that relate the surface forms of sentences to one another in a systematic fashion. Suppose further that we permit empty nodes, such as the NP node in the *by* phrase in diagram 11, to be generated freely in the surface structures of English, subject to the general condition that an empty node must be replaced by some syntactic transformation to permit that structure to qualify as well formed. When we think of matters in these terms, it is immediately obvious that we can simply take the structure in diagram 11 to be one of the possible surface P-markers that will be generated by the PS rules for English. Furthermore, if the rules of agent postposing and NP preposing are obligatory, in a sense that will be specified shortly, the structure in diagram 11 will automatically be converted into a passive sentence of the form NP-V-PP. If we generate a structure exactly like diagram 11 except that it lacks a *by-φ* phrase, then no rules will be applicable and the correct surface form of the corresponding active sentence will be produced.

If this reinterpretation of the Chomsky-Emonds analysis of the passive is correct, the problem of "motivating" the empty *by-φ* phrase disappears completely, since the only motivation that is required for generating a node in some position in a P-marker is that the node in question actually occur in that position in some surface form of English. The function of the phrase-structure rules in any given language L is thus simply and solely to characterize the surface form of the sentences of L. We can then think of the transformational rules of L, redefined along the lines suggested above, as constituting a set of general syntactic conditions (as opposed to specific lexical restrictions) on the insertion of lexical items on a surface P-marker. In a theory of this sort the problem of accounting for the derived constituent structure of passive sentences in English simply does not arise, since the domain of application of the transformational rules is explicitly restricted to the surface constituent structure of sentences. From this point of view the whole problem of assigning derived constituent structure which has plagued transformational grammar since its inception is simply the consequence of an incorrect and inadequate definition of the notion 'transformational rule.'

As I suggested earlier, the classical theory of transformations is both too strong and too weak. It is too strong in that it defines the domain of application of transformational rules and the set of possible elementary operations far too narrowly. At the same time, it is too weak in that it places virtually no constraints whatsoever on possible base forms. This conclusion follows directly from the fact that transformational derivations can be of unbounded length and complexity, thus permitting virtually any abstract base form to be converted into a well-formed surface structure by means of some sequence of transformational rules. That this particular defect raises serious questions concerning the explanatory power of transformational grammar has been realized for some time. Thus Hilary Putnam pointed out as early as 1961 that the class of languages generated by a transformational grammar of the then current variety was not even recursive; in fact, it is equivalent in weak generative capacity to an unrestricted rewriting system. But as Chomsky himself has noted on a number of occasions (see, for example, Chomsky 1961:130), unrestricted rewriting systems are of little empirical interest, since they do no more than claim that a language is generable by some set of rules. More recently (1971) Stanley Peters and R. W. Ritchie have demonstrated that even within the constraints on recoverability of deletion proposed by Chomsky in 1965, a transformational grammar of the *Aspects* variety is still weakly equivalent to a Turing machine. As a corollary, they were able to demonstrate that the so-called universal base hypothesis (which claims that all languages have the same set of base rules) cannot be proven false.

It is of course possible that these results can be circumvented if the power of deletion transformations is constrained still further. Thus Peters (1971) been shown that a transformational grammar that has what he terms the ''survivor'' property is recursive, and further constraints of an elaborate sort have been proposed by Chomsky (1973). On the other hand, it seems equally possible that this whole approach is misguided, and that it might be more fruitful to attempt to constrain the form of grammars, as has been suggested here. One reason for thinking so is that ultimately it is not weak generative capacity that is of primary linguistic interest, but strong generative capacity. To be of empirical interest, a linguistic theory must constrain not only the class of languages that can in principle be generated, but also the class of possible structural descriptions that can be assigned to the sentences of a language. If the constraints on the power of transformational derivations suggested here are correct, it may be possible for the first time to begin to approach the question of strong generative capacity in a systematic manner, especially if such constraints are combined with those on the set of possible base rules suggested by Chomsky in 1970. The reason is that the weak generative capacity of the theory to be outlined in Chapter 2 is not essentially greater than that of a context-sensitive phrase-structure grammar (though a CS PS grammar would itself be descriptively inadequate, for reasons that are familiar), since the transformational rules are constrained in such a way that they may state restrictions on the occurrence of lexical items and phrase types only within the limits provided by a set of context-free phrase-structure rules. The occurrence of empty nodes cannot increase the (weak or strong) generative capacity of the grammar because of the general constraint requiring that all empty nodes be filled lexically or replaced by some other constituent at some point in a derivation. If this can be shown to be true, it follows automatically that a grammar of this type is recursive. (To prove this assertion, it would be necessary to discuss in detail the role of deletion transformations in a grammar of this type. I think it can be shown, however, that all of the nonstylistic deletion rules that produce unbounded numbers of deletions, such as equi-NP deletion and relative clause formation, can in fact be replaced by movement rules of the kind to be defined shortly. If that is so, the standard conditions on recoverability of deletion should be sufficient to ensure that the grammar is recursive.)

More important, however, is the fact that a theory of this type imposes heavy constraints on the strong generative capacity of grammars. In particular cases, it can even be shown that the theory is explanatorily adequate, in the sense that given some subset of the sentences of a language, the simplest possible grammar consistent with the constraints imposed on the transformational rules by the theory will characterize just the class of actually occurring constructions of a certain type, along with the correct structural descriptions of the sentences of that class. (See Chapter 4 for arguments to this effect in the case of complement-infinitive constructions in English.) There is thus some hope that with a theory of this form, supplemented by universal conditions on the class of possible phrase-structure rules, the class of possible morphological rules, and so on, it may be possible to approach the goal of explanatory adequacy in the sense of Chomsky's *Aspects of the Theory of Syntax,* particularly if progress is made toward an understanding of the semantic constraints on the form of grammar.[1]

1. Not everyone (Chomsky in particular) would agree, of course, that there *are* any significant semantic constraints on the form of syntactic rules. It is implicit in the theory proposed here, however, that the "syntactic" and "semantic" motivation for particular rules of grammar are, in principle, inseparable. In fact, I believe it can be shown that the inadequacies of the classical theory of transformations derive ultimately from Chomsky's consistently held belief that some significant part of syntax is learned independently of semantic considerations. See, for example, the remarks in Chomsky 1973, in which it is stressed that transformational rules apply "blindly" to the proper analysis of the terminal string of a P-marker, regardless of semantic and lexical considerations. In particular, Chomsky emphasizes repeatedly that the passive transformation behaves in this fashion. Chomsky's view, however, is extremely difficult to reconcile with the existence of a number of well-known "exceptions" to the passive transformation. As we shall see later on, the existence of exceptions to the passive transformation, as it is formulated by Chomsky, provides strong support for the view that *no* syntactic analysis that assumes that the passive applies blindly to underlying strings of a certain type, regardless of semantic and lexical considerations, can account adequately for the relationship between active and passive sentences in English. (See Postal 1974 for further arguments against Chomsky's position.)

2 Co-occurrence Transformations

2.1 Redefining the Notion 'Transformational Rule'

We shall now consider in more detail how to go about redefining the notion 'transformational rule.' As I have indicated, I assume that the PS rules for any given language characterize the class of possible surface structure configurations of that language. I also assume, following Emonds (1976), that major phrase-node categories as well as lexical categories may dominate the null terminal symbol. We refer to nodes that dominate the null terminal symbol as *empty* nodes and nodes that dominate actual lexical items as *filled* nodes. The occurrence of empty nodes in surface P-markers is constrained by the following general condition:[1]

(1)   Any P-marker containing an empty node that has never been filled
       in the course of a derivation is rejected as ill formed.

This condition simply guarantees that every empty node generated by the PS rules will get filled in at some point in the course of a derivation. It is a general constraint on derivations, that is, a part of the theory of grammar, not a part of the description of English or any other particular language. As such it does not contribute to the complexity of the grammars of particular languages, but rather is a universal condition governing the form of grammar.

1. The notions developed in this section derive basically from the proposals in Emonds 1976, further elaborated in Bowers 1973. As will become evident, however, the interpretation that I give to these proposals diverges quite considerably from what Emonds himself had in mind. In general, I am indebted to Emonds's work in ways that are so numerous and varied that it would be pointless to attempt to catalog them all.

Given this basic terminology, we now define the notion *co-occurrence transformation* (CT) in the following manner:

(2)   A co-occurrence transformation is a rule that (1) fills an empty
       node *B* with a constant; (2) fills an empty node *B* with the contents
       of a filled node *A* of the same category;[2] (3) removes the contents of
       a filled node, leaving an empty node behind in its place.

We may assume, in addition, that a CT leaves an empty node behind it in the position that was occupied by the replacing node *A*. There is no general constraint on the number of times a node may be filled other than those imposed by the rules of a particular grammar. By convention, all empty nodes that remain at the end of a derivation that have been filled at least once are deleted.

In order to be able to state formally CTs of the sort just defined, I shall introduce the following notation. A filled node is indicated by an expression of the form '*A*:*a*,' where *A* is a category and *a, b, c, ...* are expressions. To indicate arbitrary expressions, I use the variables *x, y, z, ...* An empty node is one that contains the null terminal symbol ϕ; hence an empty node of the category *A* would be specified by the expression '*A*:ϕ.' To indicate that an empty node *A* has been filled with the contents *x* of some filled node *B*, we simply replace the expression *A*:ϕ with the expression *A*:*x* and leave the empty node *B*:ϕ in the position where *B* was in the structural description. As I suggested in Chapter 1, the input expressions to the CTs are full P-markers. The class of P-markers to which a CT applies is given by a structural description, specified in terms of filled and empty nodes, variables, dominating categories, and specified terminal symbols. For the sake of convenience I adopt two further conventions governing the use of variables. Suppose we wish to indicate a phrase of category *A* which immediately dominates a phrase of the category *B*, along with anything else. We shall symbolize this dominance by an expression of

2. The distinction between operations of type 1 and type 2 has no formal significance. See Reichenbach 1976 for a formal argument to this effect.

the following sort: [$_A$ ... *B* ... $_A$]. But suppose we wish to indicate that the category *A* dominates *B*, along with anything else. In that case, we use the conventional symbols *X, Y, Z*, and so on as variables for arbitrary subtrees in the following manner: [$_A$ *X-B-Y$_A$*]. Using these notations, we may state a rule that fills an empty subject NP with the contents of the direct object node in the following manner:

(3) *X* -[$_S$ NP:ϕ [$_{VP}$ V:*x* NP:*y* ... $_{VP}$] $_S$]-*Y*
  X -[$_S$ NP:*y* [$_{VP}$ V:*x* NP:ϕ ... $_{VP}$] $_S$]-*Y*

Equivalently, rather than repeating the whole structural description in indicating the output of a rule, we may simply draw an arrow from the contents of the filled node to the null symbol in the empty node:

(4) *X* -[$_X$ NP:ϕ [$_{VP}$ V:*x* NP:*y* ... $_{VP}$] $_S$]-*Y*

It should be noted at once the co-occurrence transformations are much more powerful in certain respects than classical transformations. First of all, since the input to a CT is a full P-marker, the grammatical relations of a constituent, as well as its linear position, may be specified in full. Second, the derived constituent structure to be assigned to the output of a CT is specified by the rule itself, since the precise position in the P-marker to which a constituent is to be moved is marked in the output of the rule by means of an empty node. The definition proposed above thus embodies the revisions suggested in Chapter 1. Notice in particular that no rules for assigning derived constituent structure to the output of a CT are necessary, since the CT itself specifies the precise structure of the output. Finally, let us consider the kinds of operations that may be performed by CTs. Definition 2, in addition to the equivalent of movement rules, also permits new constituents to be inserted and deleted in positions where nodes of the relevant category are permitted by the PS rules. Rules that insert new constituents into a P-marker are exactly the same in form as movement rules, except that in this case an empty node is replaced by some independently formed constituent of the right category.[3] Obviously, lexical insertion rules, which fill an empty category node with a lexical item of the right category in accordance with specific structural conditions, are special instances of insertion rules. Similarly, deletion rules remove the contents of filled nodes of a given category, leaving behind an empty node of that category in the position occupied by the deleted node. As we shall see, it is not in general necessary, as it is in the classical theory, to ensure that deleted nodes are uniquely recoverable. The reason is that in the theory proposed here, rules of semantic interpretation are associated directly with syntactic operations rather than with abstract underlying forms.[4]

2.2   The Passive Again

Returning briefly to the problem of the passive *by* phrase, it is immediately evident that the Chomsky-Emonds analysis discussed in Chapter 1 can be reformulated in terms of CTs of the sort just defined. In fact, rule 3 is a (somewhat oversimplified) formal statement of the rule of NP preposing. The rule of agent postposing may be stated roughly as follows:

(5) $X-[_S \text{ NP}:x \ [_{VP} \text{ V}:y \ldots [_{PP} \text{ P}:by \text{ NP}:\phi] \ldots _{VP}] \ _S]-Y \Rightarrow$
$X-[_S \text{ NP}:\phi \ [_{VP} \text{ V}:y \ldots [_{PP} \text{ P}:by \text{ NP}:x] \ldots _{VP}] \ _S]-Y$

The manner in which these two rules apply has already been discussed. It should be noted that the two rules of agent postposing and NP preposing are *intrinsically ordered*. In other words, NP preposing is applicable only after agent postposing has applied, since only then will an empty NP be available in the subject position. In fact, extrinsic ordering conditions of the sort required in the classical theory are

---

3. Implicit in this definition is the assumption that all major phrase-node categories are cyclic nodes. As we shall see in Chapter 3, independent evidence supports this assumption.

4. For a more explicit statement of the role of semantic interpretation in a theory of the kind proposed here, see Bowers and Reichenbach 1979.

generally unnecessary in the theory proposed here. This claim will be justified in more detail as we proceed.

As I have already indicated, the problem of assigning the correct derived constituent structure to the output of the passive rules does not arise in the theory proposed here. Given the formulation of agent postposing in rule 5, the correct structure of the passive *by* phrase is automatically determined by the rule itself. Furthermore, the problem of "motivating" an empty *by* phrase in the structure of passive sentences disappears, since the only nodes that can be generated in a P-marker are those that actually occur in some observable surface form of English. Thus the existence of surface passive sentences with *by* phrases (and also of *have* and *get* passives; see Chapter 3) is in itself sufficient motivation for the *by-φ* phrase that triggers the CT of agent postposing.[5]

Finally, notice that though CTs are more powerful than classical transformations, the *theory* proposed here is actually less powerful than the classical theory, because the operation of the CTs is limited by the very heavy constraints that the theory imposes on the *form* of grammar. In particular, the elimination of abstract underlying forms, along with the requirement that the PS rules generate only the class of possible surface constructions of English, automatically prohibits derivations of arbitrary length and complexity of the type permitted in the classical theory.

The remainder of this chapter is devoted to empirical arguments from English that provide evidence in favor of a theory of the sort just outlined. I shall show in each case that the classical theory of transformations requires ad hoc and unmotivated complications in the rules of

---

5. One slight problem, however, is raised by this analysis. What is to prevent sentences containing both a subject NP and a *by* phrase from being generated, thus apparently producing ungrammatical sentences of the form **the girl was Mary kissed by John?* For the moment, we shall simply follow the Chomsky-Emonds analysis and assume that verbs must be subcategorized in the lexicon to take a *by-φ* phrase. This solution, while perfectly possible within the general framework proposed here, is nevertheless undesirable, since it requires that lexical items be able to subcategorize empty nodes. As we shall see in Chapter 3, however, the need for this device can be eliminated by an appropriate reanalysis, for which there is independent motivation.

English, which can be eliminated entirely within the framework proposed here.

2.3   *There* Insertion

It is well known that there is a syntactic relationship in English between such pairs of sentences as the following:

(6)   *a*. A mouse is in my room.
     b. There is a mouse in my room.

Though the rule (or rules) relating these sentences has been much discussed in the literature, no fully satisfactory formulation has yet been proposed. The basic problem is to account for the fact that the fixed element *there* that appears in sentence-initial position is an NP. That this element is actually an NP is shown by the fact that it can undergo the process of raising:

(7)   *a*. There seems to be a mouse in my room.
     b. I believe there to be a mouse in my room.

Furthermore, the raised NP in such sentences as 7*b* can in turn be passivized, further confirming its NP status:

(8)   There is believed to be a mouse in my room.

The facts concerning raising also demonstrate, incidentally, that *there* must be a subject, since raising applies only to the subjects of infinitive complements.

It follows from these observations that the surface form of *there* sentences must be roughly as shown in diagram 9. At the same time, the related sentence 6*a* must have the form found in diagram 10. When these two structures are taken together, it is evident that the rule relating them must consist of at least two separate parts: (1) a rule moving

(9)

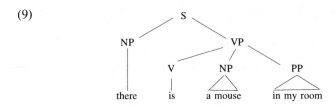

the subject NP to the right of the copula *be* (subject postposing); (2) a
rule inserting the element *there* in subject position. Clearly there is no
problem in formulating the rule of subject postposing. The problem

(10)

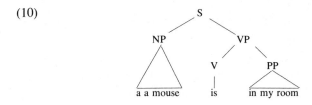

arises when we try to formulate the rule that inserts the element *there*
in the structure resulting from subject postposing. The fact is that the
classical theory of transformations offers no way to account for the fact
that *there* is a subject NP. The reason is simply that transformations,
by definition, cannot introduce new structure. Suppose, for example,
that we formulate a rule introducing the element *there* to the left of the
copula after the rule of subject postposing has moved the subject NP
the mouse to the right of it. Unless some ad hoc principle of derived
constituent structure is invented solely for the purpose of adjusting the
output of *there* insertion, the result of such a rule will be an incorrect
derived P-marker of the form found in diagram 11. The point is that the
classical theory of transformations does not permit a fixed element
such as *there* to be introduced into a string along with its dominating

(11)

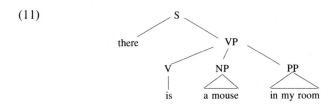

nodes. Hence there is no principled way to account for the NP status of the element *there*.

Recall that this is exactly the same problem that was encountered in the earliest formulations of the passive transformation, namely, how to assign the correct constituent structure to a transformationally inserted element such as *by*. The problem is even worse in the case of *there* insertion, because there is no plausible way to fix up the underlying structure so as to account for the NP status of *there* in derived structure. The reason is that the position where *there* is to be introduced is already occupied in the underlying P-marker by the subject NP *a mouse*. It is only after subject postposing has applied that the element *there* can be inserted.[6]

Suppose, however, that the theory of CTs proposed earlier is correct. In such a theory the problem of accounting for the derived constituent structure of *there*-insertion sentences disappears at once. Let us start out by reformulating the rule of subject postposing as a CT:

(12) Subject-postposing:

$$X-[_S \text{ NP}:x \ [_{VP} \text{ V}:y \text{ NP}:\phi \ldots \ _{VP}] \ _S]-Y \Rightarrow$$
$$X-[_S \text{ NP}:\phi \ [_{VP} \text{ V}:y \text{ NP}:x \ldots \ _{VP}] \ _S]-Y$$

The result of applying rule 12 to a P-marker such as that in diagram 10 is, by the definitions of Section 2.2.1., a structure such as that in diagram 13. Now it is a trivial matter to formulate a rule filling in the

(13)

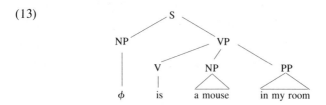

6. This is not to deny of course that some way of getting around the problem can be found. See, for example, Chomsky 1970 for one proposal. The point is that there is no *motivated* way within the classical theory of transformation to account for the derived constituent structure of *there*.

empty subject NP that is left behind as a result of the application of subject postposing with the fixed element *there,* thus accounting automatically for the fact that *there* is an NP:

(14) *There* insertion:[7]

$$X-[_S \text{ NP:}\phi \; [_{VP} \text{ V:}be \text{ NP:}x \dots {}_{VP}] \; _S] -Y \Rightarrow$$
$$X-[_S \text{ NP:}there \; [_{VP} \text{ V:}be \text{ NP:}x \dots {}_{VP}] \; _S]-Y$$

The rule of *there* insertion, then, is a clear counterexample to the classical theory of transformations. In a theory in which transformations refer to the grammatical functions of constituents, on the other hand, it is a trivial matter to account correctly for the surface form of *there*-insertion sentences and the corresponding intransitives with *be*.

2.4 Nonanaphoric *It*

Consider next the pronominal element *it* that occurs as the subject of such "weather" verbs as *rain, snow, hail,* and also in a number of other contexts, some of which will be discussed later on:

(15)
$$\text{It} \left\{ \begin{array}{l} \text{rained} \\ \text{snowed} \\ \text{hailed} \\ \text{etc.} \end{array} \right\}$$

7. Notice that *there* insertion, like a great many syntactic rules in natural languages, takes place only in the presence of specific lexical items. In this case, the main verb must be *be*, or in some dialects one of a small class of intransitive verbs including *stand, occur, take place, exist,* and perhaps a few others. In the framework proposed here, it is entirely natural to permit, as part of the statement of a rule, a specification of the set of expressions over which any given variable is allowed to range. We can do so either by stating specific syntactic or semantic properties that the expressions must have or, in cases in which the variable ranges over some heterogenous set of expressions, by simply listing the set of expressions in question. Hence, a more precise statement of rule 14 would fill the category V with a variable, say y, specifying as part of the rule that $y = \{ be, exist, stand, occur, \dots \}$.

It is clear that the element *it* in such sentences is not an anaphoric expression.[8] Rather, it is an "empty" pronoun whose only function is to fill in the obligatory subject position in English. It is equally clear that this dummy *it* is an NP, as is shown, once again, by its behavior with respect to raising and passive:

(16) *a*. It seems to have rained.
  b. I believe it to have rained.
  c. It is expected to rain.

There is no adequate way to describe the syntactic and semantic behavior of the dummy *it* in the classical theory. We would like to be able to say that at some level the structure of such sentences is simply *rained*, in other words, that such verbs as *rain* are 0-place predicates. In the classical theory, however, it is impossible to derive such sentences from underlying structures that lack a subject NP, since that would require a PS rule such as the following in the base:

(17) S → (NP) VP

That in turn would require some mechanism to exclude the countless numbers of ungrammatical sentences without subjects that would be permitted by such a rule. Furthermore, even if some appropriate way to exclude such sentences could be found, we would still face the problem, as in the case of *there* insertion, of accounting for the NP status of *it* in surface structure.

The framework proposed here offers a trivial solution to this problem. Suppose that we subcategorize such verbs as *rain* in the lexicon to take no NP arguments (as is semantically correct). Since the subject NP is an obligatory node in surface structure in English, such struc-

8. It is for this reason that proposals for deriving such sentences from the underlying forms *rain rained* and the like, which have appeared from time to time in the literature, are highly implausible, since they would appear to claim that *it* is a true referring expression, derived by a somewhat peculiar process of pronominalization from an underlying referential noun.

(18)

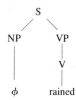

tures as that in diagram 18 will be generated by the base rules. It is now a simple matter to formulate a rule replacing the empty subject NP with the element *it* in the presence of such weather verbs as *rain*:

(19) *It* insertion:

X-[$_S$ NP:ϕ [$_{VP}$ V:x . . . $_{VP}$] $_S$]-Y $\Rightarrow$
X-[$_S$ NP:*it* [$_{VP}$ V:x . . . $_{VP}$] $_S$]-Y
x = {*rain, hail, snow, shower,* . . . }

It might be argued that the element *it* should be introduced in the base by the lexical insertion rules for verbs and that the interpretation of the sentence *it rained* as a 0-place predicate should be accounted for by a special rule of semantic interpretation assigning the pronoun *it* a nonanaphoric interpretation. One crucial fact, however, demonstrates conclusively that the empty *it* in such sentences cannot be a deep-structure element, but rather must be transformationally introduced. It happens that certain of the weather verbs can take pseudo-objects, as in the following examples:

(20) *a.* It rained on the spectators.
       b. It snowed on the houses.

Furthermore, it is possible to form pseudo-passive sentences from these examples. Now if the dummy element *it* were present in deep structure, we would expect to find pseudo-passives of the following form:

(21) *a.* *The spectators were rained on by it.
       b. *The houses were snowed on by it.

In fact, these sentences are completely ungrammatical. What we find instead are such examples as the following:

(22) *a*. The spectators were rained on.
    b. The houses were snowed on.

If at some point the structure of the sentence *it rained on the spectators* is as in diagram 18—that is, if there is simply an empty NP node in the subject position—then we can account for such passives as those in example 22 by applying the rule of NP preposing directly to a structure such as that in diagram 23. Furthermore, as long as such verbs as *rain* are subcategorized so as not to take the *by-φ* phrase that triggers the

(23)

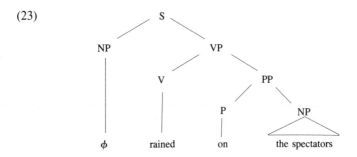

rule of agent postposing, the ungrammatical sentences in example 21 will be automatically excluded.

The situation, then, is as follows: either we may apply the rule of *it* insertion to such structures as diagram 23, producing the sentences in example 20, or we may apply NP preposing,[9] in which case we come out with such sentences as those in example 22. The crucial point is that the sentences in examples 20 and 22 cannot both be accounted for under the assumption that the dummy *it* is a deep-structure element. At the same time, there is no motivated way to introduce dummy *it* transformationally under the classical theory of transformations. In the theory proposed here, in contrast, all of these problems can be solved

9. This account is oversimplified. In Chapter 3 we shall refine the statement of the passive rules considerably.

in a natural and simple way without any ad hoc and unmotivated complications. I conclude that the facts concerning weather verbs provide another argument against the classical theory and in favor of a theory of the kind proposed here.[10]

2.5   Dative Movement

Consider next the rules of dative movement. These are the rules that are generally assumed to relate such pairs of sentences as the following:

(24)   *a*. John gave a book to Bill.
         b. John gave Bill a book.

(25)   *a*. John bought a present for Mary.
         b. John bought Mary a present.

It is immediately apparent that in the classical theory of transformations the only possible way of stating these rules is to derive the *b* sentences in examples 24 and 25 from the *a* sentences, since by definition transformations cannot introduce new structure. Thus if we were to take the *b* sentences as basic and formulate rules to move the

10. Notice, incidentally, that the ungrammaticality of the passive forms in example 21 also provide a clear counterexample to the claim that syntactic rules such as the passive apply independently of any semantic considerations, since it is clearly the nonanaphoric status of the empty *it* that accounts for the fact that it cannot undergo agent postposing. Anaphoric pronouns, in contrast, can always undergo agent postposing. Thus a purely structural condition is insufficient to account for the distribution of passive sentences in English. The syntactic rules also pay attention to the semantic properties of the constituents in question. It is implicit in the approach to syntax advocated here that there can be no sharp separation between the "syntactic" and the "semantic" motivation for particular rules of grammar. That is not to say, however, that there is no distinction between syntax and semantics, as some recent writers have urged. On the contrary, if the rules of syntax cannot be determined on purely formal grounds, in isolation from semantic considerations, it becomes even more crucial to discover general principles for deciding, with reference to a given grammar, where the division between syntax and semantics falls for that particular grammar.

indirect object to the right of the direct object, simultaneously introducing the prepositions *to* and *for,* the result would be incorrect derived constituent structures such as diagram 26. But if the sentences with PPs are taken as basic, there is no problem, since the necessary transformations destroy rather than create structure.

(26)

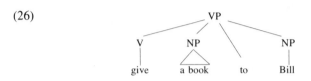

Unfortunately, certain problems inherent in this approach to dative movement have never been satisfactorily resolved. The main difficulty is that some *to* and *for* phrases meet the structural description of the dative-movement rules but nevertheless cannot be preposed. Consider, for example, the following sentences:

(27) *a.* John sent a book to London.
    b. John got a book for Christmas.
    c. Bill sold the house for a lot of money.
    d. Bill rolled the ball to the house.
    e. John carried the bucket for Mary.

all of which should be able to undergo the dative-movement rules but in fact cannot:

(28) *a.* *John sent London a book.
    b. *John got Christmas a book.
    c. *Bill sold a lot of money the house.
    d. *Bill rolled the house the ball.
    e. *John carried Mary the bucket.

It has sometimes been suggested that we might account for these "exceptions" to dative movement by imposing the appropriate selectional restrictions on the object of the *to* or *for* phrase. In particular, it has been suggested that the NP that is to undergo dative movement must be animate. This is, however, neither a necessary nor a sufficient condition. That it is not sufficient is shown by such a sentence as 27e. That it is not necessary is shown by the fact that such a sentence as *John sent London the necessary information* is fine, as long as 'London' designates a receiver rather than a destination. The point is, of course, that it is not merely the intrinsic semantic features of the NP that are relevant in determining whether or not it can undergo dative movement but rather its *relation* to the verb. Furthermore, unless we are willing to introduce labeled relations into syntactic representations at some level, it is apparent that the difference between, say, a dative *to* phrase and a directional *to* phrase cannot be represented in a phrase-structure grammar without considerable artificiality.

None of these problems would arise, of course, if the *b* forms with indirect objects could be taken as basic. The reason is simply that whereas any indirect object can be shifted into a *to* or *for* phrase, the reverse is not true. In the framework proposed here, the solution just suggested is perfectly feasible. Thus we may formulate a rule of *to*-dative movement in the following fashion:

(29) *To* dative movement:

$$X - [_{VP} \ V{:}x \ NP{:}y \ NP{:}z \ [_{PP} \ P{:}\phi \ NP{:}\phi \ _{PP}] \ \ldots \ _{VP}] - Y \Rightarrow$$
$$X - [_{VP} \ V{:}x \ NP{:}\phi \ NP{:}z \ [_{PP} \ P{:}to \ NP{:}y \ _{PP}] \ldots \ _{VP}] - Y$$
$$x = \{give, \ sell, \ send, \ldots\}$$

Rule 29 will apply to a tree of the form shown in diagram 30, converting it in the manner indicated into the sentence *John gave a book to*

(30)

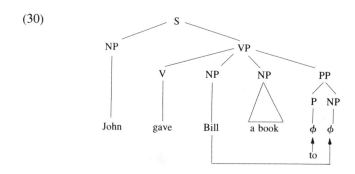

65

Bill. Such a sentence as *John sent a book to London,* in contrast, derives from a totally different structure. Hence there is no possibility of producing such ungrammatical sentences as those in example 28.

Obviously *for* dative movement can be reformulated in a similar fashion. Thus the sentence *John bought a present for Mary* will be derived in the manner shown in diagram 31, whereas such a sentence

(31)

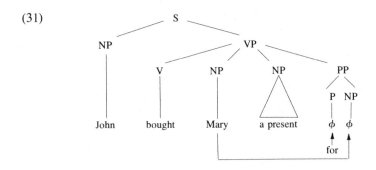

as *John got a present for Christmas* will be derived from an entirely different structure. I conclude, then, that the facts of dative movement provide further support for a theory of the sort proposed here, in which transformations state co-occurrence relations in surface structure.

2.6 Postposition in Nominals

Chomsky (1970) has argued that certain syntactic processes that apply in sentences have analogues in the domain of the NP. In particular, it is the rules of agent posposing and NP preposing that apparently account for such alternations as the following:

(32) *a.* the enemy's destruction of the city
  b. the destruction of the city by the enemy
  c. the city's destruction by the enemy

Notice, however, that the rule of agent postposing in nominals, as Chomsky formulates it, produces the wrong derived constituent structure for the passive *by* phrase, just as it does in sentences. There is a similar difficulty with Chomsky's rule of *of* insertion. This is a rule that inserts the unmarked preposition *of* between a nominal and its direct object in a great many contexts, including such nominals as those in example 32. As Chomsky formulates this rule, however, it will produce uniformly incorrect derived constituent structures of the form shown in diagram 33. The problem, once again, is that in the

(33)

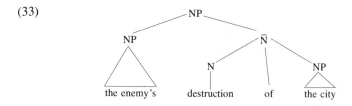

classical theory there is no way for transformations to create new structure. In the framework proposed here, such problems simply do not arise. Thus we may reformulate the rules of agent postposing and *of* insertion as CTs in the following manner:

(34) Agent postposing (nominals);

$$X-[_{NP} \text{ NP}:x \ [_{\bar{N}} \text{ N}:y \ldots [_{PP} \text{ P}:\phi \text{ NP}:\phi \ _{PP}] \ _{\bar{N}}] \ _{NP}] -Y \Rightarrow$$
$$X-[_{NP} \text{ NP}:\phi \ [_{\bar{N}} \text{ N}:y \ldots \ [_{PP} \text{ P}:by \text{ NP}:x \ _{PP}] \ _{\bar{N}}] \ _{NP}]-Y$$

(35) *Of* insertion:

$$X-[_{\bar{N}} \text{ N}:x \ [_{PP} \text{ P}:\phi \text{ NP}:y \ _{PP}] \ldots \ _{\bar{N}}]-Y \Rightarrow$$
$$X-[_{\bar{N}} \text{ N}:x \ [_{PP} \text{ P}:of \text{ NP}:y \ _{PP}] \ldots \ _{\bar{N}}]-Y$$

These two rules will then operate as shown in diagram 36 in the derivation of a nominal such as 32*b*.

Similar problems arise with still another postposing rule. I have shown elsewhere (Bowers 1975a) that there must be a rule analogous to subject postposing which moves the subject of a nominal in a wide

(36)

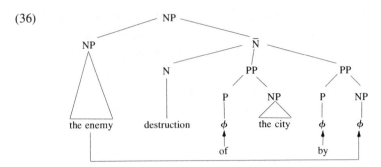

variety of contexts into an *of* phrase in postnominal position. It is this rule that accounts for such alternations as the following:

(37) *a.* the ball's movement
     b. the movement of the ball

(38) *a.* Bill's death
     b. the death of Bill

(39) *a.* the sun's brightness
     b. the brightness of the sun

(40) *a.* God's love
     b. the love of God

(41) *a.* the hunters' shooting
     b. the shooting of the hunters

As in the case of agent postposing, it is clear that the postposed subject must be a PP in surface structure. Under the classical theory of transformations, it is impossible to state subject postposing in nominals in such a way that the correct derived constituent structure will result. If we formulate it as a CT, however, the problem is nonexistent.

Let us consider next a somewhat different problem. Chomsky (1970) has noted that the rule of agent postposing in nominals apparently requires that a trace be left behind in subject position in the form of the definite article. Exactly the same is true of the rule of subject postposing just mentioned. This fact is rather difficult to account for in the classical theory, since genitive NPs and articles cannot co-occur in prenominal position. Chomsky's solution to this problem, as in the case of the inserted element *there,* is to increase the power of grammatical theory by allowing feature complexes to be associated with nonterminal nodes. Thus he would permit feature complexes of the form [+ def, + NP] in subject position in nominals. The NP could then be postposed, leaving behind the feature [+ def], which would then be realized phonologically as the definite article *the.* Aside from the fact that there appears to be little independent motivation for such an innovation in the theory of grammar, it is far from clear what sorts of constraints could be put on the use of this device. What, for example, is to prevent genitive NPs from being associated with other features such as [− def], [+ demonstrative], and so forth? Likewise, what is to prevent the subjects of sentences from being associated with such irrelevant features as [+ def]? Furthermore, notice that the motivation for use of such a device in one case totally contradicts the motivation for its use in another. In the case of the definite article in nominals, we want to be able to move the NP away, leaving the other feature behind. In the case of *there* insertion, we want to have a feature complex of the form [+ there, + NP], in order to ensure that *there* gets treated as an NP, as it is in the case of raising, for example. In short, this solution, far from solving the problem, only raises a host of new problems without really shedding any light on the matter. Let us see, therefore, whether a more insightful approach is possible.

It is generally assumed in the literature of transformational grammar that there is a special category 'Article' to which belong the definite and indefinite articles, demonstratives, and perhaps other elements of the determiner as well. This analysis, however, leaves a number of facts unexplained. Notice, for example, that the demonstrative articles behave in a number of respects exactly like nouns. In particular, they agree in number with the head noun (*this book, these books; that book, those books*), and can stand alone in positions where NPs can occur, as in *I like this, that is good.* The indefinite articles *some, any,* and *much* can also stand alone in positions where NPs occur. Furthermore, various quantifiers that are nominal in form, such as *a few* and *a good many*, occur in the same position as the articles and demonstratives, and of course, as we have just seen, possessive NPs, including the possessive pronouns, never co-occur with the articles. What these observations suggest is that the articles and demonstratives simply *are* NPs with no internal structure, just as the fixed element *there* that occurs in existential sentences is an NP that happens to have no internal structure. This proposal would account for the failure of articles and demonstratives to co-occur with genitive NPs in prenominal position and at the same time would explain the other facts just noted.

Now, however, we can easily account for the required presence of the definite article *the* in nominals with postposed genitive subjects. All we need to do is formulate the rule of subject postposing (for instance) in such a way that it fills in the empty NP left in subject position with the article *the*:

(42)   Subject postposing (nominals):

$$X-[_{NP} \text{ NP}:x \; [_{\bar{N}} \text{ N}:y \; [_{PP} \text{ P}:\phi \text{ NP}:\phi \; _{PP}] \ldots \; _{\bar{N}}] \; _{NP}]-Y \Rightarrow$$
$$X-[_{NP} \text{ NP}:the \; [_{\bar{N}} \text{ N}:y \; [_{PP} \text{ P}:\phi \text{ NP}:x \; _{PP}] \ldots \; _{\bar{N}}] \; _{NP}]-Y$$

(The empty P node will of course be filled in by *of* insertion.) Similarly, we can reformulate agent postposing slightly, so that the article *the* is obligatorily left behind in the empty NP node in subject position. Note that since *the* and *a* are not nouns, but rather noun phrases, they will never be able to meet the conditions for lexical insertion in positions where nouns normally occur, just as the element *there* can never occur freely in positions that are subcategorized by heads of phrases. The demonstratives and other indefinite articles, on the other hand, we may categorize as nouns, thus accounting for the fact that they can occur freely in NP positions.

In contrast, let us consider briefly the behavior of true possessive genitives. Genitive subjects that are possessive in meaning, in contrast to those that are the subjects of derived nominals, can appear in postposed position with the full range of articles:

(43)

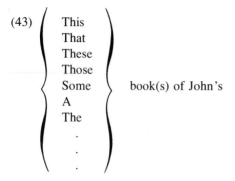

$$\left(\begin{array}{c} \text{This} \\ \text{That} \\ \text{These} \\ \text{Those} \\ \text{Some} \\ \text{A} \\ \text{The} \\ . \\ . \\ . \end{array}\right) \quad \text{book(s) of John's}$$

Only if no article is in subject position can a possessive genitive appear in subject position. Hence the simplest way to explain their distribution is to generate them in postnominal position and write a rule that moves a genitive NP into an empty NP in subject position.

(44)   Genitive preposing:

$$X-[_{NP} \text{ NP:}\phi \; [_{\bar{N}} \text{ N:}x \ldots [_{PP} \text{ P:}of \text{ NP:}y + \text{ 's }_{PP}] \; _{\bar{N}}] \; _{NP}] -Y \Rightarrow$$
$$X-[_{NP} \text{ NP:}y + \text{ 's } [_{\bar{N}} \text{ N:}x \ldots [_{PP} \text{ P:}\phi \text{ NP:}\phi \; _{PP}] \; _{\bar{N}}] \; _{NP}]-Y$$

Notice, incidentally, that the rule of NP preposing, which preposes object NPs into subject position in such sentences as example 32*c*, as well as in such nominals as *John's photograph* (in the sense of *the photograph of John*), is quite distinct from that of genitive preposing. The former applies to object NPs in an *of* phrase which are not marked with the genitive marker *'s*. Such phrases, however, are similar to possessive phrases in being able to occur with the full range of articles:

(45)

$$\left(\begin{array}{c} \text{This} \\ \text{That} \\ \text{These} \\ \text{Those} \\ \text{Some} \\ \text{A} \\ \text{The} \\ . \\ . \\ . \end{array}\right) \quad \text{photograph(s) of John}$$

The genitive forms thus appear to be derived by means of a preposing rule in this case also.

The behavior of nominals, then, provides strong support for the theory of transformations proposed here, since even the simplest post-posing rules cannot be stated adequately unless transformations are permitted to refer to grammatical relations. At the same time we have shown that the transformational relationships between classes of nominal expressions that have been dealt with in the literature can be described perfectly adequately at the level of surface structure without the need to assume abstract underlying forms. Finally, we have shown that the definite article that is required when the subjects of derived nominals are postponed can actually be handled more simply in a theory that limits transformations to stating distributional relations between surface forms than it can in the classical theory.

2.7 Transitive and Intransitive Verbs

We turn next to a somewhat different type of problem. It has frequently been observed in the literature (notably in Hall 1965 and Fillmore 1968) that there are in English (as in a great many other languages) pairs of sentences such as the following, in which the subject of the intransitive has a semantic relation to the verb similar to that of the object of the transitive:

(46) *a*. The police dispersed the crowd.
    b. The crowd dispersed.

(47) *a*. John rolled the ball down the hill.
    b. The ball rolled down the hill.

(48) *a*. We melted the ice.
    b. The ice melted.

A natural way to account for the relationship between these pairs in the classical theory of transformational grammar would be to derive the intransitive sentences in 46*b*, 47*b*, and 48*b* from underlying forms with a direct object and no subject. The transitive *a* sentences would contain both a subject and an object. If there were a rule that moved the objects of intransitives into subject position, the relationship between the subject of the intransitives and the object of the transitives could be explained in a simple and natural way.

Unfortunately, this solution is impossible within the classical theory, as was first pointed out by Hall (1965). The reason is that in order to generate subjectless deep structures of the form [$_S$ ϕ [$_{VP}$ *disperse –the crowd*]], it would be necessary to assume a base rule for S containing an optional subject NP:

(49) S → (NP) VP

But this rule immediately raises insuperable difficulties, since it would permit *any* verb in English to occur in an intransitive sentence, including *hit, guard, send, kill,* and innumerable other transitive verbs. Thus some new mechanism would be required to prevent all verbs except those that do in fact have intransitive forms from occurring in deep structures lacking a subject NP. But the only motivation for this new mechanism is that it accounts for the difficulties that are created by PS rule 49, permitting subjectless base forms. The obvious conclusion is that rule 49 is incorrect, in which case we are left once again with no way to account for the relationship between the transitive and intransitive pairs in examples 46–48.

2.7.1 Three Possible Solutions

At least three solutions to this problem have been proposed, none of which is entirely satisfactory. Since all of these proposals have been extensively discussed and criticized in the literature, I shall survey them only briefly, pointing out the most obvious difficulties with each.

2.7.1.1 *The causative solution.* It has been argued by George Lakoff (1965), and subsequently by many others, that the transitive *a* sentences should be derived, in analogy with constructions of the form *the police caused the crowd to disperse, John caused the ball to roll down the hill,* and so on, from underlying structures of the form:

(50) [s The police–CAUSE [s the crowd–disperse]]

Here the element CAUSE is intended to represent a so-called abstract verb,[11] which may be realized either by the lexical item *cause* (or perhaps some set of roughly synonymous lexical items, depending on its precise feature composition) or by the transitive verb *disperse*. The latter possibility is said to come about as the result of a process known as predicate raising, which raises the intransitive verb in the embedded clause into the matrix clause and combines it with the element CAUSE in a manner that has never been made formally precise. Other syntactic operations, which need not be spelled out in detail here, accompany this operation, and the net result is the transitive sentence *the police dispersed the crowd.*

Deep structures such as form 50, then, are intended to underlie both simple transitive sentences such as the one just cited and paraphrases of them, such as *the police caused the crowd to disperse.* Aside from the fact that the introduction of abstract verbs into the theory of grammar increases enormously the power of a theory that is already far too powerful, there is a fundamental defect in all such proposals that attempt to derive *words* (such as *disperse*) from underlying *phrases* (such as *cause to disperse*). The problem, as has been exposed most clearly by Jerry Fodor (1970), is that words and phrases, simply by virtue of their very different syntactic properties, tend to have different properties of co-occurrence accompanied by corresponding differences in semantic interpretation. The only way that these differences (which

11. In later elaborations of this theory it is claimed that such elements as CAUSE are actually semantic primitives and that such abstract underlying structures as 50 represent, in effect, the semantic interpretation of the surface forms they underlie. Space precludes a detailed critique of the theory of "lexical decomposition," which has been elaborated in numerous recent publications by Lakoff, McCawley, Postal, and a host of others. Suffice it to say that this approach has failed to win general acceptance, despite the extensive claims that have been made for it.

tend to multiply on closer inspection) can be accounted for in theories of this sort is by the addition of more and more conditions of an ad hoc and syntactically unmotivated kind to the transformations mapping the abstract underlying structures onto their surface forms. The obvious alternative is simply to admit that words and phrases, though often closely related in meaning, are not identical either syntactically or semantically, in which case the whole approach either collapses or is reduced to a notational variant of standard interpretive theories (see Katz 1971 for an explicit argument along these lines). In short, this approach, though it has prompted interesting and valuable empirical investigations of a wide variety of syntactic and semantic phenomena, contains inherent difficulties that have yet to be resolved in a satisfactory manner. From the point of view advocated here, this conclusion is hardly surprising, since all approaches of this kind are merely extensions of the classical theory of deep structure.

2.7.1.2 *Case grammar.*   I pointed out earlier that the fundamental reason that the relationship between transitive and intransitive Verbs cannot be accounted for in the classical theory of deep structure is that it has no way of generating the subjectless deep structures that one would like to assume underlie intransitive sentences. The causative solution discussed in Section 2.7.1.1 attempts to get around this problem by adding additional clauses at the level of deep structure while preserving the basic SVO word order of English. The solution proposed by Charles Fillmore (1968) is somewhat different. Faced with the fact that subjectless deep structures cannot be economically generated at the level of deep structure, he concludes that the notion 'subject of' is a purely surface grammatical function that has no role to play in underlying structure and attempts to derive *both* transitive and intransitive sentences from underlying subjectless structures. Although the nature of his approach is somewhat obscured by his belief that a universal system of 'case' relations underlies the surface forms of particular languages, nevertheless the general idea is quite clear, namely, to reduce all of the surface forms of English to underlying subjectless structures.

While Fillmore's theory has some initial plausibility, its attractiveness diminishes considerably on closer inspection. First of all, his theory apparently places no significant constraints on the possible systems of underlying case relations. In fact, as case grammars become more elaborate, the number of basic case relations tends to increase at an alarming rate. Fillmore's notion that a rather small set of universal case relationships underlies the surface forms of all languages is thus cast in doubt. Second, there are notorious difficulties with the semantic definitions that Fillmore attempts to provide for his basic case relationships. Third, many of the paraphrase relations on which Fillmore bases his arguments have turned out on closer inspection to be less straightforward than he supposed. In fact, Fillmore himself suggests that it may be necessary to permit the rules mapping underlying case structures onto surface forms to contribute to the meaning of sentences. But this possibility vitiates considerably the explanatory power of his theory, suggesting that such "surface" grammatical functions as subject and object do in fact contribute significantly to the meaning of sentences. Finally, Chomsky has pointed out (1972a) that Fillmore's proposals can be accommodated rather easily in an interpretive theory of the usual kind if the direction of his rules is simply reversed. Chomsky argues further that in those cases in which the direction of his rules cannot be reversed, Fillmore's analyses are empirically wrong, suggesting once again that surface grammatical functions play a significant role in determining semantic interpretation. In addition to these general arguments, in a number of clear cases (see Dougherty 1970) Fillmore's assumption that the notion 'subject of' is a superficial surface relation leads to a loss of generality in the statement of syntactic rules of English, such as the passive.

Despite these difficulties, Fillmore's arguments contain one important point: that the relationship between transitive and intransitive sentences is just as much a 'syntactic' relationship as the relationship between active and passive sentences. Any theory of syntax that attempts to handle the one ought also to be able to handle the other by means of the same sorts of syntactic mechanisms. This is a point that I shall elaborate on directly, in connection with the third solution to the problem of transitive and intransitive verbs which has been proposed recently in the literature.

2.7.1.3 *Lexical redundancy rules.* The third of the classical theory's solutions to the problem of transitive and intransitive verbs is due to Chomsky (1970). Chomsky, in contrast to Lakoff and Fillmore, simply accepts the conclusion that transitive and intransitive verbs cannot be related to one another by means of syntactic transformations of the same type that are assumed to relate active and passive sentences, and proposes to account for such relationships by means of an entirely new kind of rule. These rules, which he calls 'lexical redundancy rules,' were originally rather restricted in scope. Recall that in *Aspects,* the subcategorization and selectional properties of lexical items are represented by a set of contextual features associated with each entry in the lexicon. As in phonology, however, a great many of the binary features assigned to lexical items in this manner are in fact predictable. For example, any English verb that takes manner adverbials can also occur without a manner adverb, though the converse is not true. Thus, given the information that a verb has the contextual feature [+ _____ . . . Manner], the fact that it also has the feature [+ _____ . . .] is entirely predictable and should not have to be mentioned explicitly in the lexical entry for verbs. Proceeding on analogy with phonology, Chomsky proposes to incorporate this generalization into the grammar by eliminating all of the "redundant" (i.e., predictable) contextual features from the lexical entries for specific lexical items. The lexical redundancy rules operate on sets of contextual features before lexical insertion, filling in the redundant features on the basis of the features contained in these reduced lexical entries. In the case just discussed we would have a rule in the lexicon of roughly the following form:

(51) [+ _____ . . . Manner] → [+ _____ . . .]

Rule 51 is to be interpreted as an instruction to add the contextual feature on the right of the arrow to a distinctive feature matrix containing the feature on the left.

All of the examples of lexical redundancy rules discussed in *Aspects* are of this rather limited and uninteresting sort. Recently, however, Chomsky has suggested that this mechanism should be extended to account for such relationships as the one between transitive and intransitive verbs. More specifically, suppose that English has a lexical redundancy rule stating that certain verbs with the contextual feature [+ _____ NP] may also appear in the context specified by a feature of the form [+ _____]. If at the same time the rule is formulated in such a way that it systematically revises the selectional features associated with these lexical items so that the features associated with the object of the transitive verb are transferred to the subject of the intransitive verb, we may simply eliminate the latter feature from the lexical entries of the verbs in question, simplifying the lexical representation of these verbs and thereby reflecting the generalization that for certain verbs the existence of an intransitive form is predictable.[12]

While the relationship between transitive and intransitive verbs can certainly be described in this manner, there are some rather serious difficulties with Chomsky's proposal. The main problem is that it seems to provide no reliable criteria for deciding what sorts of syntactic relationships are to be described by means of transformations and which are to be described by means of lexical redundancy rules. Why, for example, should the two components of the passive not be treated as lexical redundancy rules? Lexical redundancy rules certainly have the necessary power, since they can, in effect, "move" selectional features to other positions in a P-marker.

More generally, it appears that exactly the same sort of evidence that is used to motivate such transformational rules as the passive is also used to motivate lexical redundancy rules. The following criteria, for example, are all relevant in both cases: (1) the systematic nature of the

12. For further applications and extensions of this idea, see Jackendoff 1975 and Ruwet 1972.

relationship; (2) the fact that the rules are structure-dependent; (3) the existence of identical selectional restrictions; (4) the fact that (under the lexicalist hypothesis, at any rate) there is a systematic morphological relationship between the verbs in the related pairs of sentences; (5) the existence of systematic semantic relationships between the pairs in question (e.g., *John hit Bill* implies *Bill was hit,* but not vice versa, just as *John rolled the ball* implies *the ball rolled,* but not vice versa). In fact, the only thing that appears to differentiate such "purely syntactic rules" as the passive from such "lexical redundancy rules" as the one relating transitive and intransitive sentences is the theoretical assumption (which is actually simply an artifact of the classical theory of transformations) that the latter must apply in a block before the application of any of the purely syntactic transformations.

The crucial question, then, is whether there is any empirical motivation for maintaining a distinction between syntactic transformations and lexical redundancy rules. I do not believe that there is. In fact, I shall argue that it is a defect of the classical theory that it forces syntactic processes to be arbitrarily divided in this way into two separate rule types. I shall demonstrate this defect by showing (see Section 3.6.1) that the rule relating transitive and intransitive verbs actually enters into the derivation of passive sentences in English. Thus if the analysis of the passive that I shall propose in the next chapter is correct, there can be no principled way of distinguishing between syntactic transformations and lexical redundancy rules.

2.7.2 A New Approach

The three solutions to the problem of transitive and intransitive verbs just discussed have one feature in common: they all take for granted the correctness of the classical theory of transformations. Furthermore, all three fail to come to grips with the basic problem pointed out at the beginning of this section, which is that the classical theory of transformations makes it impossible to account for the relationship between transitive and intransitive verbs in a natural and simple way. The most obvious and straightforward way of accounting for the systematic syntactic relationship between transitive and intransitive sentences in English is to assume that at the point where lexical items are inserted into a P-marker, the object of the transitive and the subject of the intransitive occupy the same syntactic position. Furthermore, the simplest way of doing so is to assume that the subject of the intransitive derives from the object position. This solution, however, is not available in the classical theory for reasons that have already been discussed.

These observations suggest that it is not merely a matter of finding some more sophisticated syntactic analysis (as is assumed by the first two solutions) or of patching up the classical theory in some way (as is assumed by the third solution), but rather that there are fundamental defects in the basic assumptions that underlie the classical theory of transformational grammar. The basic problem, I have suggested, lies in the definition of the notion 'transformation'. It is therefore of some interest that under the revised definition of transformation suggested earlier, it is a simple matter to account for the relationship between transitive and intransitive verbs. In fact, the rule that is needed to do so, NP preposing, has already been stated in Section 2.2.1.

Let us suppose that the structural condition for the insertion of such an intransitive verb as *disperse* has the following form:

(52) *disperse*: ____ NP

Form 52 is to be interpreted as an instruction to fill an empty verb node with the lexical item *disperse,* just in case the sentence contains an object NP and no subject NP.[13] Since the subject NP in English is obligatorily generated by the PS rules, the structural condition specified in form 52 can be met only if an empty NP node is generated in the subject position. Hence the result of inserting the verb *disperse*

13. I assume as a general convention that empty nodes, unless explicitly mentioned in the structural description of a rule, are to be overlooked. Also, since lexical insertion transformations are local, in the sense of Chomsky 1965, we may simply omit reference to the dominating VP and S nodes in the statement of lexical insertion rules. Likewise, unless there is some specific reason for mentioning the category to which a lexical item belongs, I shall generally omit reference to that also in the statement of lexical insertion rules.

(53)

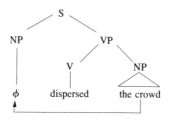

will automatically be a P-marker of the form shown in diagram 53. If no further operations were applied to this structure, it would be rejected as ill formed by the general convention (see Section 2.2.1) requiring that all empty nodes be filled at least once in the course of a derivation. Notice, however, that the rule of NP preposing is applicable to form 53. Informally, this rule says: ''Replace an empty subject NP with a filled object NP.'' The effect of this operation (indicated by the arrow in diagram 53) is of course to produce the correct surface form of the intransitive sentence *the crowd dispersed.*

Consider, in contrast, what happens in the case of the transitive verb *disperse.* Transitive sentences with *disperse* must contain both a subject and an object. Hence, the structural condition for insertion of transitive *disperse* must be as follows:

(54) *disperse*: NP ＿＿ NP

Assuming that transitive *disperse* selects the same class of object NPs as intransitive *disperse* (and in particular that it imposes the same selectional restrictions), the result of applying condition 54 will be a P-marker of the form shown in diagram 55. Here NP preposing is inapplicable, since the subject NP is already lexically filled, and diagram 55 therefore remains as it is.

(55)

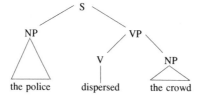

We have thus succeeded in accounting in a simple and natural way for the relationship between sentences containing the transitive and intransitive forms of such verbs as *disperse, roll,* and *melt.* At the point in a derivation where verbs are inserted into P-markers, an NP such as *the crowd* must appear in the object position, whether the verb is transitive or intransitive. Hence the selectional restrictions, and other semantic conditions, governing the objects of transitives and the subjects of intransitives need be stated only once in the lexicon. In the particular case in which the same phonological form can occur in both transitive and intransitive sentences, a simplification can be achieved in the lexicon, since the subcategorization conditions for the two forms of the verb can be collapsed into a single lexical entry.[14]

2.7.3   Causatives vs. Derived Intransitives

The analysis of related transitive and intransitive verbs proposed in Section 2.7.2 is, as far as it goes, an improvement on the solutions available within the classical theory; but the facts are actually rather more complicated than I indicated there. There is strong evidence that in many languages, including English, transitive and intransitive verbs can be syntactically related to one another in at least two ways, depending on whether the transitive or the intransitive verb is the more basic form. I have discussed examples of the first type to some extent elsewhere (Bowers 1973), and have shown that such intransitive sentences as the following:

(56) *a*. The book reads well.
      b. The clothes will wash without any trouble.
      c. Those books lend for only three weeks.
      d. That apartment rents for $200 a month.

---

14. In many languages the operation of NP preposing in intransitive sentences is accompanied by the addition of a special morphological mark. See Babby 1975 for an interesting discussion of a situation of this sort in Russian, and Epée 1975 for a similar situation in Duala.

must be derived syntactically from the basic transitive verbs *read, wash, lend, rent,* and so on, since derived intransitives, in contrast to basic intransitive verbs, invariably have an implied (though not an understood) agent. To say that a book reads well necessarily presupposes that books are the sorts of things that are read by someone. Likewise, to say that clothes will wash easily seems to make sense only under the assumption that washing clothes is an action performed by an active, purposive agent (or alternatively, perhaps, by some machine capable of performing agentive-like actions). Basic intransitive verbs do not necessarily imply the presence of an agent (though in many cases an agent *could* be involved). All of the intransitive verbs mentioned in the preceding section seem to be of this type. Such sentences as the following, for example:

(57) *a*. The ball rolled down the hill.
     b. The crowd dispersed rapidly.
     c. The ice melted.
     d. The coach turned into a pumpkin.

simply describe events that affect the subject NP; no agent is implied. As has been pointed out so frequently, the related transitive forms of these verbs can usually be paraphrased by means of a causative construction, so that *John rolled the ball down the hill* means, roughly, "John caused the ball to roll down the hill"; *the police dispersed the crowd* means something like "the police caused the crowd to disperse"; and so on. The same is not true, however, of the derived intransitives in example 56. Thus we cannot adequately paraphrase the sentence *John read the book* by means of the sentence **John caused the book to read.*[15] These observations strongly suggest that the transi-

---

15. This test does not invariably work. There is nothing wrong with the sentence *John causes that apartment to rent for $200 a month,* though I maintain that it still sounds rather odd, if it is intended as a paraphrase of the sentence *John rents that apartment for $200 a month.* In general, it is not always possible to decide for sure whether a given verb is a derived intransitive or a basic intransitive; there are always unclear cases. This is hardly surprising, however, particularly in such a language as English, in which none of these relationships are morphologically marked.

tive forms of such verbs as *roll, disperse,* and *melt* are derived from basic intransitive forms, whereas just the opposite is true in the case of such verbs as *read, wash,* and *lend.*

Furthermore, in some cases a derived intransitive can be formed from a transitive verb that has itself been derived from a basic intransitive verb (though the reverse process is apparently never found, a fact that will be explained by the analysis to be proposed shortly). In other words, the two processes can be applied in sequence. Consider, for example, the verb *gallop,* as in the following sentences:

(58) The horse gallops.

From a basic intransitive sentence of this kind, we may form the derived intransitive:

(59) The cowboy galloped the horse.

Example 59 is of course a causative sentence, meaning roughly "the cowboy caused the horse to gallop." But now we can use the derived transitive verb *gallop* to form a derived intransitive sentence such as the following:

(60) The horse gallops well.

This sentence is, in fact, ambiguous. Under one interpretation, it means simply that the horse is good at galloping, and there is no implication that he is caused to do so by an outside agent. Under the other interpretation, an agent is implied, just as in the sentences in example 56, and the sentence means that the horse is good (for someone) to gallop, or the like. Ambiguities of this sort can be accounted for only if at least two syntactic processes relate transitive and intransitive verbs and if, furthermore, the two processes can, in certain cases, be applied sequentially.

The next question is how these processes can be represented explicitly in the grammar of English. Consider first the process of causativization. Essentially, this is a process that turns basic one-place predicates into two-place predicates. (In languages with more extensive systems of causativization, two-place predicates can also be turned into three-place predicates.) The simplest way to describe this process would be to formulate a rule that takes an intransitive sentence and adds a new NP argument in the subject position, simultaneously moving the subject of the intransitive verb into the direct-object position. Such a rule cannot even be formulated in the classical theory of transformations, despite the fact that it is the most obvious and straightforward approach to the whole problem. In the framework proposed here, however, it is a simple matter to formulate the necessary rule. By definition 2, CTs are allowed to fill empty nodes with the contents of some filled node of the same category. Nothing in this definition, however, requires the filled node to be one that is already present in the input tree. Hence we may formulate causativization as a combination of two operations, (1) postposing of the subject of an intransitive sentence into the direct-object position and (2) introduction of a new NP in the empty subject position. We may state such a rule in the following fashion:

(61) Causativization:
$X-[_S \text{ NP}:x \, [_{VP} V:y \text{ NP}:\phi \ldots _{VP}] \, _S] -Y \Rightarrow$
$X-[_S \text{ NP}:z \, [_{VP} V:y \text{ NP}:x \ldots _{VP}] \, _S]-Y$
$y = \{roll, \, disperse, \, melt, \, gallop \ldots \}$

Rule 61 will then take a structure such as that shown in diagram 62 and convert it directly into a transitive structure of the form shown in diagram 63. Consider next the inverse process of detransitivization. Once again,

(62)

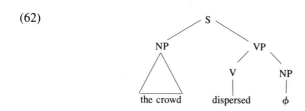

(63)

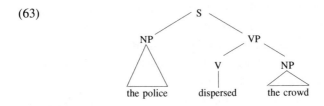

the simplest way to represent this process is to formulate a rule that simultaneously removes the subject NP in a transitive sentence and moves the former direct object into the vacant subject position. Just as in the case of causativization, such a rule is completely impossible to formulate in the classical theory. Notice, in particular, that detransitivization involves an instance of unrecoverable deletion. In the classical theory of deep structure such a rule would be impossible, since it would predict incorrectly that every derived intransitive sentence is infinitely ambiguous. However, in a theory in which semantic interpretation is associated directly with syntactic rules, rather than with abstract underlying structures, such a rule may be formulated with no difficulty. We may state the process in question as a CT of the following form:

(64) Detransitivization:

$X - [_S$ NP:x $[_{VP}$ V:y NP:z ... $_{VP}]$ $_S] -Y \Rightarrow$
$X - [_S$ NP:z $[_{VP}$ V:y NP:ϕ ... $_{VP}]$ $_S] -Y$
$y = \{read, lend, rent, gallop, ... \}$

Rule 64 will then take structures such as the one shown in diagram 65 and convert them directly into intransitive sentences of the form shown in diagram 66. Notice that in our formulation of the processes of

(65)

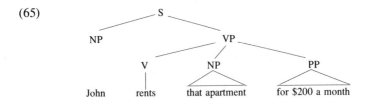

(66)

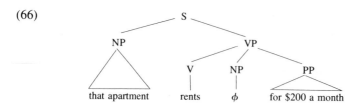

causativization and detransitivization we have already accounted for the ambiguity of sentence 60, because the verb *gallop* happens to be one that permits both processes. Assuming that *gallop* is listed in the lexicon as a basic intransitive verb, we may first form an intransitive sentence such as *the horse gallops well*. We may then apply rule 61, producing such a sentence as *the cowboy gallops the horse well,* after which we may apply rule 64, producing once again the sentence *the horse gallops well,* but now with an entirely different interpretation.

To conclude this section, I shall discuss very briefly an example of causativization in a language that has a more extensive system of causativization than English. I shall take my examples from Duala, a Bantu language spoken in the Cameroons.[16] Duala is particularly convenient for our purposes, since it is similar to English in a number of respects. In particular, it has a fixed SVO word order, and indirect objects, as in English, occur between the main verb and the direct object (the significance of this fact will become obvious shortly). Duala differs from English, however, in having an extensive system of voice markers. Among them is the causative morpheme -*isε*, which is obligatorily added to the verb whenever a basic intransitive sentence is converted into a derived transitive. Hence Duala must have a rule virtually identical to rule 61, the only difference being that the rule in Duala also adds the morpheme -*isε* to the main verb.

A further difference between Duala and English is that in Duala, as in most languages that have a productive, morphologically marked causative construction, the causative morpheme can be added not only

16. See Epée 1976, chap. 2, for a detailed discussion of the causative, and many other voice phenomena, including detransitivization, in Duala.

to basic intransitive verbs, but also to basic transitive verbs.[17] The result, of course, is a sentence with a derived three-place predicate with a new subject, the so-called causative agent. Suppose now that we modify slightly the causativization rule for Duala, writing it in the following manner:

(67) Causativization (Duala):

$$X - [_S \ NP:x \ [_{VP} \ V:y \ NP:\phi \ \ldots \ _{VP}] \ _S] \ -Y \Rightarrow$$
$$X - [_S \ NP:z \ [_{VP} \ V:y \ + \ is\epsilon \ NP:x \ \ldots \ _{VP}] \ _S]-Y$$

If we assume that the range of the variable y includes both transitive and intransitive verbs and that the PS rules for Duala generate VPs of the form $[_{VP} \ V \ NP \ NP \ \ldots \ _{VP}]$, rule 67 immediately predicts that the subject of a basic intransitive verb should appear in the indirect-object position in its causative form. This prediction is of course correct, as the following examples demonstrate:

(68) *a*. baboledi   ba   longi   milongi

       workers   they   build   houses

       'The workers built the houses.'

    b. janea   di   longisε   baboledi milongi

       chief   he   build + Cause   workers   houses

       'The chief had the workers build the houses.'

Though each language has its own variations, the facts of causativization in Duala are quite similar to those in a wide range of typologically unrelated languages that have productive causative constructions. If the analysis of causatives suggested here is correct, it seems likely

---

17. In many languages with a productive causative construction—Turkish, for example—it is possible for derived transitives, as well as basic transitives, to be causativized. In such cases, the causative morpheme may be added twice to the verb, creating a so-called double causative. Obviously such double causatives are easily accounted for in the framework proposed here.

that the analogous facts in other languages can be accounted for in an equally simple and straightforward manner. In particular, it is unnecessary to assume, as many recent writers have done, that causatives are syntactically derived from underlying bisentential structures containing a "causative verb" in the matrix clause and a one- or two-place predicate in the embedded clause.[18] Instead, the surface forms of causative sentences can be generated directly, the altered grammatical relations in causativized sentences being accounted for by CTs similar in form to those proposed above.[19]

2.7.4   Object Detransitivization

We have just seen that the relation between transitive and intransitive verbs in English is not bidirectional. Detransitivization is the process of deriving intransitive sentences from transitive sentences containing a basic transitive verb by suppression of the subject. The inverse process of transitivization derives transitive sentences from intransitive sentences containing a basic intransitive verb by addition of a new subject. If sentences can be derived by addition or suppression of

18. See, for example, Aissen 1974 for a recent analysis of the Turkish causative along these lines.

19. Such rules as 45 are doubtless language-specific manifestations of universal syntactic processes, as are such other familiar "voice" phenomena as passivization. Thus one might attempt to formulate a universal causative rule sufficiently general to account for causativization in any natural language. While the general form of such a universal rule is intuitively clear to anyone who has examined such processes as causativization, it seems doubtful that the introduction of new notational conventions for "capturing generalizations" will be of much help. What is needed, rather, is a linguistic metatheory in which syntactic processes of a general kind can be stated without reference to language-specific rules. One of the persistent problems with the classical theory is the fact that the "level" of deep structure is somehow meant to be language-specific and at the same time is meant to incorporate certain concepts of universal grammar—relational notions, universal categorial notions, and so on. The notion of deep structure has thus served to obscure in an important way the crucial distinction between the theoretical and metatheoretical use of basic linguistic concepts. There is some hope, once the basic methodological unsoundness of the notion 'deep structure' has been exposed, of beginning the task of constructing a linguistic metatheory in which such universal processes as causativization can be formulated in a rigorous and empirically verifiable manner.

subjects, it is logical to suppose that they can be formed by addition or suppression of other constituents as well. In particular, we might expect to find processes that involve the addition or suppression of objects. At least one of these processes has been discussed to a certain extent in the literature of transformational grammar. That is the process of object deletion, which is meant to relate such pairs as the following:

(69) *a.* John ate his dinner.
     b. John ate.

(70) *a.* Bill writes books.
     b. Bill writes.

(71) *a.* John cooks the meals.
     b. John cooks.

(72) *a.* Bill buys equipment for the company.
     b. Bill buys for the company.

As this rule is usually formulated, it requires an underlying abstract object NP, which is supposed to mean (in the case of sentence 69*b*, for instance) something like "unspecified food." This abstract constituent is then optionally deleted by the rule of object deletion.

Obviously what we have here is a process for deriving intransitive sentences from basic transitive sentences by suppression of an object. In the framework proposed here it is unnecessary to posit some abstract underlying object. Instead, we can relate the pairs in examples 69–72 directly to one another by a detransitivization process that removes objects. This process, which I shall term object detransitivization, may be formulated in the following manner:

(73) Object detransitivization:

$$X-[_{VP} \text{ V}:x \text{ NP}:y \ldots _{VP}] -Y \Rightarrow$$
$$X-[_{VP} \text{ V}:x \text{ NP}:\phi \ldots _{VP}]-Y$$
$$x = \{eat, \ write, \ cook, \ldots \}$$

Notice that as we have formulated it, this rule will apply not only to direct objects but to indirect objects as well. This is correct, since indirect objects may also be suppressed.

(74) *a.* John paid the money.
     b. Bill sold the car.
     c. Mary teaches French.
     d. John gives lessons.

Semantically, sentences of this type necessarily presuppose the presence of an indirect object. Thus sentence 74*c*, for example, makes sense only under the supposition that Mary teaches *people* French. Likewise, money that is paid is necessarily paid *to* someone. Rule 73 is not yet adequate, however, for notice that we can have sentences containing an overt indirect object and a suppressed direct object:

(75) *a.* John paid Bill.
     b. Mary teaches people.
     c. Bill wrote his friend.
     d. John promised us.
     e. Mary asked me.

In each case there is necessarily an "understood" direct object of some sort, because verbs of this type are basic three-place predicates.

These observations suggest that the suppression of direct objects and indirect objects are distinct processes, for which separate rules are required. We may formulate the two rules in question in the following manner:

(76) Direct-object detransitivization:

$$X-[_{VP} \; V{:}x \; (NP{:}y) \; NP{:}z \ldots _{VP}] - Y \Rightarrow$$
$$X-[_{VP} \; V{:}x \; (NP{:}y) \; NP{:}\phi \ldots _{VP}] - Y$$
$$x = \{eat, \; write, \; cook, \; pay, \; teach, \ldots \}$$

(77) Indirect-object detransitivization:

$$X-[_{VP} \; V{:}x \; NP{:}y \; NP{:}z \ldots {}_{VP}] -Y \Rightarrow$$
$$X-[_{VP} \; V{:}x \; NP{:}\phi \; NP{:}z \ldots {}_{VP}]-Y$$
$$x = \{pay, \; sell, \; teach, \; rent, \ldots \}$$

Further confirmation of the correctness of this approach can be derived from the fact that there are sentences in which *both* a direct and an indirect object have been suppressed:

(78) *a*. John paid in full.
      b. Mary teaches.
      c. John wrote every day.
      d. They rent at exorbitant rates.
      e. The company ships free of charge.

This fact could not be accounted for if there were a single rule of object detransitivization such as 73. If there is a detransitivization process for both grammatical relations, however, the existence of such sentences is predictable. Notice, incidentally, that since CTs apply in random sequential order, it should be possible to find sentences to which *to* dative movement has applied, followed by direct-object detransitivization. This prediction too is borne out by the facts, as such examples as the following show:

(79) *a*. Bill sells only to his friends.
      b. John rents mainly to college students.
      c. Bill writes to his friends regularly.
      d. They give generously to charity.

Let us consider, finally, the relation between object detransitivization and the processes discussed in Section 2.7.3. Since CTs are hypothesized to apply in random sequential order, we should expect to find cases in which object detransitivization has applied in a transitive sentence that was itself derived by means of causativization. As a matter of fact, the verb that was used earlier, *gallop,* can also be used to illustrate the existence of such processes. Consider the following sentence:

(80) John gallops fantastically.

This sentence is quite different in meaning from the sentence *the horse gallops fantastically*. It does not mean that John runs on all fours in the manner that horses do. Rather, it is the derived intransitive form of such a sentence as *John gallops horses fantastically,* derived by the application of direct-object detransitivization. Hence we have the following sort of derivation:

(81) the horse gallops well → John gallops the horse well → John gallops well

Other examples of the same sort are easy to construct. Thus from the sentence *the dice rolled* we may first form the transitive sentence *John rolled the dice*. To this derived transitive sentence we may apply either subject or object detransitivization. Applying the former gives us such a sentence as *these dice roll badly*; applying the latter gives us such a sentence as *John rolled*. In fact, the sentence *John rolled* is ambiguous, as it may be interpreted as a basic intransitive or as a derived intransitive.

2.7.5   Object Transitivization

Let us consider, finally, the possibility of deriving a transitive sentence from a basic intransitive sentence by the addition of a new object. A priori one might suppose that such cases would be hard to distinguish from instances of causativization. As it turns out, however, in numerous cases it can be shown very easily that a derived transitive could not have been derived by the addition of a subject. Consider the following sentences:

(82) *a*. John $\left\{\begin{array}{l} \text{walked} \\ \text{rushed} \\ \text{ran} \\ \text{marched} \\ \text{rowed} \\ \text{punted} \\ \quad . \\ \quad . \\ \quad . \end{array}\right\}$ the papers over to the dean's office.

b. The men crowded Bill over to the edge.
c. John reached the papers up (over, across, etc.) to Bill.
d. John shouted Bill out the door.
e. Bill called John over to the house.
f. Bill yelled obscenities at the Provost.
g. John is talking nonsense to them.

Corresponding to each of these examples, we find a sentence with a basic intransitive verb—*walk, run, crowd, shout, call,* and so on. It is not the *object* of the transitive verb that appears as the subject of the intransitive, however, as it is in instances of causativization, but rather the *subject*:

(83) *a*. John $\left\{\begin{array}{l} \text{walked} \\ \text{rushed} \\ \text{ran} \\ \text{marched} \\ \text{rowed} \\ \text{punted} \\ \quad . \\ \quad . \\ \quad . \end{array}\right\}$ over to the dean's office.

b. The men crowded over to the edge.
c. John reached up (over, across, etc.) to Bill.
d. John shouted out the door.
e. Bill called over to the house.
f. Bill yelled at the provost.
g. John is talking to them.

Furthermore, it would be impossible to derive such sentences by means of causativization, because in every instance it is impossible for the object of the derived transitive to appear as the subject of the basic intransitive from which it is derived:[20]

(84) *a.* *The papers $\left\{ \begin{array}{l} \text{walked} \\ \text{rushed} \\ \text{ran} \\ \text{marched} \\ \text{rowed} \\ \text{punted} \\ \cdot \\ \cdot \\ \cdot \end{array} \right\}$ over to the dean's office.

   b. *Bill crowded over to the edge.
   c. *The papers reached over to Bill.
   d. *Bill shouted out the door.
   e. *John called over to the house.
   f. *Obscenities yelled at the president.
   g. *Nonsense is talking to them.

These observations, then, show quite conclusively that there must be a process of object transitivization, as well as a process of object detransitivization. This process forms transitive sentences from intransitive sentences by adding an NP argument in the object position. We may state a formal rule to represent this process:

(85) Direct-object transitivization:
$X - [_{VP} \text{ V:}x \text{ (NP:}y) \text{ NP:}\phi \ldots \text{ }_{VP}] - Y \Rightarrow$
$X - [_{VP} \text{ V:}x \text{ (NP:}y) \text{ NP:}z \ldots \text{ }_{VP}] - Y$
$x = \{walk, run, crowd, reach, yell, \ldots \}$

As in the case of object detransitivization, it is necessary to ask whether indirect objects as well as direct objects can be added to a

20. Examples 84*d* and 84*e* are of course not actually ungrammatical. They have the wrong semantic interpretation, however, since their subjects cannot be interpreted as the "shoutee" or "callee," respectively, as would be the case if they were the forms from which the transitives in example 82 were derived.

transitive sentence to form a new sentence with a three-place predicate. Once again, the answer appears to be yes. Consider the following pairs of sentences:

(86) *a.* John bought a book.
    b. John bought Mary a book.

(87) *a.* Bill wrote an article.
    b. Bill wrote the newspaper an article.

(88) *a.* I found a nice ring.
    b. I found Mary a nice ring.

(89) *a.* John promised that he would go.
    b. John promised Mary that he would go.

(90) *a.* Bill asked a question.
    b. Bill asked me a question.

(91) *a.* They got a ticket on the place.
    b. They got him a ticket on the plane.

The verbs in these sentences, in contrast to the three-place predicates discussed earlier, do not seem to need an understood indirect object in the transitive *a* forms in order to make sense. Writing an article, for instance, does not conceptually presuppose a benefactee. As a matter of fact, it appears to be generally the case that benefactive indirect objects that can bemoved into a *for* phrase by the rule of *for* dative movement (see Section 2.5) are added to a basic two-place predicate, whereas indirect objects that move into *to* phrases may or may not be basic. Hence we may formulate a rule of indirect-object transitivization of the following sort:

(92) Indirect-object transitivization:

$$X - [_{VP} \text{ V}:x \text{ NP}:\phi \text{ NP}:y \ldots _{VP}] - Y \Rightarrow$$
$$X - [_{VP} \text{ V}:x \text{ NP}:z \text{ NP}:y \ldots _{VP}] - Y$$
$$x = \{buy, write, promise, ask, \ldots \}$$

Are there basic intransitive verbs that can undergo both direct-object and indirect-object transitivization? In fact, there are. A number of the sentences in example 82 can occur with benefactive indirect objects:

(93) *a.* Run me those papers over to the Dean's office, would you?
   b. I'll row you the boat down to the point.
   c. Reach me down those papers, please.
   d. Call me that taxi over to the house, would you?

Thus such a sentence as 93*b*, for example, would be derived in the following fashion:

(94) I'll row down to the point → I'll row the boat down to the point → I'll row you the boat down to the point

2.7.6   Other Grammatical Relations

Before we leave the general topic of voice relations, it is perhaps worth pointing out that other grammatical relations besides subject, direct object, and indirect object can be either basic or derived. Consider, for example, predicate adjectives and nouns. In such sentences as the following:

(95) *a.* John seems tired.
   b. Bill looks cold.
   c. I consider Harry a nut.
   d. I find you strange.
   e. He is a friend of mine.

the predicate adjective or noun is clearly basic, as is shown by the fact that it cannot be omitted.

(96) *a.* *John seems.
   b. *Bill looks.
   c. *I consider Harry.
   d. *I find you.
   e. *He is.

But in such sentences as:

(97) *a*. They feed them the meat raw.
  b. They always bring you the coffee cold.
  c. They eat the meat raw.
  d. The coffee always comes cold.

the predicate adjective is added to the basic transitive and intransitive verbs *feed, bring, come,* and so on. In the framework proposed here it would be natural to account for this difference by writing a rule to insert an AP or NP in the position reserved for predicate adjectives and nouns after verbs of the latter type, whereas verbs of the first kind would have to be subcategorized in the lexicon to take a predicate AP or NP.

The same is true of PP complements of various kinds. For example, it appears that the *from* phrase in such a sentence as *John bought a book from Bill* is basic (though it can be omitted). The concept of buying apparently requires that two people be involved, the person who is doing the buying and the person from whom the article is being bought. An instrumental phrase of the sort that occurs in *John hit Bill with a stick,* however, does not appear to be a necessary part of the meaning of the verb *hit*. In a theory that has only one device available to it for the expression of relations between lexical items—parenthesization, for instance—this difference cannot be expressed, since both of these phrases are optional. In the theory proposed here, however, these PP complements would be derived by deletion and insertion, respectively:

(98) *a*. John bought a book from Bill → John bought a book
  b. John hit Bill → John hit Bill with a stick

thus reflecting the fact that *buy* is a basic three-place predicate, whereas *hit* is a basic two-place predicate.

2.8   Concluding Remarks: Grammatical Processes

The arguments in this chapter show that even the most basic syntactic processes cannot be adequately stated within the limits imposed by the classical theory of transformations. Worse yet, many of the most fundamental syntactic processes, such as causativization and detransitivization rules of various kinds, cannot be stated at all within the framework of the classical theory. The phenomena examined in this chapter show that syntactic processes must be defined over *surface grammatical relations*. The classical theory fails because it is both too weak and too strong. It is too weak in that it does not permit transformations to refer to grammatical relations. It is too strong in that it permits abstract underlying structures whose reality cannot, in general, be verified empirically. The problem is that no matter how hard one tries to constrain underlying forms, the power of transformational derivations is such that one will always be able to construct absurd and incorrect analyses that are just as compatible with the data as the correct ones.

Underlying these defects, however, is a more fundamental one. If the classical theory in any of its various forms were correct, it would be possible, in principle, to select the correct analysis for any syntactic problem solely on the basis of formal criteria, that is, without taking into account the meaning of the sentences in question. This assumption is fundamentally wrong, for the most important characteristic of grammatical processes in general and of syntactic processes in particular is that they are the reflection, and indeed the manifestation in form, of relationships in meaning. That is why syntactic processes must be defined in terms of grammatical relations, because it is the grammatical relations between constituents that determine (in part) the meaning of sentences. It is precisely because the classical theory does not permit grammatical processes to refer to grammatical relationships that it is forced to resort to the artifice of using abstract underlying forms. The process of causativization, to take a concrete example, cannot be stated directly in the classical theory in terms of surface grammatical relations as a relationship between transitive and intransitive sentences. Hence the only solution is either to relate the transitive and intransitive forms in question indirectly, through some underlying causative structure, or to resort to lexical redundancy rules. The first solution is wrong because it opens the way to all sorts of absurd and unverifiable analyses; the second is wrong because such grammatical processes as causativization are not merely lexical, but syntactic and semantic as well.

The theory proposed here, in contrast, takes it as axiomatic that grammatical processes, by their very nature, are simultaneously syntactic, semantic, and lexical, and that differences in form tend to reflect differences in meaning. It thus does not separate as the classical theory does, the process of forming a sentence from the process of interpreting it semantically. On the contrary, both take place simultaneously. In the succeeding chapters we shall enlarge the scope of our inquiry to take account of complex as well as simple sentences and of mood and topic-comment relationships as well as voice relationships. In every instance we shall see that a theory in which grammatical processes are stated in terms of surface grammatical relations permits a simpler and more elegant description of the facts than is possible in the classical theory.

3 Verb-Phrase Complements

3.1 Introduction

So far I have avoided discussing the so-called passive auxiliary. In this section I shall show that the element *be* + EN is not a transformationally inserted discontinuous constitutent, as is maintained in the classical theory, but rather must consist of the main verb *be* plus a nonsentential (VP) verbal complement. More generally, I shall argue that all of the elements of the auxiliary, except for the element 'Tense,' have a structure of this sort, though I shall present explicit arguments in support of this view only for the passive and progressive auxiliaries, these being the clearest cases.

Generally speaking, tbe arguments against the classical analysis of the auxiliary verbs are parallel to the arguments in chapter 2. In particular, it is possible to show that the classical theory fails to account correctly for the derived constituent structure of sentences containing auxiliary verbs. Furthermore, in a number of clear cases the classical analysis makes it impossible to incorporate linguistically significant generalizations into the grammar of English. After establishing the correct surface form of the passive and progressive auxiliaries, I shall return to the problem of relating the active and passive forms of sentences, and show how this problem relates to the analysis of transitive and intransitive verbs proposed in Chapter 2.

3.2 The Passive Auxiliary

According to the classical analysis of the passive, the auxiliary element *be* + EN is a discontinuous constituent consisting of the unanalyzed verbal element *be* plus the past participial morpheme -EN. This element is introduced immediately to the left of the main verb by the passive transformation itself, accompanied by the permutation of the subject and object and the introduction of the preposition *by*. Implicit in this analysis are a number of dubious claims. First of all, there is no relationship, under this analysis, between the verbal element *be* and all of the other lexical items in English that belong to the category Verb. On morphological grounds alone, this claim is suspect, because *be* takes exactly the same range of verbal affixes as all other members of the category Verb—tense markers, -*ing*, -EN, -ϕ (in infinitives), and so forth. Thus any theory of morphology based on this analysis will necessarily have to assign the same set of verbal affixes to a heterogeneous and unrelated set of categories and unanalyzed elements. In such a theory, it is a complete accident that the passive and progressive auxiliaries behave morphologically like any other member of the category Verb, a conclusion that is surely unacceptable. (The same remarks apply, of course, in the case of the other elements of the auxiliary.) It might still be argued that the auxiliary verbs should be analyzed differently from "normal" verbs at the level of deep structure, even if they behave the same in surface structure. Even if this view could be supported by syntactic evidence, however, it would be of no help to the classical analysis: the classical theory of transformations offers no way of assigning the unanalyzed elements of the auxiliary to the category Verb by a transformational rule, since the transformations cannot introduce new structure, as we have already had occasion to observe.

The view that the auxiliary verbs are unanalyzed 'grammatical morphemes' is further contradicted by the fact that they can occur as the main verb in a wide range of sentence types. In particular, the verb *be* occurs as the main verb in such "copular" sentences as *the book is on the shelf, John is my friend,* and *Bill was happy.* In some treatments, this problem is solved by the introduction of *be* under the special category Copula. This "solution," however, only raises further problems. If *be* belongs to the category Copula in such sentences as those just cited, why does it not also belong to that category when it occurs as an element of the auxiliary? Furthermore, it will now be necessary to assign such verbal affixes as Tense to *three* kinds of elements: verbs, copular elements, and the unanalyzed auxiliary morphemes *be* and *have*. Once again, the fact that all three kinds of elements happen to take the same set of verbal affixes is purely accidental in such a theory.

The third claim made by the classical analysis of the passive auxiliary is that it is introduced by the passive transformation. Notice that the previous claim—that is, that the auxiliary verb *be* is an unanalyzed grammatical morpheme that is related neither to other members of the category Verb nor to the copula *be*—is in fact a corollary of this claim, since transformations cannot introduce new constituent structure. We have already seen the consequences of this sort of analysis for the theory of derived constituent structure in the case of the element *by*, which is introduced by the passive transformation. We might therefore expect to encounter similar problems in the case of the passive auxiliary.

In fact, that is precisely what happens. It is well known that English has, in addition to the normal *be* passive, passive forms with the auxiliary verb *get*:

(1) *a*. John got arrested by the police.
     b. The letter got mislaid.

Sentences of this type have always been a source of embarrassment for the classical analysis of the passive, since there is no non–ad hoc way to account for the obvious parallelism between these examples and such "normal" passive forms as *John was arrested by the police* and *the letter was mislaid*. Worse yet is the fact that transitive verbs as well as intransitive verbs may occur in passive constructions of this sort. Consider, for example, such sentences as the following:

(2) *a*. We got John examined by the doctor.
     b. I had a book stolen from me by a thief.
     c. I saw the building demolished by the workmen.

It might be tempting to try to get around this difficulty by finding some "deeper" source for the sentences in example 1 and 2. One possibility might be to derive the complements in such cases from underlying infinitive complements by means of a rule deleting the element *to be*, as has sometimes been suggested for such similar pairs as *I consider John a fool* and *I consider John to be a fool*.[1] This proposal is easily demolished, however, since the putative underlying forms are in every case either different in meaning from the sentences in question or ungrammatical. Thus the infinitival forms *John got to be arrested by the police* and *we got John to be examined by the doctor* are quite different in meaning from 1*a* and 2*a*, respectively. The sentence **the letter got to be mislaid*, in contrast to 1*b*, is ungrammatical. Likewise, there are no infinitival forms corresponding to either 2*b* or 2*c*: **I had a book (to) be stolen from me by a thief, *I saw the building (to) be demolished by the workmen*. Hence it is impossible to maintain that the *get* and *have* passives are merely reduced forms of underlying infinitive constructions.[2] Finally, notice that even if such a derivation were possible, it would still fail to account for the parallelism between *have* and *get* passives and the normal *be* passives, unless the latter could also be derived from an infinitive construction in deep structure. There is in fact an infinitive construction with *be* in English, but it is quite different in meaning from an ordinary passive form. Thus compare *John was examined by the doctor* and *John was to be examined by the doctor*. Once again, the obvious conclusion is that passive forms cannot be considered to be reduced forms of underlying infinitive complements.

The only systematic attempt that I know of to account for all of the passive forms of English in a unified way is that of Kinsuke Hasegawa

1. For such a proposal, see Rosenbaum 1967. I have argued elsewhere, however (Bowers 1973, chap. 2), that there is no syntactic justification for a rule of *to be* deletion, even in apparently straightforward cases of this sort.

2. This is not to say, of course, that an ''abstract'' sentential complement that always occurs in reduced form in surface structure could not be set up as the ''underlying'' form of these sentences. It is in the nature of things that the classical theory will always be able to invent some hypothetical underlying form in such cases. The point is that there would be no independent syntactic motivation for such an abstract underlying form. It is precisely the aim of the theory proposed here to restrict syntactic representations in such a way that it will be impossible, in principle, to set up abstract deep structures of this sort.

(1968). Hasegawa argues that the *be* passives, like the *have* and *get* passives, should be derived from a bisentential underlying form of the following sort:

(3)　[s John–be [s the police–arrest–John]]

According to this proposal, the underlying active form is contained in a sentential complement of the main verb *be*. The passive rule applies on the lower cycle, after which the usual rule of equi-NP deletion applies obligatorily, deleting the subject of the complement under identity with the subject of the main verb *be*.[3] Clearly, Haswgawa's proposal is an improvement on the classical analysis. In particular, the parallelism of the various passive forms is no problem for him, since the *have* and *get* passives can be derived from exactly the same sort of underlying structure as the *be* passives, the latter differing from the former only in the choice of the matrix verb.

One crucial argument, however, shows that Hasegawa's analysis cannot be correct. Chomsky has observed (1970) that object NPs that are parts of idioms can in certain cases be passivized, producing such passive forms as the following:

(4)　*a*. Tabs were kept on John by the police.
　　b. Advantage was taken of Bill by Harry.

In Hasegawa's analysis, passives of this sort must be derived from underlying forms containing the nouns *tabs* and *advantage* in the matrix sentence as subjects of the verb *be*. But the nouns *tabs* and *advantage* (in the relevant sense) can never be subjects in deep structure, since they occur only in the fixed expressions *keep tabs on, take advantage of,* and the like. As Chomsky notes (p. 220): "Such facts are difficult to reconcile with the proposal that the passive derives from

---

3. Note that the identity condition must, in fact, be met if a grammatical sentence is to result, since there are no sentences of the form *John was Bill arrested by the police*. Presumably it could be argued that this gap is filled by such transitive passive forms as *John had Bill arrested by the police*.

a matrix proposition with an embedded complement.'' The point is that some ad hoc statement will have to be made in order to ensure that parts of idioms occur as subjects only if the main verb is *be*, if there is a complement that has undergone passivization, and so forth, None of these problems arise, of course, if object NPs are moved directly into subject position by a passive rule of the usual kind.

It seems, then, that we are faced with a dilemma. The classical analysis of the *be* passive fails to account for the obvious relationship between *be* passives and *have* and *get* passives. At the same time, any analysis that derives both types of passive from underlying bisentential structures runs into equally serious difficulties of another sort. I shall propose shortly an analysis of the passive auxiliary that escapes both of these difficulties, but before doing so I shall discuss briefly the progressive auxiliary, where problems of a similar nature arise.

3.3   The Progressive Auxiliary

The progressive auxiliary, like the passive auxiliary, is generally assumed to consist of a discontinuous constituent containing the verbal element *be* plus an affix, which in this case is the element *-ing*. Thus the underlying structure of the sentence *John is running* is, according to the classical theory, roughly as follows:

(5)   John-Tns-be-ing-run

The affix *-ing* is attached to the main verb, *run,* and likewise the element *Tns* is attached to the auxiliary verb, *be*, by the familiar rule of affix hopping. We note at once that exactly the same morphological problems arise in the case of the progressive auxiliary as in the case of the passive auxiliary. Hence the criticisms along these lines raised in Section 3.2 are equally applicable here.

More important is the fact that other verbal constructions in English are obviously closely related to the ''progressive aspect'' forms of the verb but have to be treated in an entirely different way from the *be* progressive. In fact, at least three main classes of verbs, plus a few others, require progressive complements. They are: (1) verbs of perception; (2) verbs of temporal aspect; (3) verbs of imagining and remembering; (4) the verbs *have, find, catch, leave, get,* and perhaps a few others. I discuss each of these classes in turn.

Consider first the complements that occur in such examples as the following:

(6) *a*. I heard him walking toward the door.
  b. I felt someone touching my arm.
  c. We smelled the stew burning.
  d. We watched them operating the machines.
  e. They observed us removing the stones.
  f. I saw John entering the room.

It is immediately apparent that there is a close syntactic and semantic connection between sentences of this type and such *be* progressives as *John was walking toward the door, someone was touching my arm,* and *the stew was burning.* Just as the objects of the verbs of perception in example 6 are understood to be in the process of performing the actions described in the *-ing* complements, so the subjects of the corresponding *be* progressives are understood to be in the process of performing those actions. Insofar as these examples have been dealt with at all in the literature, it seems to have been assumed that they should be derived from an underlying form containing a sentential complement whose verb is in the progressive aspect.[4] There are serious difficulties with such a proposal. First of all, these complements, unlike all other sentential complements, can never co-occur with other elements of the auxiliary. Nor can they even occur with the auxiliary

4. An exception is Rosenbaum 1967. Rosenbaum, for reasons that will shortly become apparent, chose to assume a special "progressive" complementizer in such cases. This solution, however, is clearly ad hoc, since every other kind of complement he discusses is derived from one of the three complement types *that, for-to,* and poss-*ing*. Furthermore, Rosenbaum's proposal fails completely to elucidate the relationship between these progressive complements and the progressive-aspect forms with *be*. Other defects inherent in any approach that assumes bisentential structure for these complements will be discussed shortly.

verb *be*, which normally must accompany the progressive affix -*ing* in complements of all types. Thus we find no such forms as the following:

(7)   *a*. *I heard him be walking toward the door.
      b. *I felt someone have been touching my arm.
      c. *We smelled the stew could be burning.
      d. *We watched them could have been operating the machines.

This fact alone is sufficient to cast doubt on the notion that these complements could be derived from underlying sentences, since there would be no non–ad hoc way of *preventing* them from occurring with the elements of the auxiliary under the classical analysis.

Second, observe that none of the usual complement types can serve as the source of such sentences, since all either are ungrammatical or differ in meaning. Thus there are no infinitive complements of the form **I heard him to be walking toward the door, *we smelled the stew to be burning, *we watched them to be operating the machines.*[5] Similarly, sentences containing *that* complements—*I heard that he was walking toward the door, I felt that someone was touching my arm, they observed that we were removing the stones,* and so on—are quite changed in meaning from the sentences in example 6, or in some cases are simply ungrammatical: **we watched that they were operating the machines.* Finally, these complements could not be gerundives, because they cannot occur with the possessive marker *'s*, as in **I felt someone's touching my arm.*[6] Furthermore, if Emonds (1976) is correct in arguing that all true gerundive complements are dominated by NP, then we would expect to find grammatical passive forms of the sentences in example 6. Such passive forms, however, are invariably

5. The sentence *I felt someone to be touching my arm* is possible, but is subtly different in meaning from *I felt someone touching my arm*. The latter is a direct perception, whereas the former is more in the nature of an inference, analogous to the sentence *I felt that someone was touching my arm*.

6. Again, if the sentence *they observed our removing the stones* is possible, it does not have the interpretation of direct perception that is associated with 6*e*, but rather is analogous to *they observed that we were removing the stones*.

ungrammatical: *him walking toward the door was heard by everyone*, *the stew burning was smelled by John*, *them operating the machines was watched by us*.

In the light of these facts, it seems evident that the case for deriving the progressive complements of verbs of perception from underlying full sentences is extremely weak. Any such analysis would have to choose arbitrarily some underlying complement type, whose complementizer would then have to be deleted obligatorily in all cases, or alternatively to invent some new "abstract" complement type (see footnote 2) for which no independent syntactic motivation exists. At the same time, the underlying progressive auxiliary *be* would have to be deleted obligatorily in all cases. And finally, there would have to be a set of restrictions preventing any of the elements of the auxiliary, except for the progressive marker *be* + *ing*, from occurring in the complement sentence.

Similar arguments can be constructed for the other classes of verbs that take progressive complements. Consider verbs of temporal aspect—*begin, start, stop, cease, quit, keep*—which occur in such intransitive sentences as the following:

(8)

$$
\text{John} \left\{ \begin{array}{l} \text{began} \\ \text{started} \\ \text{stopped} \\ \text{continued} \\ \text{ceased} \\ \text{quit} \\ \text{kept} \end{array} \right\} \text{eating his dinner.}
$$

as well as in a few transitive forms:

(9) *a*. They kept the men working until midnight. (Cf. the men kept working until midnight.)
  b. We started him talking about Africa. (Cf. he started talking about Africa.)

As in the case of the verbs of perception, the progressive complements to the verbs of temporal aspect cannot co-occur with any other elements of the auxiliary, as readers may verify for themselves. Furthermore, there is once again no plausible sentential source for such complements. Peter Rosenbaum (1967) analyzes these sentences as instances of intransitive verb-phrase complementation and assumes that they have a poss-*ing* complementizer in deep structure. As such, they occupy a rather anomolous place in Rosenbaum's system, since they are the only examples of poss-*ing* complementation (as Emonds observed in 1976) that are not NP complements. Furthermore, Emonds (1976) has argued persuasively that *all* gerundives (= Rosenbaum's poss-*ing* complements) should be derived from sentences that are dominated by NP. If Emonds is correct, then either the sentences in examples 8 and 9 are NP complements or they must be derived in some other way. But if they are NP complements, it is impossible to explain the fact that originally motivated Rosenbaum's decision to analyze them as verb-phrase complements, namely, the fact that they cannot undergo the passive or appear in focus position in cleft and pseudo-cleft sentences. It would appear that the only alternative, within Rosenbaum's system, is to regard them as instances of verb-phrase complementation with a special -*ing* complementizer. Again, this "solution" seems ad hoc, since there is no limit to the number of special deep-structure complementizers that can be invented to take care of such refractory cases.

It seems that we are left once again with no syntactically motivated deep-structure source for the progressive complements to verbs of temporal aspect. At the same time, it is clear that there is a systematic relation between the progressive complements of these verbs and sentences with the progressive aspect marker *be + ing*. Just as the sentence *John is eating his dinner* asserts that John is in the process of eating his dinner, so each of the sentences in example 8 asserts something about the process in question. Thus *John began (started) eating his dinner* says something about the point at which the process of eating dinner was initiated. Likewise, *John stopped (ceased, quit) eating his dinner* states something about the end point of this process. And finally, *John continued (kept) eating his dinner* asserts that the process of eating dinner was maintained by John.

Exactly the same remarks hold for the third class of verbs that take progressive complements, the psychological verbs of imagining and remembering. Consider the following examples:

(10)   I $\left\{\begin{array}{l} \text{imagined} \\ \text{remembered} \\ \text{visualized} \\ \text{pictured} \end{array}\right\}$ John feeding the pigeons.

Here again it is clear that the object of the matrix verb is in the process of carrying out the action described in the complement. Only in this case the process in question is a mental event taking place in the mind of the person who is the subject of the matrix verb. Exactly the same arguments as before work against a deep-structure sentential source for these sentences, since the progressive complement may not co-occur with any of the elements of the auxiliary and since there is no plausible deep-structure source for these complements. Rosenbaum (1967) also treats these complements as instances of intransitive VP complementation with a POSS-*ing* complementizer. In addition to the arguments against such a view mentioned in connection with the verbs of temporal aspect, there is another argument against treating complements of this sort as instances of POSS-*ing* complementation. Many people find these sentences are possible with the possessive marker:

(11)   I $\left\{\begin{array}{l} \text{imagined} \\ \text{remembered} \\ \text{visualized} \\ \text{pictured} \end{array}\right\}$ John's feeding the pigeons.

There is a subtle difference in meaning, however, between examples 10 and 11. The sentences in example 10 seem, as we might expect, to refer to the direct perception of an ongoing event, though of course the event as well as the perception of it are in this case purely mental acts. The sentences in example 11 seem to refer to the mental reconstruction of a static scene rather than an ongoing process. If this observation is correct (though I myself find the sentences in example 11 interpretable only on analogy with those in example 10, then we have a direct argument in this case against a POSS-*ing* source for the complements to verbs of remembering and imagining.

Consider finally the somewhat miscellaneous set of verbs that occur with progressive complements in such examples as the following:

(12) *a*. She found a bear sleeping in her bed.
     b. They caught him sneaking around the halls.
     c. We left Bill standing in the rain.
     d. I got the children playing hopscotch.
     e. We had Bill stirring the soup for us.

First of all, the semantic connection between these examples and the progressive aspect is even clearer than in the previous cases, since each of the sentences in example 12 actually implies the corresponding sentence with a *be* progressive. Thus if it is true that she found a bear sleeping in her bed, it follows logically that a bear was sleeping in her bed. Likewise, *they caught him sneaking around the halls* necessarily implies *he was sneaking around the halls; we had Bill stirring the soup for us* implies *Bill was stirring the soup for us*; and so on. In addition, all of the syntactic arguments used in the previous cases hold here as well. Thus we do not find other auxiliary elements co-occurring with the progressive complement, nor do we find the auxiliary verb *be*, which is normally required with the progressive affix -*ing*: **they caught him (to) be sneaking around the halls*, **we left Bill (to) have been standing in the rain*, **I got the children can (be) playing hopscotch*, and so on.[7] Furthermore, none of the standard complement

---

7. Notice that we do find the sentence *she found a bear to be sleeping in her bed.* Furthermore, the perfect auxiliary can occur in infinitive complements of this type; for example, *she found a bear to have been sleeping in her bed.* Once again, there is a difference in meaning between these examples and sentence 12*a*. The latter refers to direct perception, whereas the former is an inference, analogous to *she found that a bear was sleeping in her bed.* There is a similar difference in meaning between *I observed Bill feeding the pigeons* and *I observed Bill to be feeding the pigeons,* where the former refers to direct perception and the latter to an inference, paraphrasable as *I observed that Bill was feeding the pigeons.* It should be clear by now that whenever a verb happens to take both an infinitive complement and a progressive complement,

types provides a reasonable sentential source for these progressive complements either. It is interesting to note, incidentally, that the verbs *have* and *get*, which occur in passive constructions of the sort discussed in Section 3.2, also occur in progressive constructions, as in sentences 12*d* and 12*e*.

Summarizing briefly, I have argued in this section (1) that a clear semantic and syntactic connection exists between verbs in the ''progressive aspect'' and the progressive complements to at least four semantic classes of verbs, and (2) that we cannot account for this relationship adequately by deriving all progressive complements from underlying sentential complements containing a verb in the progressive aspect. Note that under the classical analysis of the progressive auxiliary in English, a derivation of the sort that we have just rejected for the progressive complements to verbs of perception, verbs of temporal aspect, and so on, is in fact the only possible way of accounting systematically for the relationship between progressive complements and the *be* progressive. The fact that there is no syntactic motivation for such a derivation thus strongly suggests a fundamental defect in the classical analysis of the progressive auxiliary, just as the existence of the *get* and *have* passives discussed earlier, which likewise cannot reasonably be derived from underlying complements containing a passive sentence, strongly suggests a fundamental defect in the classical analysis of tbe passive auxiliary. I shall show shortly that the only way out of this situation is simply to abandon the classical analysis altogether and to try instead to find some way of relating progressive complements and the progressive-aspect marker to one another directly through the assignment of the proper surface forms to these sentences. But before proceeding to do so, I shall discuss briefly yet a third class of complements that cannot be economically derived from underlying sentential complements.

------

there is a difference in meaning of varying degrees of subtlety. This fact provides a direct argument against the derivation of progressive complements from underlying infinitives by a rule of *to be* deletion.

3.4   Bare-Infinitive Complements

Let us return for a moment to the verbs of perception discussed in Section 3.3. Corresponding to each of the sentences in example 6 (with the exception of 6*e*) is another sentence that contains a complement whose verb is in the infinitive form but lacks the marker *to* that is usually associated with infinitive complements:

(13)   *a.* I heard him walk toward the door.
     b. I felt someone touch my arm.
     c. We smelled the stew burn.
     d. We watched them operate the machines.
     e. I saw John enter the room.

Insofar as these complements have been dealt with at all in the literature, they seem to have been assumed to be merely infinitive complements that have undergone an idiosyncratic rule deleting the underlying infinitive marker *to* (see Rosenbaum 1967:97 for a brief discussion of such a possibility). The logic of this argument, however, is at best dubious. Unlike most "low-level" rules that allow some grammatical morpheme to be deleted optionally for stylistic reasons, the rule of *to* deletion is obligatory. In fact, the putative underlying forms are not even marginally acceptable:

(14)   *a.* *I heard him to walk toward the door.
     b. *I felt someone to touch my arm.
     c. *We smelled the stew to burn.
     d. *We watched them to operate the machines.
     e. *I saw John to enter the room.

Furthermore, there is obviously a close connection between the "bare infinitive" complements in example 13 and the corresponding progressive complements in example 6. In each case the matrix verb refers to a direct perception of some event, as opposed to an inference, as in such a sentence as *I saw that John was entering the room.* The only difference between them is that in the case of the progressive complement the perception in question appears to refer to a part of an ongoing action, whereas in the case of the bare infinitive the perception refers to the whole event. Thus it seems anomolous to say: "I saw John enter the room, but I don't know whether he actually got inside," whereas it does seem possible to assert: "I saw John entering the room, but I don't know whether he actually got inside (because my attention was distracted at just that moment)."

Now we have already seen that in the case of the progressive complements, there are good reasons to suspect that a derivation from an underlying sentential complement is syntactically unmotivated. But if, as I have just argued, a close syntactic and semantic connection exists between progressive complements and bare-infinitive complements, it seems likely that bare-infinitive complements also should not be derived from underlying sentences. In fact, exactly the same arguments that were brought forward in the preceding sections apply here as well. In particular, bare-infinitive complements may not occur with any other elements of the auxiliary, as is shown by the ungrammaticality of such examples as the following:

(15) *a*. *I heard him have walked toward the door.
       b. *I felt someone be touching my arm.
       c. *We watched them can operate the machines.
       d. *I saw John have been entering the room.

Furthermore, the only plausible source for bare infinitives in this case, an underlying infinitive complement, is suspect, partly because there is no independent motivation for an obligatory rule of *to* deletion and partly because a parallel source for the closely related progressive complements is impossible. Hence, it seems that we have found yet another complement type that cannot be plausibly derived from an underlying sentence structure.

A few other verbs in English require a bare-infinitive complement. In particular, the causative verbs *make, let,* and *have* all require a bare infinitive and are ungrammatical if the element *to* is present:

(16) *a*. We made the doctor (*to) examine John.
  b. I let him (*to) leave the house.
  c. I had someone (*to) steal a book for me.

Not surprisingly, these complements cannot occur with any other members of the auxiliary either:

(17) *a*. *We made the doctor have examined John.
  b. *I let him be leaving the house.
  c. *I had someone should (can, will, etc.) steal a book from me.

Once again, it seems that a derivation of these forms from underlying sentential complements with a *for-to* complementizer, while certainly possible in a theory permitting abstract underlying forms, would fail completely to illuminate the special nature of these complements and would in fact lead to unmotivated complications in the grammar.

In the preceding sections, it was shown that corresponding to the progressive and passive auxiliary elements are progressive and passive complements to verbs other than *be* that cannot plausibly be derived from underlying sentential complements of any of the usual types. We have now found a third complement type that seems to have much the same properties as the progressive and passive complements but is infinitival in form. Let us inquire, therefore, whether there is any corresponding element of the auxiliary that requires the following verb to have the form of a bare infinitive. Of course there are such elements: the "modal auxiliaries" invariably require the verb following them to have the unmarked (i.e., *to*-less) infinitival form of the verb:

(18) *a*. You could *be* right.
  b. He should *be* careful.
  c. They may *have* left already.
  d. You can certainly *do* it.

It is interesting to note, moreover, that the only structural difference between the modals and the verbs that take bare infinitives is that the former are intransitive, the latter transitive.

Can it be an accident that corresponding to each of the auxiliary elements modal, progressive, and passive there are complement structures of exactly the same form that exhibit properties quite different from those of normal sentential complements? Such a conclusion hardly seems likely. Furthermore, the only verbal element traditionally assigned to the auxiliary for which we have not found a corresponding complement type is the perfect auxiliary *have* + EN. Despite its very different syntactic and semantic properties, however, the auxiliary verb *have* still requires the verb following it to have the morphological form of a past participal, just as the passive auxiliary *be* does.[8] It is worth pointing out, in fact, that the verbal affixes that occur in the three nonsentential complement types that we have just discussed—namely, the bare infinitive, the progressive form with *-ing*, and the past participial form with -EN—are the *only* affixes, aside from the tense morphemes, that may be attached to a main verb in English.

We are thus left in the following situation. The classical theory picks out three verbal elements (the modal, progressive, and passive auxiliaries) which it treats as unanalyzed grammatical morphemes, despite the fact that each of these elements has a corresponding productive complement type consisting of a verb plus a verbal complement whose head takes the affix $-\phi$ (i.e., the bare infinitive), *-ing*, or -EN—that is, one of the three affixes that are required by the corresponding "auxiliary verbs." The only possible way of accounting for the systematic relationship between the auxiliary verbs and the corresponding complement types is to derive the latter from underlying sentential structures containing the relevant auxiliary elements. In every case, however, there are strong syntactic arguments against deri-

---

8. Even in the case of the perfect auxiliary, there is some evidence of a corresponding construction with *be*. In standard English, only a trace of this construction remains in such a sentence as *John is gone*, in which *gone* is neither a passive adjective (since it doesn't take degree modifiers: **John is very gone, *John is extremely gone, *John is more gone than Bill,* and the like) nor a passive sentence of the usual sort. In many dialects of English, however, the perfect *be* is found with a wide range of intransitive Verbs: *John is left, John is disappeared, Bill is died,* and so forth. A similar situation exists in modern German, of course, in which the perfect auxiliary is either *haben* or *sein,* depending on the type of verb that it accompanies.

vations of this sort, as we have seen. In particular, there is no plausible sentential source among the usually recognized complement types for the progressive, passive, and bare-infinitive constructions. In addition, any such bisentential analysis fails completely to account for the severe co-occurrence restrictions imposed on these constructions. The classical theory thus fails to account adequately either for the so-called auxiliary verbs or for the complement types to which they are syntactically and semantically related.

3.5 A New Proposal

The remarks in the preceding sections strongly suggest that rather than attempt to derive passive, progressive, and bare-infinitive constructions from underlying complement sentences containing passive, progressive, or infinitival auxiliary elements, we might more fruitfully adopt the opposite approach and treat the so-called auxiliary elements as special cases of the passive, progressive, and bare-infinitive constructions. Furthermore, since there is little motivation for treating any of these complement types as underlying sentences, let us try instead to characterize the surface form of these constructions directly, as we have already done in other cases.

What is the surface form of these constructions? For the three complement types just discussed, we have roughly the following structures:

(19) a. NP–V + Tns–(NP)–V + EN–(NP)–(PP)– ...
      b. NP–V + Tns–(NP)–V + ing –(NP)–(PP)– ...
      c. NP–V + Tns–(NP)–V + ϕ–(NP)–(PP)– ...

In all three cases we find a subject NP followed by a tensed verb plus an optional object NP (depending on whether the tensed verb is transitive or intransitive), followed in turn by a second verb with one of the affixes -EN, -ing, -ϕ. This second verb may itself be followed by various complement structures, including NPs, PPs, Ss, and so forth. Furthermore, it is easy to demonstrate that the string consisting of the second verbal element plus its various complements is a constituent. For example, it may be deleted as a unit under identity with another constituent, as in such examples as the following (see Sag 1977 for further discussion):

(20) *a*. John was arrested by the police, but I don't think that Bill was (arrested by the police).
  b. John is going to the movie, but I don't think that Bill is (going to the movie).
  c. John may buy it, but I don't think you should (buy it).

(21) *a*. John got arrested by the police, but I don't think that Bill did (get arrested by the police).
  b. John began eating his dinner right away, but Bill didn't start (eating his dinner) until 8:00.
  c. I will let you borrow my book, but I won't let him (borrow my book).

Also, it may be placed in focus position in pseudo-cleft sentences with *do* (see Bowers 1973, chap. 4, for further discussion), unless it is a passive complement:

(22) *a*. What I am doing is building an airplane.
  b. What I may do is buy an airplane.
  c. What I saw John doing was eating his dinner.
  d. What I made John do was take out the garbage.

Finally, Emonds (1976) has observed that the passive and progressive forms with *be* may be preposed as a unit around *be*:

(23) *a*. Arrested by the police was a well-known businessman.
  b. Coming into the home stretch is Purple Heart.

Since the second verbal element with the complement structures following it is a constituent, and since the head of this constituent is a verb, it makes sense to assume that the whole phrase is simply a VP.

Furthermore, since the first verb may or may not take an object NP, and since the type of verbal complement that may occur to the right is obviously one of its lexical properties, it also makes sense to assume that the main verb, plus object and VP complement, is itself a VP. Putting these observations together, we conclude that the surface form of a progressive complement such as *I saw John entering the room* must be as shown in diagram 24. The structure of such a sentence as

(24)

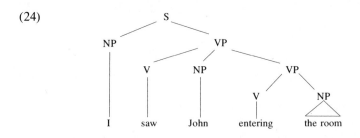

John began eating his dinner is just the same, except that in this case there is no object NP, since the main verb, *begin,* is intransitive (see diagram 25). Consider, finally, the structure of a sentence containing the so-called progressive aspect, such as *John is eating his dinner.*

(25)

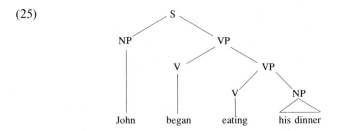

Obviously the only difference between this sentence and sentence 25 is that the main verb is *be* rather than *begin.* Hence we may assign such progressive-aspect sentences a structure of the form shown in diagram 26. The same analysis can be used to account for the relation between *be* passives and *have* and *get* passives. The only difference is that in this case the head of the embedded VP complement must be in the past participial form. Thus we may assign the structure shown in diagram

(26)

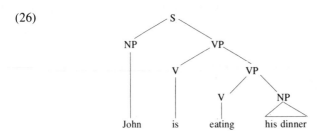

27 to the two passive sentences *John was arrested by the police* and *John got arrested by the police*. For a transitive complement, such as *we had John arrested by the police*, we will have a structure such as that shown in diagram 28.

(27)

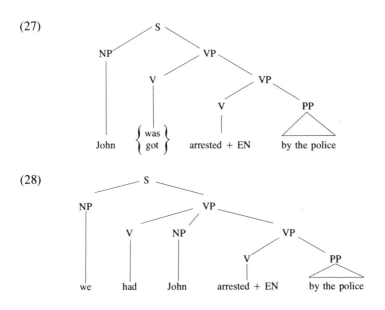

(28)

Consider, finally, the bare infinitives discussed in Section 2.6.3. For such transitive verbs of perception as *see, hear, watch*, as well as for the causative verbs *make, let*, and *have*, we shall have a structure identical to 24 and 28, except that in this case the verb in the embedded VP complement must have the unmarked infinitive form (see diagram 29). Similarly, the intransitive modal verbs, such as *can, will, shall*,

(29)

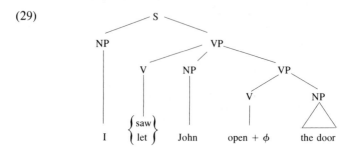

may, might, could, will be assigned a structure of the sort shown in diagram 30.

(30)

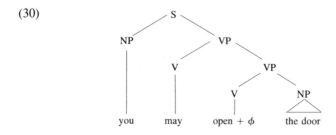

3.6   Arguments in Support of VP Complements

If the structures proposed in Section 3.5 are correct, then the problems with the classical analysis of the auxiliary verbs discussed in Sections 3.2–3.4 disappear completely. First of all, the close syntactic and semantic connection between the auxiliary verbs and the corresponding complement constructions becomes transparent under the VP analysis proposed here. The only difference between the *be* and *get* passive, for example, lies in the choice of the main verb. Otherwise, their structures are identical. Likewise, the only difference between the *be* progressive and the other progressive complements discussed earlier lies, once again, in the choice of the main verb. Second, if we assume that the ability to occur with a VP complement is a lexical property of particular verbs and that the choice of affix associated with the head of a VP complement is determined by the verb in the immediately dominating VP node, then the co-occurrence restrictions noted earlier can easily be accounted for in the lexicon. Third, let us suppose that the elements Tns, POSS, and *to,* which occur in true sentential complements, are generated as the only auxiliary elements by means of a PS rule of the following form:[9]

(31)
$$S \rightarrow NP \ (\ \left\{ \begin{array}{l} \text{Tns} \\ \text{POSS} \\ \text{to} \end{array} \right\} \ ) \ VP$$

We can then explain immediately why all of the true sentential complements can occur with the so-called perfect, progressive, and passive auxiliaries, and at the same time exclude the possibility of deriving VP complements from sentential structures. In addition to these general arguments, a number of specific arguments support a VP analysis for the auxiliary verbs. In particular, it is necessary to discuss the consequences of such an analysis for such matters as the active/passive relation, agentless passives, and *there* insertion. I take up each of these matters in turn.

3.6.1 The Relationship between the Active and the Passive

If the analysis of passive complements proposed in Section 3.5 is correct, then active and passive sentences differ markedly in structure. A passive sentence such as *John was kissed by Mary* has a biverbal structure of the sort shown in diagram 32, whereas its active counter-

---

9. It is necessary to assume that the complementizer elements *Tns,* POSS, and *to* are optional for a number of reasons. Both subjunctive complements, as in *I request that you be on time,* and imperatives, such as *(you) be on time,* require the unmarked infinitival form of the verb. Furthermore, it seems likely that the modals should be regarded as tenseless also, since such alternations as *can/could, may/might,* and *will/ would* do not seem to correspond in any systematic way with the normal present/past alternations of the verb. Finally, a number of modals—*must, ought, better,* and so on—do not alternate at all, and in such cases there is certainly no motivation for assigning some underlying tense marking. The fact that *to* always occurs with that infinitival form and POSS with the *-ing* form can be stated as a general co-occurrence restriction on base forms.

(32)

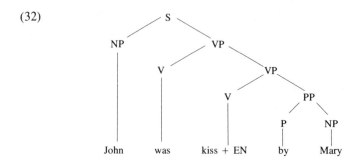

part, *Mary kissed John,* has a simpler structure containing only a single VP, as in diagram 33. The question that now arises is how the syntactic relationship between these two sentence types can be ac-

(33)

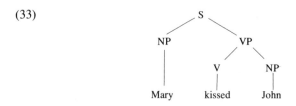

counted for in a theory of the sort proposed here, in which no level of deep structure exists. What we have to account for, basically, is the fact that though the NP *John* in diagram 32 is the grammatical *subject* of the passive sentence *John was kissed by Mary,* it is nevertheless the grammatical *object* of the verb *kiss.* In other words, we have to explain the fact that the NP arguments *John* and *Mary*, though they have different grammatical functions within active and passive sentences, nevertheless bear the same grammatical relation to the verb *kiss* in both cases.

The simplest way to account for these facts is the following. Let us assume that the verb *kiss* is invariably subcategorized in the lexicon to take a subject and an object. Thus we shall write a lexical insertion condition for *kiss* of the following form:

(34) *kiss*: NP _____ NP

We shall also assume that the grammar of English contains two CTs, which I shall call agent postposing and object preposing. Both of these rules apply only in the presence of a verb marked with the passive morpheme -EN. The first rule has the effect of moving the subject of a passive verb into an empty PP and simultaneously supplying the preposition *by*. We may state this rule formally in the following manner:

(35) Agent postposing:

$$X-\text{NP}:x \; [_{\text{VP}} \; V:y + \text{EN} \ldots [_{\text{PP}} \; P:\phi \; \text{NP}:\phi \; _{\text{PP}}] \ldots _{\text{VP}}] -Y \Rightarrow$$
$$X-\text{NP}:\phi \; [_{\text{VP}} \; V:y + \text{EN} \ldots [_{\text{PP}} \; P:by \; \text{NP}:x \; _{\text{PP}}] \ldots _{\text{VP}}]-Y$$

The second rule, object preposing, simply moves an object NP into the subject position to the left of a passive VP.

(36) Object preposing:[10]

$$X-\text{NP}:\phi \; [_{\text{VP}} \; V:y + \text{EN}-Y-\text{NP}:x-Z \; _{\text{VP}}] -W \Rightarrow$$
$$X-\text{NP}:x \; [_{\text{VP}} \; V:y + \text{EN}-Y-\text{NP}:\phi-Z \; _{\text{VP}}]-W$$

Suppose now that we insert the lexical item *kiss* in a tree of the type that is required for passive sentences with *be*. Recalling that it is a lexical property of *be* that it must occur with a passive VP complement, we see that the application of these two lexical insertion rules will result in a structure of the form shown in diagram 37. Clearly, both agent postposing and object preposing are applicable, in sequence, to the structure in diagram 37 and will apply automatically in

10. As Chomsky has noted (1973), there must be a condition ensuring that the sequence V(+ EN)-Y constitutes a semantic unit, in some sense that has yet to be made precise. A natural way to incorporate this observation into the grammar might be to require that any expression $y-y'$, where y' is any (non-null) expression associated with the variable Y, has the property of being listed in the lexicon as a whole. Thus all "idiomatic" fixed expressions that permit pseudo-passive forms—*take advantage of, pay heed to, look up to, look at,* and so on—would have to be specified fully in the lexicon with their constituent structures and inserted into P-markers as units. See Katz 1973 for a general treatment of idioms along these lines.

(37)

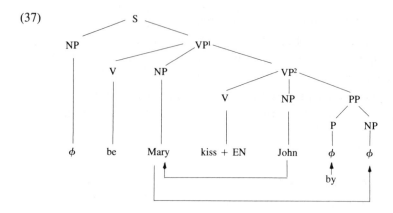

the manner indicated. The result is a P-marker of the form shown in diagram 38. Now all we have to do to produce the correct form of the passive sentence *John was kissed by Mary* is get the NP *John* in the

(38)

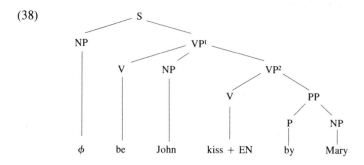

subject position before *be*. Recall, however, that we formulated a rule in Chapter 2 that will accomplish just this result. That is the rule of detransitivization, which moves an object NP into the subject position. What we have here is simply the special case in which the variable in subject position is null. Note that if we had inserted the transitive verb *have*, along with its subject, detransitivization would be inapplicable at this point and we would come out with the sentence *I had John kissed by Mary*. Finally, notice that if the main verb in VP[1] is *get*, we can produce either sentence *I got John kissed by Mary* or, by the application of detransitivization, the intransitive passive form *John got kissed by Mary*.

Consider next what happens if the VP complement is a progressive or bare-infinitive complement. In such cases, the rules of agent post-posing and object preposing will be inapplicable, since they apply only in the presence of a passive -EN morpheme. Such a sentence as *John is eating his dinner* would therefore be derived in the manner shown in diagram 39. Here the only applicable rule is detransitivization, which

(39)

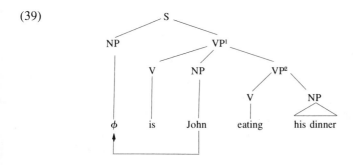

moves the NP *John* into subject position, producing the progressive sentence *John is eating his dinner*. Note that if we had inserted in VP¹ such a transitive verb as *see,* detransitivization would be inapplicable and we would come up with a sentence such as *we saw John eating his dinner*.

Finally, let us consider a complex sentence such as *the ducks were being fed by the kids*. Such a sentence will be derived by the rules we now have from a structure of the sort shown in diagram 40. On the VP²

(40)

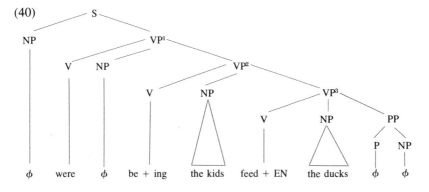

cycle agent postposing and object preposing will apply, producing the string $\phi - were - \phi - the\ ducks - feed + \text{EN} - by - the\ kids$. On the VP[1] cycle, detransitivization applies, moving the NP *the ducks* in front of the progressive verb *be + ing*. Finally, on the S cycle detransitivization is applicable once again and moves *the ducks* into its final position as the subject of the sentence. Obviously these rules, along with the appropriate lexical insertion rules for verbs, will produce an indefinite number of complex sentences of various kinds, containing VP complements.

If derivations of this sort are correct, we can immediately deduce several important conclusions. First of all, we have accounted correctly for the syntactic relationship between active and passive sentences without having to assume the existence of a level of deep structure. Even though the *structures* of active and passive sentences differ radically, the conditions for insertion of such a transitive verb as *kiss* are the same in both cases. Thus at the point where the verb *kiss* is actually inserted into a P-marker, we have the same subject and object whether we are dealing with an active structure or a passive structure. If the semantic relationship between the verb and its arguments is determined by the structure at the point where heads of phrases such as verbs are actually inserted, the analysis proposed above accounts completely for the relationship between active and passive forms without forcing us to assume that actives and passives are structurally identical at some more abstract level of syntactic representation.

Second, if the derivation of passive sentences proposed here is correct, there can be no principled way of distinguishing between such "syntactic" rules as the passive and such "lexical" rules as detransitivization. The reason is simply that the rule of detransitivization, which in the classical theory must be treated as a lexical redundancy rule, actually enters into the derivation of passive sentences. As we have already seen, the classical theory fails completely to account for the relationship between "normal" *be* passives and other passive constructions with *have* and *get*. The analysis proposed here does not suffer from this defect. But in order to achieve this result, it is necessary to give up the in any case rather arbitrary distinction between syntactic and lexical rules. Putting the matter slightly differently, we may say that any theory that treats passivization as a syntactic phenomenon and the relationship between transitive and intransitive verbs as a lexical phenomenon must necessarily fail to account for the syntactic and semantic relationship between *be* passives and *have* and *get* passives, thus failing to capture an important generalization of English syntax.

Third, notice that implicit in the analysis proposed above is the assumption that the VP node, like the nodes S, NP, and AP, is cyclic. In the derivation of passive sentences, the lexical insertion rule for *kiss* must be applied on the VP^1 cycle, whereas the lexical insertion rule for *be* must be applied on the S cycle. In fact, we may assume, without loss of generalization, that *all* of the major category nodes are cyclic nodes, and that the lexical insertion rules for heads of phrases, as well as the CTs, apply on each syntactic cycle. Since it is the lexical insertion rules for heads of phrases that (in part) determine the semantic interpretation of sentences, the resulting theory is one in which the process of generating a well-formed surface structure and assigning it a semantic interpretation are carried out simultaneously at every point in a derivation. Hence there is no strict separation, as there is in the classical theory, between the process of forming a sentence and the process of assigning it a semantic interpretation. This theory does not imply, of course, that there is no distinction between syntax and semantics. What it does imply, however, is that there can be no principled way of separating the semantic and the syntactic "motivation" for particular rules of grammar. In other words, no evaluation procedure for syntax is independent of semantic considerations.

3.6.2 *Agentless Passives and Stative Passives*

It is well known that the *by* phrase that occurs in passive sentences in English is completely optional. English is not peculiar in this respect. In every language that has a productive process of passivization, an explicit agent phrase is optional. Furthermore, in a great many languages, passives without agent phrases are preferred, and in some it is very difficult to get informants to accept explicit agent phrases at all. The only way that the optionality of the agent phrase in passive sentences can be accounted for in the classical theory is by hypothesizing an abstract, underlying subject NP for all agentless passive sentences, which is then deleted optionally after the application of the passive rules. In many cases this analysis is not too implausible. Thus such a sentence as *Mary was kissed* can be paraphrased by one with an explicit agent, such as *Mary was kissed by someone*, suggesting that there really is an ''understood'' agent lurking beneath the surface of all agentless passives. Yet the evidence for a deleted agent phrase is purely semantic and could be handled equally well by rules of implication. Thus the basis for the feeling that there is an understood agent in such sentences as *Mary was kissed* could rest simply on the fact that any sentence containing an explicit agent phrase, such as *Mary was kissed by John*, logically implies the truth of the sentence *Mary was kissed* (though the opposite, of course, is not true). Hence there is certainly no need to assume the existence of a syntactic rule of agent deletion.

Furthermore, there are good reasons to suppose that no analysis that derives passives from underlying actives can account adequately for the distribution of the passive *by* phrase. Notice, first, that quite a few verbs in English can appear *only* in the passive: *be rumored, be said, be made,* and so on. In order to account for such cases, these verbs must be marked with an ad hoc role feature requiring that they undergo the passive obligatorily. Worse yet is the fact that there are passive verbs that can never have an explicit agent phrase and for which an understood agent cannot even be posited on semantic grounds. Consider the verb *be born,* as in *John was born on May 1.* Not only can this verb not take a *by* phrase of any sort, but there are not even any semantic grounds for supposing that there is a deleted agent. In particular, notice that the active verb *bear,* as in *she bore three children,* is not a paraphrase of the passive form just cited. If only a few idiosyncratic verbs such as *be born* had this property, this would not constitute a particularly strong argument against agent postposing, since some ad hoc device could always be invented to account for these exceptional cases. It happens, however, that there is a productive class of such agentless passive forms in English. Consider examples of the following sort:

(41) *a*. The city is now destroyed.
      b. The door is closed.
      c. The painting is practically finished.
      d. That patch is obviously not painted.
      e. The window should be fixed by now.
      f. The last time I saw it, the vase was broken.
      g. The job is almost done now.

Passives of this kind, which I shall refer to as "stative passives," are clearly different in meaning from the corresponding passives with agent phrases:

(42) *a*. The city has been destroyed by the enemy.
      b. The door is closed every day (by the janitor).
      c. The painting that Bill started was finished by John.
      d. That patch has obviously never been painted by anyone.
      e. The window should be fixed (by someone).
      f. The vase was broken in front of my very eyes.
      g. That job is done by the maid.

The sentences in example 41 refer to completed states, whereas the normal passive sentences in example 42 describe actions. Furthermore, a stative passive, unlike a normal passive, can never take an explicit *by* phrase:

(43) *a*. *The city has been destroyed by the enemy for a week now.
      b. *The door is practically closed by Bill.
      c. *The painting is practically finished by the artist.
      d. *That patch is obviously not painted yet by anyone.
      e. *The window should be fixed by the workmen by now.
      f. *The last time I saw it, the vase was broken by Bill.
      g. *The job is almost done now by the maid.

nor can it be interpreted as having an understood agent.

It is important to observe that in English stative passives are *not* adjectives. In particular, they differ from such passive adjectives as *amused, frightened, tired, upset,* in that stative passives, unlike passive adjectives, can never occur with the set of degree modifiers, such as *so, too, very, enough,* comparatives, equatives, and so forth, that characteristically appear in the specifier of APs. Thus the following sentences with passive adjectives are grammatical:

(44) *a.* Bill is very tired.
     b. Mary was so upset that she couldn't speak.
     c. I was more amused than Bill was.
     d. John wasn't as frightened as I was.
     e. He was too astonished to say a word.

whereas similar sentences containing stative passives are impossible:

(45) *a.* *The door is very closed.
     b. *The job is more done than I thought it was.
     c. *This painting isn't as finished as that one.
     d. *That patch is obviously so painted that it's impossible to see the color underneath.
     e. *The book will probably be too stolen to sell.

Another fact that reveals that stative passives are not APs is that they cannot appear after the verb *seem,* which takes only predicate APs:

(46) *a.* *The door seems closed. (Compare *the door seems to be closed.*)
     b. *The job seems done.
     c. *The painting seems finished.
     d. *That patch doesn't seem painted.
     e. *That book seems stolen.
     f. *The city seems destroyed.
     g. *The window seems fixed.
     h. *The vase seems broken.

whereas passive adjectives may appear freely in this position:

(47) *a*. Bill seems tired.
    b. Mary seems upset.
    c. The children seem amused.
    d. They seem frightened.
    e. She seemed astonished at the news.
    f. The place seems very run-down.
    g. This room seems very neglected.
    h. They seem interested in our plan.

The point is that we have found a productive class of passive sentences that can never take an explicit *by* phrase and for which there is not even the possibility of assuming an abstract underlying indefinite agent phrase. The existence of these stative passive forms thus provides a compelling argument against any theory that has to derive passives from underlying actives, since there is simply no plausible source for them.

All of these problems disappear at once if passive sentences are assigned a structure different from that of active sentences. First of all, verbs that have no active form, such as *be rumored*, do not have to be marked as obligatorily undergoing the passive transformation, but can simply be listed in the lexicon with an -EN form. Thus *rumor* will have a lexical entry of the following form:

(48) *rumor*: NP ____ + EN NP

Normal transitive verbs, in contrast, which have both active and passive forms, will be entered in the lexicon in the following fashion:

(49) *kiss*: NP ____ (+ EN) NP

Notice that we now have a mechanism that can be used to account for the behavior of such impassivizable verbs as *resemble, cost,* and *weigh* as well. A verb that is transitive in form but lacks a passive, such as *resemble*, will simply be entered in the lexicon as follows:

(50) *resemble*: NP _____ NP

thus ensuring that it is inserted only into active structures.

Consider next how we are to describe stative passives. As we observed above, stative passives simply lack an agent phrase altogether. Hence we may account for this fact by listing verbs that have a stative passive form, such as *destroy*, with a lexical entry of the following form:

(51) *destroy*: _____ + EN NP

This procedure will permit us to construct P-markers of the form shown in diagram 52, to which object preposing and detransitivization

(52)

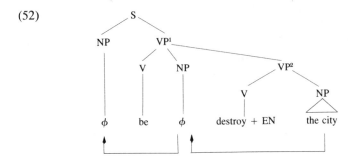

will apply, producing *the city is destroyed*. Furthermore, since at the point where *destroy* was inserted there was no subject NP, it will be interpreted correctly as a stative passive. Note that such a verb as *be born* will have an entry of exactly the same form. The only difference between *be born* and *destroy* is that the latter also has a lexical entry of the form indicated in item 49, whereas the former is more limited in its distribution. (Actually, of course, the verb *bear* does have a lexical entry of the form NP _____ NP, as in *she bore the child*; what it lacks is an entry of the form NP _____ + EN NP.)

Let us consider finally how we might account for the agentive interpretation of agentless passive forms, that is, the interpretation of *the city was destroyed* as "someone (or something) destroyed the city."

Actually, we have already had occasion to deal with a situation of this sort in Chapter 2. Recall that in order to account for the interpretation of such derived intransitives as *that apartment rents for $200 a month,* I proposed a rule of detransitivization that converted basic transitive sentences into intransitive sentences with an agentive interpretation. What we have now is a similar situation. Basically, passivization is a process whereby a sentence with a basic two-place predicate is converted into one with a one-place predicate. The difference between passivization and detransitivization is that in the first case the subject of the transitive verb can either be deleted or be demoted into a PP, whereas in the second case it can only be deleted. As we noted earlier, many languages have a strong preference for the agentless form of the passive and in some cases deletion of the agent is actually obligatory. These observations suggest that the simplest way to account for agentless passives is to reformulate the rule of object preposing so that it is parallel in its effect to detransitivization. More concretely, suppose that we reformulate object preposing in the following way:[11]

(53) Object preposing:

$$X-NP:z \; [_{VP} \; V:y \; + \; EN-Y-NP:x-Z_{VP}] -W \Rightarrow$$
$$X-NP:x \; [_{VP} \; V:y \; + \; EN-Y-NP:\phi-Z \; _{VP}]-W$$

Stated in this fashion, object preposing will now convert a structure of the form shown in diagram 54 into an agentless passive structure such

---

11. Given the strong similarity of object preposing and detransitivization, we might consider the possibility of actually combining the two rules into a single rule. Whether or not we can do so depends on the status of derived intransitives of the following form:

(*a*) John takes advantage of easily.
(*b*) Mary talks to without any trouble.
(*c*) The child won't give in to easily.

The question is whether detransitivization can apply to the same range of objects and pseudo-objects as passivization can. If it can, it would appear that the two rules are generalizable. If not, the two rules are probably distinct, though parallel in form and function.

(54)

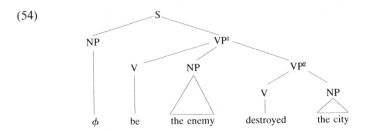

as that in diagram 55, to which detransitivization will apply in the usual fashion, producing the sentence *the city was destroyed*, correctly

(55)

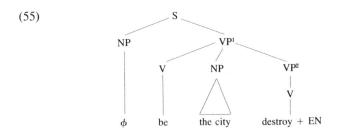

interpreted as agentive rather than stative. If we want to produce passive sentences with explicit agents, we must first apply agent postposing, after which object preposing will be free to apply as usual.

3.6.3   There *Insertion*

I have argued in the preceding sections that the so-called progressive and passive auxiliaries *be* + *ing* and *be* + EN are not discontinuous constituents at all, but rather are base forms consisting of the intransitive verb *be* plus a progressive or passive VP complement. An analysis of this sort requires a stage in the derivation of passive and progressive sentences at which we have a structure of the following form:

(56) [$_{NP}$ ϕ]–be–NP–VP

We might therefore ask whether any real evidence supports the assumption that the subject of *be* occurs in object position at some stage in the derivation of passive and progressive sentences. I have already pointed out that the relationship between transitive and intransitive *get* provides evidence in support of such a derivation, since we can then account for the relationship between these transitive and intransitive passive and progressive forms in exactly the same way we have accounted for the relationship between other transitive and intransitive forms, namely, by the rule of detransitivization. It happens that in the case of the passive and progressive with *be,* however, there is actually direct evidence for the existence of an intermediate stage of the form indicated in item 56.

It is well known that in English, existential sentences with *there* can be formed not only with the "copula" *be*, but also with the *be* of the passive and progressive. Thus we find such sentences as the following:

(57) *a*. There were some kids playing a baseball game in the vacant lot.
  b. There were many demonstrators arrested by the police.

It should be noted immediately that sentences of this kind pose very serious problems for the classical theory of transformations, since no reasonable derived constituent structure can be assigned to them. Either the subject NP must be inserted between the passive or progressive auxiliary and the main verb or the auxiliary *be* must be moved to the left of the subject NP. The first alternative produces a highly implausible derived constituent structure in which the subject NP ends up being dominated by the node Aux (or perhaps by VP). The rule required by the second alternative bears some resemblance to the rule of subject-auxiliary inversion, which is involved in the formation of questions. It is easy to show, however, that the two rules differ. Subject-auxiliary inversion moves the first element of the auxiliary, no matter which auxiliary it is, whereas the rule involved in the existential sentences must take the progressive or passive auxiliary, along with any preceding elements of the auxiliary: *there have been many people arrested by the police, there must have been many people arrested by the police,* and so on. Worse yet, such an analysis necessarily claims that the element *there* is not the subject. But then it is impossible to explain the fact that subject-auxiliary inversion applies over *there*, just as it does over other subject NPs: *were there many people arrested by the police?*, *have there been many people arrested by the police?*, *were there some kids playing baseball in the vacant lot?*, *could there have been some kids playing baseball in the vacant lot?*, and so forth. No matter how we choose to formulate the rules involved in the formation of existential sentences, the classical theory necessarily assigns absurd and incorrect derived constituent structures to such sentences as those in example 57.[12]

Notice, however, that if the analysis of passive and progressive sentences proposed here is correct, the sentences in example 57 can be derived immediately by the rule of *there* insertion, discussed in Section 2.3. Furthermore, if we assume that the rule inserting *there* in the empty subject node applies directly to the hypothesized intermediate stage (form 56), we can eliminate entirely the need for a rule of subject postposing, thereby simplifying the grammar considerably. Thus consider the passive sentence *many demonstrators were arrested by the police*. According to our analysis, the structure of this sentence just before the application of detransitivization on the final S cycle is as shown in diagram 58. Suppose now that we simply allow the rule of

(58)

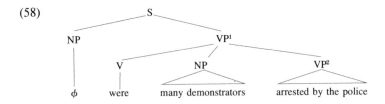

there insertion optionally to fill in an empty subject NP with the fixed element *there*, just in case it is followed by the verb *be*, plus an object

---

12. It might be possible to rescue the classical theory from these consequences by the introduction of feature complexes of the form [+ there, + NP], as Chomsky proposes (1970). As there is very little motivation for weakening the theory in this way, however, the necessity of introducing such devices into the classical theory is merely a symptom of the inadequacy of its theory of transformations.

NP. Formulated in this manner, *there* insertion will apply automatically to such a structure as 58, producing the correct derived constituent structure (diagram 59). If we choose not to apply *there* insertion, then

(59)

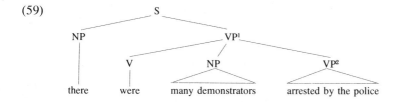

detransitivization will necessarily apply, producing the sentence *many demonstrators were arrested by the police*. Obviously, exactly the same rules will apply in progressive structures, accounting for such sentences as 57*a*.

These observations suggest, naturally enough, that a rule of subject postposing is unnecessary in the derivation of existential sentences with the ''copula'' *be* as well. In particular, if we assume a structure of the sort shown in diagram 60 for the sentence *a mouse is in my room*,

(60)

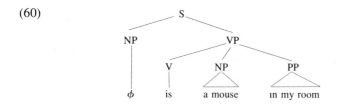

we may apply either *there* insertion, in which case we get the existential sentence *there is a mouse in my room,* or detransitivization, producing the sentence *a mouse is in my room*. Hence we may simply eliminate entirely the rule of subject postposing, thus simplifying the grammar significantly.

This observation suggests, incidentally, a convenient way of removing an otherwise ad hoc restriction on *there* insertion. It has frequently been noted (though never explained) that *there* insertion fails to apply when the copula is followed by a predicate AP or NP: **there is some-*

one my friend, *there is someone angry,* and the like. Notice, however, that if sentences with a predicate AP or NP were to be derived from structures of the form NP-*be* $\{^{NP}_{AP}\}$, then under the analysis just proposed, it would be impossible to produce existential forms for these constructions, since there would never be an empty node in the subject position into which *there* could be inserted.

If these arguments are correct, the hypothesized intermediate stage in the derivation of passive and progressive sentences (form 56) actually shows up in existential sentences with *there,* thus providing direct evidence in support of the proposed analysis. The rule of *there* insertion, however, can be used to provide still another sort of argument in support of a VP analysis of passive and progressive complements. Notice first that the rule of *there* insertion applies only to the *subjects* of sentences. This is shown by the fact (already mentioned in Section 2.3) that when *there* is made the subject of an infinitive complement, it can be raised and passivized just like any other subject NP. Now let us consider a sentence containing both a progressive and a passive complement, such as *a baseball game is being played in the vacant lot,* and ask at what point the rule of *there* insertion is applicable. In fact, *there* can be inserted only in the topmost subject NP, as is shown by the fact that only the first of the following two sentences is grammatical:

(61) *a*. There is a baseball game being played in the vacant lot.
      b. *There is being a baseball game played in the vacant lot.

This fact follows automatically, if the progressive complement is a VP, since the only place where the subject of a sentence occurs in such a structure is in the topmost S. As is indicated in diagram 62, the only point at which *there* insertion is applicable is on the topmost S cycle. In particular, *there* insertion is *not* applicable on the VP[1] cycle, despite the fact that it is followed by the verb *be* plus an indefinite NP, since the empty NP immediately dominated by VP[1] is not a subject NP. If the progressive VP complement in diagram 62 were derived from an underlying sentence, nothing would prevent the application of *there* insertion on the lower S cycle, followed by NP preposing on the

(62)

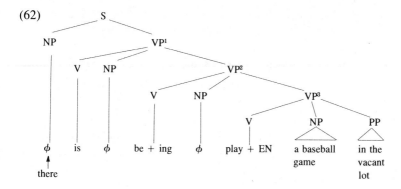

topmost S cycle, thus producing the ungrammatical sentence 61*b* (see diagram 63). Furthermore, exactly the same is true of the progressive

(63)

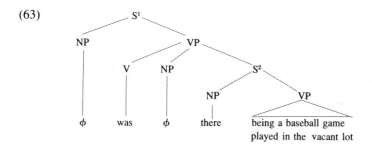

complements of verbs other than *be*. Thus all of the following sentences are ungrammatical:

(64) *a*. *I saw there being a baseball game played in the vacant lot.
 b. *There started being a baseball game played in the vacant lot.
 c. *We found there being a baseball game played in the vacant lot.
 d. *I tried to imagine there being played a baseball game in the vacant lot.

though the corresponding sentences without *there* insertion are of course perfectly acceptable:

(65) *a*. I saw a baseball game being played in the vacant lot.
 b. A baseball game started being played in the vacant lot.

    c. We found a baseball game being played in the vacant lot.
    d. I tried to imagine a baseball game being played in the vacant lot.

Again, the ungrammaticality of the sentences in example 64 follows automatically from a VP analysis of progressive complements, since the NP to which *there* insertion must be applied is not a subject NP, but rather the object of the main verbs *see, start, find, imagine.* Finally, notice that the same test can be used to demonstrate that bare-infinitive complements must also be VPs, since such sentences as the following are also ungrammatical:

(66) *a.* *I had there be a patient examined by a doctor.
     b. *I made there be someone examined by the doctor.
     c. *We let there be some people be examined by the doctor.
     d. *The students watched there be a patient examined by the
        doctor.

whereas the corresponding sentences without *there* are perfectly acceptable:[13]

(67) *a.* I had the patient be examined by a doctor.
     b. I made someone be examined by the doctor.
     c. We let some people be examined by the doctor.
     d. The students watched the patient be examined by the doctor.

13. Notice, however, that if the modals and the perfective auxiliary *have* are also analyzed as main verbs plus a VP complement, it is difficult to explain the fact that *there* insertion may apply over both of these elements (see p. 137). This is, in fact, the strongest argument I know of for considering the modals and *have* to be true auxiliary verbs rather than main verbs. In the case of perfective *have*, this conclusion is quite plausible, since (as we noted earlier) no verb other than *have* takes a perfective complement. In the case of the modals, however, this conclusion is not so happy, since some other verbs do take bare-infinitive complements. Another way to account for the fact that *there* insertion can apply over a modal would be to assume that modals take sentential complements. In that case such a sentence as *there may be a mouse in my room* could be derived by means of raising from a structure of the form [s [NP ϕ]–may [s there–be–a mouse–in my room]]. As the modals behave like main verbs that take sentential complements in other ways as well (as we shall see in Chapter 4), at least some bare infinitives may be sentences. It is quite possible, therefore, that the only VP complements are the progressive and passive complements, as well as certain of the bare-infinitive complements; that the modals require sentential complements; and that the perfective element *have* is the only true auxiliary verb.

The facts concerning *there* insertion, then, provide strong support for the analysis of the passive and progressive complements proposed in this chapter. Furthermore, the facts just discussed provide a direct argument in support of my claim that transformations must be allowed to refer to the grammatical function of constituents, and not merely to a linear string of symbols meeting the condition of analyzability. For it is crucial, if *there* insertion is to be formulated properly, that it apply only to *subjects* of sentences. But if it is to do so, we must specify not only the symbols NP–Aux–*be*–NP, but also the node that immediately dominates the first NP—in other words, specify the grammatical relation of the first NP.

3.6.4 *The* Have *construction*

To conclude this section I shall discuss in some detail a rather complex case of multiple ambiguity, and show that all of the considerations brought forward thus far combine to provide an explanation for each of the interpretations associated with the example in question. Chomsky (1965) noted that such a sentence as the following is ambiguous in at least three ways:

(68) I had a book stolen.

The various interpretations that can be assigned to this sentence can be made clear by a consideration of the following three possible elaborations (taken directly from Chomsky 1965): (1) "I had a book stolen from my car when I stupidly left the window open";[14] (2) "I had a book stolen from him by a professional thief who I hired to do the job"; and (3) "I almost had a book stolen, but they caught me leaving the library with it." Notice that the first two interpretations can also be associated with sentences containing a bare-infinitive complement, but the third cannot. Thus such a sentence as:

14. Note that in many dialects sentence 68 can be disambiguated in favor of this interpretation by the addition of a PP whose head is *on* and whose object must be coreferential with the subject of *have*; for example, *I had a book stolen on me.*

(69) I had someone steal a book from me.

can mean either (1) "someone stole a book from me" or (2) "I hired someone to steal a book from me." (Note again that this sentence can be disambiguated in favor of the first interpretation by the addition of an *on* phrase: *I had someone steal a book on me.*) We shall consider these two interpretations first, and then take up the third.

When we recall the analysis of VP complements proposed earlier, it is evident that the only difference between examples 68 and 69 is that the former requires a passive VP complement whereas the latter requires a bare-infinitive complement. If we ignore for the moment the ambiguity of these sentences, the structure of these two sentences must be roughly as shown in diagram 70. Depending on whether the verb in

(70)

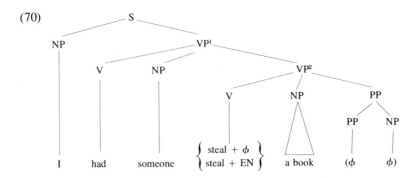

the VP complement has the passive suffix -EN or a bare infinitive, and whether or not a subject is present, we shall derive either *I had a book stolen (by someone)* or *I had someone steal a book.* Notice, however, that the grammatical relations in the VP complement at the point where lexical items are inserted is the same in both cases. Thus the NP *a book* is the object of *steal* and the NP *someone* is its agent, wherever these NPs finally end up.

Since the grammatical relation of the NPs *the book* and *someone* to the verb *steal* is obviously the same in all of these cases, the source of the first two ambiguities must lie in the relation between the verb *have* and its complement. The first interpretation can be paraphrased by

144

such a sentence as "It happened to me that a book was stolen" while the second interpretation can be paraphrased by such a sentence as "I caused a book to be stolen." The second interpretation is causative and agentive, the first interpretation is not. Notice further that sentences with progressive complements are ambiguous in exactly the same way. For example, the sentence *we have someone stealing eggs* can mean either that someone is stealing eggs from us or that we have got someone stealing eggs for us. Now observe that these sentences are disambiguated in favor of the causative interpretation when the verb *have* is put in the progressive. Thus *I am having a book stolen, I am having someone steal a book*, and so on can have an interpretation analogous only to the paraphrases "I am causing a book to be stolen," "I am causing someone to steal a book," and so forth. This observation suggests that the noncausative interpretation is analogous to tbe normal possessive meaning of *have*, as in such a sentence as *I have a book*, since the progressive is impossible with possessive *have*: **I am having a book*. We can therefore account for the first interpretation of these sentences by permitting possessive *have* to occur in such contexts as the following:

(71) *have*: NP ____ NP (VP)

When no VP complement is present, we will derive a normal possessive sentence, such as *I have a book*; when there is a VP complement, we will derive one of the sentences discussed above in the first, noncausative interpretation.

That leaves us only with the problem of accounting for the causative interpretation of these *have* sentences. Recall that in Chapter 2 I proposed to account for the causativization of intransitive verbs by means of a special syntactic rule that introduced a new (causative) agent and simultaneously demoted the subject of the intransitive verb. At the same time I pointed out that in languages with a morphological causative construction, this process typically applies to transitive verbs as well as intransitive verbs. English, however, differs from such languages in requiring a paraphrastic construction for the causative forms of transitive verbs. This paraphrastic construction is the causative *have* construction that I have just been discussing. Thus the simplest way of accounting for the second, causative interpretation of sentences 68 and 69 is to formulate a special causativization rule that has the effect of introducing an agent NP along with the paraphrastic verb *have*.[15] We may formulate such a rule in the following fashion:

(72) *Have* causativization:

$$X-NP:\phi \; [_{VP} \; V:\phi \; NP:x \; VP:y \ldots _{VP}] -Y \Rightarrow$$
$$X-NP:z \; [_{VP} \; V:have \; NP:x \; VP:y \ldots _{VP}]-Y$$

Note that it is unnecessary to specify the type of VP complement, since, as we have just seen, causative *have* can occur with all three types of VP complement. Furthermore, there appear to be no constraints on what may occur in the NP position to the right of *have*. Hence it appears that 72 is in fact a rather general rule of causativization in English.

Consider finally the third possible interpretation of sentence 68, represented by the elaboration ''I almost had a book stolen, but they caught me leaving the library with it.'' As we noted earlier, there is no ''active'' form of the complement VP corresponding to this interpretation, so that sentence 69 has no interpretation of this sort. The way to account for this third interpretation becomes obvious as soon as we recall the discussion of stative passives in Section 3.6.2. Given the fact that *have* is subcategorized to take passive VP complements and the

15. A similar paraphrastic causative construction in French uses the verb *faire*. This construction has recently received extensive discussion in the transformational literature. See Kayne 1975, Herschensohn 1979, and the references therein for discussion. From the point of view adopted here, the analyses of the *faire* construction that have thus far been proposed suffer from exactly the same defects as standard transformational treatment of causativization. In particular, it is unnecessary in the framework proposed here to assume that sentences with causative *faire* are derived from underlying bisentential structures. Instead, the verb *faire*, along with the causative agent, can simply be introduced directly into simple sentences somewhat along the lines suggested here for English. Actually, the *faire* construction in French is somewhat more like a morphological unit. This point has been demonstrated conclusively in the references cited above.

further fact that stative passives can be formed productively in normal *be* passives, the theory predicts that we should expect to find a stative passive interpretation associated with the *have* passive as well. I propose, therefore, to derive the third interpretation of sentence 68 from a structure such as that shown in diagram 73. Note that it is the possessive *have* that occurs here, because sentence 68, under this interpretation, is nonagentive and cannot occur in the progressive.

(73)

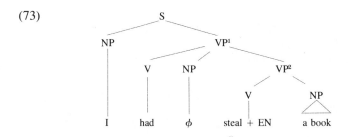

We see, then, that the third interpretation of the *have* construction is simply the transitive form, as it were, of the stative passive construction with *be*. Not only does the derivation in diagram 73 correctly predict the lack of an explicit agent phrase under the third interpretation, as well as the fact that the third interpretation has no corresponding form with an "active" VP complement (since stative passive forms never have active counterparts), but it also gives just the right semantic results. The sentence *I have the book stolen* (under the third interpretation) describes a completed state rather than an action, just as the stative passive sentence *the book is stolen* does. The only difference is that in the former the "possessor" NP is specified, whereas in the latter it is not. Further evidence that this is the correct analysis is provided by the fact that such adverbs as *now, practically, almost, for a week, by now,* which typically serve to disambiguate an agentless passive in favor of a stative interpretation, also disambiguate an agentless *have* construction in favor of the stative interpretation:

(74) *a.* We have the door closed finally.
    b. We have the job almost done now.

   c. The artist has the painting practically finished.

   d. John obviously does not have that patch painted yet.

   e. The thief we hired should have the book stolen by now.

   f. He really should have the window fixed by now.

   g. By 1965 the Americans already had most of North Vietnam's major cities destroyed.

In contrast, consider the same sentences in which the VP complement has the nonstative, agentive interpretation:

(75) *a*. We had the door closed on us (by someone).

     b. We had the job done by a professional.

     c. The artist had the painting finished by a friend.

     d. John obviously did not have that patch painted by anyone.

     e. The thief we hired should have had the book stolen by someone more competent than himself.

     f. He really should have had the window fixed by a glazier.

     g. In 1965 the North Vietnamese had most of their major cities completely destroyed by American bombers.

The sentences in example 75 differ in that in some cases the subject of *have* is agentive, in others it is not, in accordance with the first two interpretations. All of them differ from the sentences in example 74 in having a nonstative passive complement, and it will be noted that in every case the VP complement must have an agent phrase, either overt or understood. Hence the third interpretation of the ambiguous sentence 68 turns out, remarkably, to provide entirely independent motivation for the analysis of stative passives proposed earlier.

4 Infinitive Complements: On The Unity of Equi and Raising

4.1. Introduction

Up to this point I have been primarily concerned with syntactic processes that take place within the boundaries of a single clause. In this chapter I shall be concerned with the derivation of infinitive complements in English. In particular, I shall be concerned with such examples as the following, in which the infinitive complement contains no overt subject NP in surface structure:[1]

(1)   *a.* Bill tried to open the door.
      b. John seems to have left.
      c. I persuaded Harry to take out the garbage.
      d. We believe that theory to have been disproved.
      e. I expect you to arrive at 8:00.
      f. I expect to arrive at 8:00.
      g. He promised Mary to bring the book.

As is well known, the classical theory derives sentences of this sort from two radically different deep-structure sources, depending on the type of verb in the matrix clause. In the case of such verbs as *try, persuade,* and *promise,* it is assumed that the subject of the infinitive complement is deleted under identity with some underlying NP in the matrix clause. In the case of such verbs as *seem* and *believe,* the underlying matrix clause contains one less NP than appears in surface structure, and the extra NP is introduced by the rule of raising, which takes the subject of the infinitive complement and puts it in some

---

1. Infinitive complements that do contain overt subject NPs (what I shall refer to as "true *for-to* complements") will be discussed in detail in Chapter 5.

specified position in the matrix clause. Sentence 1*c*, for example, would be derived from a structure of the sort shown in diagram 2. The

(2)

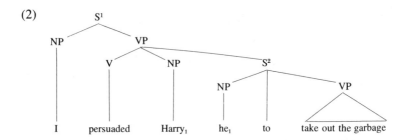

rule of equi-NP deletion then erases the pronominal subject of S^2, provided that it is coreferential with (in this case) the object of the matrix clause, *Harry*. Sentence 1*d* would be derived from an underlying structure of the sort shown in diagram 3. The rule of raising then

(3)

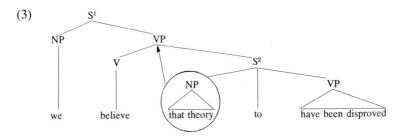

applies (as is indicated in diagram 3), removing the subject NP *that theory* from the infinitive complement S^2 and creating a derived object in the matrix clause. The result in both cases is a derived constituent structure of the following form:

(4) $[_S$ NP $[_{VP}$ V–NP $[_S$ to VP]]]

In the case of such intransitive verbs as *try* and *seem*, the derivations are similar, except that for *try* the subject of the infinitive complement is deleted under identity with the subject of the matrix clause, while for *seem* the subject of the infinitive complement is raised into the subject position.

The arguments in support of these derivations are well known and need not be repeated here. It is sufficient to observe that such an analysis explains why the surface object of such a verb as *persuade* or *believe* is the understood subject of the infinitive complement, whereas the surface subject of such a verb as *try* or *seem* is the understood subject. At the same time it explains why the surface subject of *try* and the surface object of *persuade* have a deep grammatical relation to the main verb in the matrix clause, whereas exactly the opposite is true for *seem* and *believe*.

While the details of this analysis have been the subject of much discussion, the basic observations that support it have never been questioned, and indeed are beyond dispute. They are simply facts that any theory of grammar must account for in some manner. The particular explanation for these facts that is assumed within the classical theory of transformational grammar is deficient in a number of respects. I shall try to demonstrate in this chapter not only that it is deficient, but that it is in fact untenable, if certain linguistically significant generalizations concerning the formation of infinitive complements are to be captured in the grammar of English.

I shall first take up raising and show that this rule cannot be stated adequately under the classical theory of transformations. At the same time I shall propose an alternative formulation of raising as a CT, which escapes these difficulties. I shall then discuss the relationship between equi-NP deletion and raising, and show that an analysis that splits up the process of infinitive formation into two separate rules fails to express a crucial generalization of English syntax. I shall then propose an alternative analysis that does not have this defect, and show that if it is correct, there cannot be a level of deep structure of the sort that is assumed in the classical theory of transformational grammar.

4.2. Raising

Let us start by considering the rule that raises the subject of an infinitive complement into the subject position for such intransitive verbs as *seem, happen, appear*. According to the classical theory (as represented in, say, Rosenbaum 1967), such a sentence as 1*b* is derived from a deep structure containing a *for-to* complement in the subject position (see diagram 5). The rule of extraposition then applies,

(5)

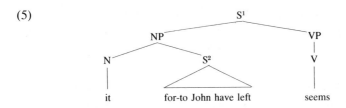

producing a structure of the form shown in diagram 6, after which raising obligatorily replaces the pronoun *it* in subject position with the subject NP *John* in the extraposed infinitive complement. Among the

(6)

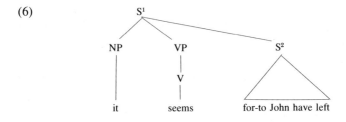

arguments in support of this derivation is the observation that there are parallel sentences containing a *that* complement which do not undergo the rule of raising:

(7)   It seems that John has left.

If such examples as 7 are also derived from underlying structures containing a subject complement, the only difference in underlying structure between 1*b* and 7 is that the former contains a *for-to* complement and the latter a *that* complement. Hence at the level of deep structure, it is claimed, these sentences share a common underlying structure.

There are serious difficulties with this proposal, however. First of all, the rule of extraposition, which in all other cases is optional (cf. *that John spoke to him surprises me, it surprises me that John spoke to him; for Bill to leave would upset Mary, it would upset Mary for Bill to leave*), must be made obligatory for just this specific class of verbs, since the hypothesized underlying forms are actually ungrammatical:

(8)   *a*. *That John left seems.
      b. *For John to leave seems.

Second, the *it* that appears in subject position in sentence 7 does not behave like the anaphoric *it* that appears in all other cases of extraposition, but rather like the "empty" *it* that occurs as the subject of weather verbs (see Section 2.4). This point can be established in a number of ways. First, anaphoric *it* can be pseudo-clefted, whereas the nonanaphoric *it* cannot. Thus the sentence *it is certain that John has left*, which is derived by means of extraposition from the grammatical sentence *that John has left is certain*, has a grammatical pseudo-cleft form, whereas sentence 7 does not:[2]

(9)   *a*. What is certain is that John left.
      b. *What seems is that John has left.

Second, notice that the subject complement of *certain* can be replaced by an indefinite pronoun and can be questioned:

(10) *a*. Something is certain.
       b. What is certain?

2. There is an apparent counterexample to this claim. Corresponding to *it happened that John saw the thief* is the pseudo-cleft form *what happened was that John saw the thief*. This is the exception that proves the rule, since the sense of *happen* in the pseudo-cleft form is quite different from the sense of *happen* in the nonclefted form. In the former, *happen* refers to the occurrence of an event and has the same sense as in the sentence *something happened* (which can of course be questioned: *what happened?*). In the latter, the sense is quite different. A rough paraphrase would be *by chance, John saw the thief*.

whereas this is not the case for the supposed subject clause in sentence 7:

(11) *a*. *Something seems.
      b. *What seems?

The same is true, of course, for the empty *it* that is the subject of such weather verbs as *rain* and *snow*:

(12) *a*. *Something rained.
      b. *What rained?

In fact, there is a close correlation between extraposability and the occurrence of anaphoric *it*. Whenever extraposition is optional, the pronoun that is left behind is anaphoric; whenever extraposition is supposedly obligatory, the pronoun that is left behind behaves like the nonanaphoric "empty" *it*.

Hence verbs of the *seem* class are exceptional in two ways. First, extraposition, which is normally optional, must be made obligatory, and second, the pronoun that is left behind must somehow be marked nonanaphoric, in contrast to the normal case, where the pronoun left behind by extraposition is anaphoric.

When we recall the discussion of nonanaphoric *it* in Chapter 2, these observations strongly suggest two conclusions: (1) that the complements of *seem, appear,* and so on are not derived by obligatory extraposition at all, but rather must be generated directly in postverbal position; and (2) that the nonanaphoric *it* that appears as the subject of such verbs is not a deep-structure pronoun, but rather is transformationally inserted. In short, the syntactic evidence indicates that the correct structure for such sentences as 1*b* and 7 is roughly as follows:

(13) [$_S$ seem [$_S$ John has left]]

where the verb *seem* is acting not as a predicate whose subject is a full proposition, but rather like a modal operator of some sort, modifying the proposition in the embedded sentential complement.

A deep structure such as form 13, however, is impossible in the classical theory for the same reason that it is impossible to derive sentences with weather verbs from underlying subjectless deep structures: because there is no way to prevent numerous other sentences from occurring without subjects if the subject node is made optional in deep structure. The only other alternative would be to derive such sentences from underlying forms containing *it* as the subject, and somehow marking this *it* as nonanaphoric. I have already shown in Chapter 2, however, that nonanaphoric *it* must be transformationally introduced in order to account for the fact that it cannot be passivized.[3]

It should now be apparent why the classical theory is forced to derive the complements of verbs of the *seem* class from underlying subject-NP complements. If we are to formulate the rule of raising without assuming underlying subjectless deep structures, there must be some element in the subject position in the matrix clause to serve as a "place holder" for the raised subject of the infinitive complement. Given such paraphrases as sentence 7, it is logical to suppose that this element is simply the pronoun *it*. The only source for epenthetic *it* in the classical theory, however, is an extraposed underlying subject-NP complement. It follows that the only possible source for the complement in such sentences such as 1*b* and 7 is an NP complement in subject position.

All of these problems can be avoided, of course, if we give up the classical theory of transformations and reformulate raising as a CT that simply replaces an empty subject NP in the matrix clause with the subject of an infinitive complement. Furthermore, if we assume that there is a rule inserting nonanaphoric *it* in subject position whenever the complement is a *that* clause rather than an infinitive complement, we can derive both sentences from a structure such as that shown in diagram 14. If the complement sentence has the complementizer *that*, then the rule of *it* insertion must apply, filling in the empty subject NP

---

3. Note that the complements of *seem, happen,* and the like cannot be treated as object-NP complements, since we would then expect to find passives of the form **that John has left was seemed (by it), *that John left was happened (by it),* and so forth.

(14)

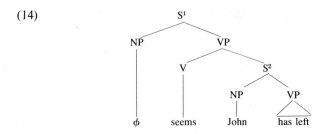

in the matrix clause with nonanaphoric *it* (see diagram 15). (If it does not apply, then of course the derivation will be rejected, since the subject NP will have no way of getting filled in.) If, however, the

(15)

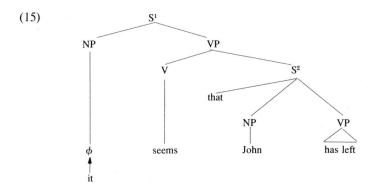

complement sentence is an infinitive, then raising must apply, replacing the empty subject NP in the matrix clause with the subject of the infinitive complement, as in diagram 16.

(16)

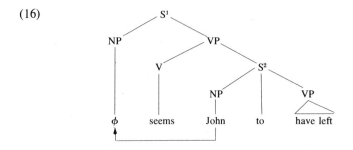

If this analysis is correct, the verb *seem* can simply be sub-categorized in the lexicon to take a sentential complement with either a *that* complementizer or an infinitival complementizer (as is semantically correct), and the rest follows automatically. Furthermore, all of the problems mentioned earlier with the classical analysis disappear completely. In particular, there is no need for an ad hoc condition making extraposition obligatory for just this class of verbs, and the lack of pseudo-cleft forms is explained automatically, since the *it* that appears as the subject of sentence 7 is the transformationally inserted nonanaphoric *it* rather than the anaphoric *it* left behind by extraposition. Finally, notice that this analysis explains neatly those cases in which the infinitive complement has no paraphrase at all with a *that* clause. Consider, for example, such a verb as *begin*, which takes an infinitive complement but not a *that* clause:

(17) *a.* John began to run.
     b. *It began that John ran.

In such cases, the classical theory is forced to assume an underlying subject-NP complement containing an anaphoric *it*, despite the fact that there is no surface evidence whatsoever for such an underlying form. Under the analysis proposed here, the only thing that needs to be said about *begin* as opposed to *seem* is that it takes only an infinitive complement. Such sentences as 17*a* will then be derived in exactly the same manner as 1*b* (see diagram 18). Thus it seems that we have found

(18)

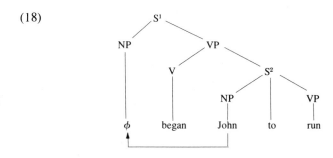

yet another case in which the classical theory of transformations forces one to assume abstract underlying structures for which there is no syntactic justification. This assumption in turn requires that ad hoc conditions be placed on the otherwise perfectly general rule of extraposition, and at the same time leaves completely unexplained the non-anaphoric interpretation of the *it* that appears in such sentences as 7.

To conclude this section, let us consider briefly raising into object position. Peter Rosenbaum (1967) attempts to formulate raising into subject and object position as a single rule by deriving such sentences as 1*d* in a manner parallel to intransitive sentences with *seem*. In particular, he assumes that the infinitive complement in such a sentence as *we believe that theory to have been disproved* is an object-NP complement in deep structure; that extraposition applies obligatorily to it; and that the pronoun *it* that is left behind by extraposition is replaced by the subject of the extraposed infinitive complement. In this case, the problems are, if possible, even worse than in the case of raising into subject position. Thus it has been pointed out by Lakoff and Ross (1966) that extraposition not only must be made obligatory, but must also be made to apply vacuously. At the same time, they argue, the application of extraposition to object-NP complements produces an incorrect derived constituent structure in which the extraposed infinitive complement is immediately dominated by S rather than by VP. These criticisms have led most scholars to assume that raising simply moves the subject of the infinitive complement directly into the object position in the matrix clause, rather than replacing the pronoun *it*. This solution, however, makes it impossible to formulate raising into subject position and raising into object position as a unitary process, a problem that has yet to be solved in a satisfactory manner within the classical theory. Later on I shall discuss this problem in detail. For the moment, it is sufficient to note that raising into object position can be naturally formulated as a CT of exactly the same type as raising into subject position. Suppose that for sentence 1*d* we assume a structure of the sort shown in diagram 19. We can then formulate raising into object position as a CT that replaces an empty object NP in the matrix clause with the subject of the infinitive complement. The only difference between raising into sub-

(19)

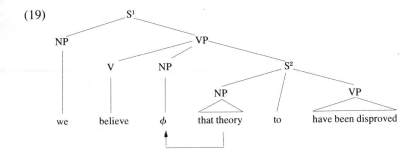

ject position and raising into object position is that in the first case the empty NP is in subject position, whereas in the second case it is in object position. We can therefore formulate raising as a CT that replaces any arbitrary empty NP in the matrix clause with the subject of the infinitive complement:

(20) *Raising*:

$$[_S X - NP:\phi - Y [_S NP:x - to - VP - Z] W] \Rightarrow$$
$$[_S X - NP:x - Y [_S NP:\phi - to - VP - Z] W]$$

Furthermore, if such a transitive verb as *believe* is subcategorized to take a subject NP and if such an intransitive verb as *seem* is subcategorized to take no NP arguments, then the raising of the subject NP into object and subject positions, respectively, will be determined automatically by the interaction of raising with the lexical insertion rules for the matrix verb.

In the absence of any other considerations, then, the theory of transformations proposed here will at the very least permit raising into subject and object position to be formulated as a unitary process, whereas such formulation is impossible under the classical theory of transformations.[4]

4. I shall not discuss here the contention in Chomsky 1973 that there is no rule of raising into object position. It should be obvious that if the theory of CTs is correct, there must be such a rule. In fact, the existence or nonexistence of such a rule is potentially crucial to a decision between the classical theory of transformations and a

4.3.   Equi-NP Deletion and Raising Are the Same Rule

We shall consider next the relationship between raising and equi-NP deletion. I shall argue that there is no syntactic motivation for splitting

---

theory that takes the domain of a transformation to be the whole P-marker. The point is that raising into object position is a rule that alters the grammatical relations within a P-marker but does not alter the linear order of the elements in the structural description. From the point of view of the classical theory, such a rule is ad hoc and unmotivated, as Chomsky observes. In fact, strictly speaking, it is not even statable, unless ad hoc conditions on the application of transformational rules are permitted. From the point of view of a theory that allows transformations to refer to grammatical relations, the analysis proposed by Chomsky is ad hoc and unmotivated, since it requires such a sentence as *Bill is believed to have left* to be derived by passivization directly "down into" the infinitive complément without regard for the grammatical relation of the NP that comes directly after the passivized main verb. In short, the evaluation measure for the classical theory of transformations will deem a grammar simpler if it has no rule of raising into object position, whereas the evaluation measure for a theory of the sort proposed here will deem a grammar simpler if it does have a rule of raising into object position. It should be noted further that the two theories make different predictions about the derived constituent structure of such sentences as *John believes Bill to have left*. If the classical theory is correct, and there is no rule of raising into object position, then there should be a major constitutent break between *believe* and *John to have left*. But if transformations must refer to grammatical relations, and there is a rule of raising into object position, then the major constituent break should come after the raised subject *John*. Hence we have a crucial case in which the two theories make different predictions about derived constituent structure. This matter has been discussed at length by Postal (1974), who brings forward a wide variety of syntactic arguments in support of the view that the major constituent break must occur after *John,* as is predicted by a theory that incorporates a rule of raising into object position. Although many of Postal's arguments are, in my opinion, inconclusive, there are enough good ones to demonstrate that there must be a rule of raising into object position. Hence Postal's arguments provide indirect support for the theory of transformations proposed here, which explicitly requires that the grammatical function of the constituents mentioned in the structural description of a transformation be specified. I believe, however, that there are more compelling theoretical and empirical arguments in support of this view (such as the many arguments brought forward in this book) than those discussed by Postal. In fact, Postal does not really come to grips with any of the fundamental problems with the classical theory of transformations (though he comes close on many occasions), at least in part because Postal, like Chomsky, believes in the existence of some sort of underlying abstract structure (though he and Chomsky disagree, of course, on the precise nature of this underlying level of representation). As I shall show shortly, however, the existence of a level of deep structure (however abstract or nonabstract one may consider it to be) is incompatible with the assumption that transformations are defined in terms of grammatical relations. Though Chomsky's up the process of infinitive formation in English into two such unrelated rules as raising and equi. Consequently, any theory that does so necessarily fails to capture an important generalization of English syntax, and is therefore inadequate.

Notice, first of all, that there is no *purely syntactic* test that can be used to distinguish the structures that are said to be derived by means of equi-NP deletion from those that are said to be derived by means of raising. In particular, the two constructions behave identically in the following respects:[5]

I. For both equi verbs and raising verbs, the infinitive complement is impassivizable:

(21) *a.* *To open the door was tried by Bill.
    b. *Harry to take out the garbage was tried by Bill.
    c. *To arrive at 8:00 was expected by everyone.
    d. *To bring the book was promised Mary by John.

(22) *a.* *To have left was seemed by John.
    b. *(For) that theory to have been disproved is believed by everyone.
    c. *(For) you to arrive at 8:00 is expected by Bill.[6]
    d. *To arrive at 8:00 is expected you by Bill.

---

conception of "deep structure" is much closer to what I would consider the correct surface form of sentences than is Postal's, Chomsky is compelled to assume a level of deep structure because of his insistence on the correctness of the classical theory of transformations. In particular, he is forced to invent an elaborate system of constraints on the application of transformational rules, most of which are completely unnecessary in a theory of the sort proposed here.

5. There are apparent counterexamples to this claim among the true *for-to* complements (i.e., infinitive complements that have overt subject NPs). I shall show in Chapter 5, however, that true *for-to* complements must be derived somewhat differently from the subjectless infinitive complements with which I am concerned here.

6. For some speakers such sentences as *I expect for you to arrive at 8:00* are acceptable, and for them such passive forms as 22*c* and such pseudo-cleft forms as 25*e* are also acceptable. This fact simply shows that the verb *expect* must be subcategorized to take either a "true" *for-to* complement or an infinitive complement of the type under discussion here that obligatorily undergoes raising. For further details, see the discussion of true *for-to* complements in Chapter 5.

II. For both transitive equi verbs and transitive raising verbs, the object NP *is* passivizable:

(23) *a*. Harry was persuaded to take out the garbage.
     b. That theory is believed to have been disproved.
     c. You are expected to arrive at 8:00.

III. For neither equi verbs nor raising verbs can the infinitive complement be pseudo-clefted:

(24) *a*. *What Bill tried was to open the door.
     b. *What Bill persuaded Harry was to take out the garbage.
     c. *What Bill persuaded was (for) Harry to take out the garbage.
     d. *What John promised Mary was to bring the book.

(25) *a*. *What John seems is to have left.
     b. *What we believe that theory is to have been disproved.
     c. *What is believe is (for) that theory to have been disproved.
     d. *What I expect is to arrive at 8:00.
     e. *What I expect is (for) you to arrive at 8:00.

IV. Both equi verbs and raising verbs *can* be pseudo-clefted by use of the "pro-verb" *do* (see Ross 1972, Emonds 1970, and Bowers 1973 for further discussion of such pseudo-cleft forms):

(26) *a*. What Bill tried to do was to open the door.
     b. What Bill persuaded Harry to do was to take out the garbage.
     c. What I expect to do is to leave town.
     d. What he promised Mary to do was to bring the book.

(27) *a*. What Bill seems to have done is to have left.
     b. What we believe him to have done is to have disproved that theory.[7]
     c. What I expect you to do is to leave town.

---

7. There are various irrelevant restrictions on pseudo-clefting with *do* (e.g., *what we believe that theory to have done is to have been disproved*) which are explainable under the assumption that *do* is a "real" verb (see Ross 1972 and Bowers 1973 for discussion).

V. The object NP of both transitive equi verbs and transitive raising verbs can be reflexivized:

(28) *a*. I finally persuaded myself to take out the garbage.
     b. I believe myself to have been cheated.
     c. Mary expects herself to be on time.
     d. I promised myself to eat a peach.

VI. For neither the equi verbs nor the raising verbs under discussion here is it possible for the infinitive complement to have an overt subject NP with *for:*

(29) *a*. *Bill tried for Harry to open the door.
     b. *I persuaded Bill for Harry to take out the garbage.
     c. *He promised Mary for Bill to bring the book.

(30) *a*. *John seems for Harry to have left.
     b. *We believe Harry for John to have taken out the garbage.
     c. *I expect you for John to arrive at 8:00.

VII. For neither equi verbs nor raising verbs is it possible for an overt subject NP to be in the infinitive complement that is coreferential with the relevant NP in the matrix clause:

(31) *a*.   *Bill$_1$ tried for $\left\{ \begin{array}{l} \text{him}_1 \\ \text{himself}_1 \end{array} \right\}$ to open the door.

     b.   *I persuaded Harry$_1$ for $\left\{ \begin{array}{l} \text{him}_1 \\ \text{himself}_1 \end{array} \right\}$ to take out the garbage.

     c.   *I expect for $\left\{ \begin{array}{l} \text{me} \\ \text{myself} \end{array} \right\}$ to arrive at 8:00.

     d.   *He$_1$ promised Mary for $\left\{ \begin{array}{l} \text{him}_1 \\ \text{himself}_1 \end{array} \right\}$ to bring the book.

(32) *a*.   *John$_1$ seems for $\left\{ \begin{array}{l} \text{him}_1 \\ \text{himself}_1 \end{array} \right\}$ to have left.

     b.   *We believe that theory$_1$ for $\left\{ \begin{array}{l} \text{it}_1 \\ \text{itself}_1 \end{array} \right\}$ to have been disproved.

     c.   *I expect you$_1$ for $\left\{ \begin{array}{l} \text{you}_1 \\ \text{yourself}_1 \end{array} \right\}$ to arrive in time.

VIII. For both equi verbs and raising verbs, reflexivization can apply "down into" the infinitive complement:

(33) *a*. Bill$_1$ tried to shave himself$_1$.
    b. I persuaded Harry$_1$ to shave himself$_1$ (*myself).
    c. I expect to shave myself.
    d. I promised Mary to shave myself (*herself).

(34) *a*. John$_1$ seems to have shaved himself$_1$.
    b. I believe John$_1$ to have shaved himself$_1$ (*myself).
    c. I expect you to shave yourself (*myself).

Furthermore, if the matrix clause has more than one NP, the embedded reflexive can be coreferential only with the "controller" NP (in the sense of Postal 1970).

What is the relevance of these observations? The point is simply that as far as the *syntax* of these infinitive complements is concerned, there is no need to assume two derivations, one via equi-NP deletion and the other via raising. All of the facts just mentioned can be explained adequately under the assumption that there is either a single rule of raising or a single rule of equi. None of them requires both equi and raising.[8] Furthermore, it seems obvious that it would be simpler to have only a rule of raising, rather than only a rule of equi, since the latter would require an additional constraint ensuring that the deleted subject NP is always coreferential with the controller NP at the point where equi is applicable. If there is only a single rule of raising, no such constraint is necessary.

This discussion brings me directly to the main defect in the classical theory of infinitive complementation, which is that it fails to draw any connection between the rules of raising and equi-NP deletion. Formally, these two rules are as different as, say, dative movement and relative-clause formation. Yet it is clear that the operations they per-

---

8. In addition, it is reasonable to assume that all of the complements in question are VP complements, in the sense of Rosenbaum 1967, in order to account for the fact that they cannot be passivized and pseudo-clefted.

form are not only parallel but indeed identical in their effects. Consider first the verbs *try* and *seem*. Both verbs are intransitive in form. In the case of *try*, equi states a relationship between the subject of the matrix clause and the (hypothesized) subject of the infinitive complement. In the case of *seem*, the rule of raising performs exactly the same function, namely, to state a relationship between the subject of the matrix clause and the (hypothesized) subject of the infinitive complement. Furthermore, the effect of the two rules is also exactly the same. In both cases, the effect of the rule is to suppress the appearance of a subject NP in the infinitive complement and at the same time to ensure that an overt subject NP does appear in the matrix clause. The only difference between the two rules is that in one case (equi) the embedded subject NP is deleted under identity with the subject of the matrix clause, whereas in the other case (raising) the embedded subject NP is moved into the subject position in the matrix clause.

Precisely the same parallelism holds, of course, in the case of such transitive verbs as *persuade* and *believe*, except that here it is the function of the two rules of raising and equi to relate the (hypothesized) subject of the infinitive complement to the object of the matrix verb. In neither case is the parallelism between the two rules expressed in the grammar. They are simply two unrelated rules of English grammar.

Clearly any analysis of this sort fails to express a rather deep generalization about the process of infinitive formation in English. This generalization may be stated as follows:

(35) To form an infinitive complement in English, remove the subject
      of the infinitive and put it in a position in the matrix clause that
      is determined by the particular matrix verb in question.

Any syntactic theory that fails to express this generalization is, I claim, inadequate. The classical theory of infinitive complementation, in particular, is inadequate in this respect. As a first step toward removing this inadequacy, I therefore propose the following hypothesis:

(36) Equi-NP deletion and raising are the same rule.

I shall show shortly how this hypothesis can be implemented. Before doing so, however, I must discuss the arguments that have been put forward in support of the view that two separate syntactic rules are involved in the process of infinitive formation.

4.4. The Arguments for Raising and Equi-NP Deletion

We have just seen that as far as the syntax of infinitive complements is concerned, there is no particular justification for assuming the existence of two separate and unrelated rules of equi and raising. What, then, are the arguments in favor of such an assumption? They are of two sorts.

The first argument has to do with selectional restrictions. It has been observed that whereas equi verbs impose selectional restrictions on the controller NP (that is, on the NP that is used to erase the subject of the infinitive complement), no such restrictions are imposed on the raised subject of the infinitive complement by the raising verbs. Thus consider such contrasts as the following:

(37) *a*. I persuaded John to move the table.
     b. *I persuaded the table to be moved by John.

(38) *a*. I believe John to have moved the table.
     b. I believe the table to have been moved by John.

The verb *persuade* requires an animate object NP, so that sentence 37*a* is acceptable, whereas 37*b* is not. The verb *believe*, in contrast, imposes no selectional restrictions on its object NP, and therefore both 38*a* and 38*b* are acceptable sentences. Similarly, consider the parallel contrast between the verbs *try* and *seem*:

(39) *a*. John tried to move the table.
     b. *The table tried to be moved by John.

(40) *a*. John seems to have moved the table.
       b. The table seems to have been moved by John.

Another way of demonstrating the same point is to consider the behavior of these verbs with respect to such items as *there* and
nonanaphoric *it*, which are transformationally inserted and therefore
are incapable of satisfying selectional restrictions of the type imposed
by such verbs as *persuade* and *try*:

(41) *a*. *I persuaded there to be an explosion.
       b. I believe there to have been an explosion.

(42) *a*. There tried to be an explosion.
       b. There seems to have been an explosion.

(43) *a*. *I persuaded it to rain.
       b. I believe it to have rained.

(44) *a*. *It tried to rain.
       b. It seems to have rained.

Since *persuade* and *try* impose selectional restrictions on their object
and subject NPs, respectively, such sentences as 41*a*, 42*a*, 43*a*, and
44*a* are anomolous for exactly the same reason that such simple sentences as the following are:

(45) *a*. *I persuaded there. (Cf. I persuaded John.)
       b. *There tried. (Cf. John tried hard.)
       c. *I persuaded it. (Cf. I persuaded John.)
       d. *It tried. (Cf. John tried.)

The verbs *seem* and *believe* do not impose selectional restrictions on
their subject and object NPs, respectively, and such sentences as 41*b*,
42*b*, 43*b* and 44*b* are therefore perfectly acceptable.[9]

---

9. Note, however, that *there* and *it* cannot appear in simple sentences with *believe*
and *seem*, either; e.g., *I believe there, *there seems, *I believe it* (where *it* is not, of

The second type of argument in favor of having both an equi rule and a raising rule has to do with truth conditions. Consider the following pairs of sentences:

(46) *a.* The doctor tried to examine John.
      b. John tried to be examined by the doctor.

(47) *a.* The doctor seems to have examined John.
      b. John seems to have been examined by the doctor.

(48) *a.* I persuaded the doctor to examine John.
      b. I persuaded John to be examined by the doctor.

(49) *a.* I believe the doctor to have examined John.
      b. I believe John to have been examined by the doctor.

As has frequently been noted, the pairs in examples 47 and 49 are synonymous, whereas those in examples 46 and 48 are not. This difference can be explained in a systematic way if at some level *try* and *persuade*, but not *seem* and *believe*, are assigned subject and object NPs, respectively. The classical theory claims that it is precisely at the level of deep structure that such conditions are met. Thus if the NPs *the doctor* and *John* are the deep-structure subjects of sentences 46*a* and 46*b,* respectively, the nonsynonymity of these sentences is accounted for immediately. Likewise, if the same two NPs are the deep-structure objects in sentences 48*a* and 48*b*, respectively, the nonsynonymity of these examples is also accounted for. If, however, the subject and object NPs in examples 47 and 49, respectively, have no deep-structure grammatical relation to the matrix verb, the synonymity of these pairs can be explained equally easily.

---

course, a referring expression), **it seems.* In the case of *there*, the ungrammaticality is simply due to the fact that the conditions for insertion of *there* are not met in such sentences. The third example is anomalous because *believe* does, in fact, impose selectional restrictions on its object NP in simple sentences: *I believe John, I believe that proposition,* but **I believe meat, *I believe clouds,* and so on. Finally, *seem* does in fact permit insertion of nonanaphoric *it*, as we have seen in Section 4.2, but only when the verb is subcategorized to take a sentential complement.

If it is assumed (1) that it is the deep-structure grammatical relations that determine the semantic interpretation of sentences, and (2) that selectional restrictions are also stated at the level of deep structure, then the two types of arguments just presented seem to converge in a satisfying way and together dictate that sentences containing the verbs *seem* and *believe* must differ radically in underlying structure from sentences containing the verbs *try* and *persuade*. These underlying structures must then be converted, in the manner described earlier, into surface forms that are syntactically indistinguishable from one another.

The crucial point to be observed, however, is that all of the arguments in favor of separate rules of equi-NP deletion and raising ARE PURELY SEMANTIC ARGUMENTS. Those involving truth conditions are obviously semantic: they have to do with the semantic interpretation of sentences, not with their formation. Furthermore, theorists of all persuasions are by now agreed that selectional restrictions are fundamentally semantic rather than syntactic. Both Ray S. Jackendoff and James D. McCawley, for instance, have argued that there is no sensible way of distinguishing "syntactic" selectional restrictions from "semantic" selectional restrictions, and that all such restrictions should be considered semantic.

We have, then, the following situation. There are no purely syntactic arguments for assuming the existence of separate rules of equi and raising. In fact, there are compelling arguments against any theory that breaks up the process of infinitive formation into two unrelated rules, since such a theory fails to express the unity of the syntactic process in question. At the same time, there are equally strong semantic arguments that seem to favor the classical theory's approach. There is no way of resolving this dilemma within the classical theory of deep structure. In particular, it is impossible to implement the hypothesis (tentatively proposed in Section 4.3) that equi and raising are the same rule without giving up the possibility of explaining the semantic facts in a coherent way. If we get rid of raising and keep equi, it will be impossible to account correctly for the interpretation of the verbs *seem* and *believe*. But if we keep raising and get rid of equi, we will be unable to account for the interpretation of sentences containing the verbs *try* and *persuade*.

The question, then, is whether it is possible to modify the classical theory in some way so that infinitive formation in English can be stated as a unified process. At the same time we want to be able to account in a systematic way for the observed differences of interpretation between *persuade* and *believe, try* and *seem*, and so on. In Section 4.5 I shall show that these two goals can be achieved, but only if raising is stated as a CT of the kind proposed here and only if the notion that there is a level of deep structure distinct from the level of surface structure is abandoned.

4.5. Why There Can't Be a Level of Deep Structure

Let us assume for the moment that the hypothesis proposed in Section 4.3 is correct, and that equi and raising are in fact the same rule. I shall now show that the contrasting interpretations of *persuade* and *believe* sentences (and likewise of *try* and *seem* sentences) can be accounted for only if the following two assumptions are correct:

I. Lexical insertion rules apply cyclically.

II. Lexical insertion rules may both precede and follow raising on the same syntactic cycle.

If assumptions I and II are correct, it follows immediately that there cannot be a level of deep structure, since it is crucial, if such a notion is to make sense, that there be some fixed point in each syntactic derivation at which all lexical items have been inserted and after which only such ''purely syntactic'' rules as raising and passive are applicable.[10]

---

10. Note that neither I nor II alone would be sufficient to prove that no level of deep structure exists. Suppose one were to propose a theory in which lexical insertion is cyclic, but in which all of the lexical insertion rules precede all of the syntactic rules on each syntactic cycle. Such a theory would be a mere notational variant of a deep-structure theory, as Chomsky has pointed out (1971). Similarly, one might propose to allow certain ''prelexical'' transformations in the theory of grammar, including certain rules that are similar to such purely syntactic transformations as raising and passive. Unless it can be demonstrated, however, that raising, for example, is both preceded and followed by lexical insertion transformations *on the same syntactic cycle*, then it will always be possible to reformulate such a theory as a deep-structure theory, taking

Let us assume, in addition, that raising is formulated, as in Section 4.2, as a CT that replaces some empty NP in the matrix clause with the subject of an infinitive complement. Notice first of all that if we were to get rid of raising and assume that there is only a single rule of equi in the grammar of English, assumptions I and II would not help us in the least. Thus suppose that we start out with a structure of the form shown in diagram 50. Lexical insertion is, by hypothesis, cyclic. Let us

(50)

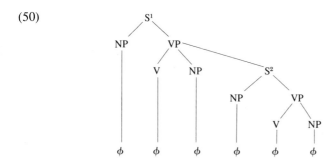

therefore insert into S^2 the lexical items he_1, *kill*, and *Harry*. We now have the structure shown in diagram 51. Moving up to the S^1 cycle, suppose we now insert the lexical items *John*, *persuade*, and $Bill_1$,

(51)

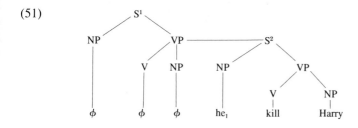

producing the structure shown in diagram 52. Equi may now apply, deleting the subject of the infinitive complement (as indicated in dia-

---

the prelexical applications of raising to be interpretive semantic rules and the postlexical applications of raising to be syntactic rules. Certain proposals of McCawley, Postal, Lakoff, and others have been criticized on just these grounds by (among others) Chomsky and Katz.

gram 52) and thereby producing the correct surface form. Furthermore, the sentence will be correctly interpreted, since the NP *Bill* is in fact the object of *persuade* and at the same time the subject of *kill*.

(52)

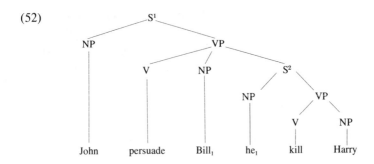

But now let us return to the stage represented by diagram 51. How can we derive the sentence *John believes Bill to have killed Harry?* In fact, we cannot, or at any rate we cannot derive it without getting the wrong interpretation. The reason is simply that equi, by its very nature, requires the object NP in S^1 to have already been filled in by the lexical insertion rules before it can apply. Therefore, we must fill in the lexical items *John, believe,* and *Bill$_1$*, producing a structure identical to that in diagram 52, except that in place of the main verb, *persuade*, in S^1, we have the verb *believe*. This derivation gives us the wrong semantic results, since *believe*, unlike *persuade*, does not have a grammatical relation to the object NP, *Bill*.

Rather than try to get rid of raising, suppose we eliminate equi from the grammar of English. Let us assume that the only syntactic rule involved in the derivation of infinitive complements is the rule of raising, which replaces some empty NP in the matrix clause with the subject of the infinitive complement. In addition, let us assume (as is semantically correct) that the lexical insertion rule for *persuade*, but not for *believe*, requires an object NP. Hence we shall have the following subcategorization conditions for these two verbs:

(53) *a. persuade:* NP ____ NP   S
      b. believe: NP ____   S

172

We start out, as before, with a tree of the form shown in diagram 50. Suppose that on the S² cycle we insert the lexical items *Bill, kill,* and *Harry,* producing in the structure shown in diagram 54. No further

(54)

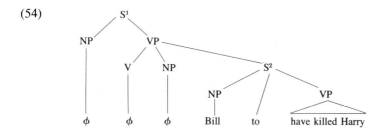

syntactic rules are applicable on the S² cycle, and we therefore move up to the S¹ cycle. Recall now that by hypothesis II, lexical insertion may either precede or follow raising. Suppose that we choose to apply a lexical insertion rule first. It is immediately evident that at this point the conditions for insertion of *believe* are met, whereas the conditions for insertion of *persuade* are not. We may therefore insert *believe,* along with its subject NP, producing the structure shown in diagram 55. Now raising must apply, moving the subject of the infinitive com-

(55)

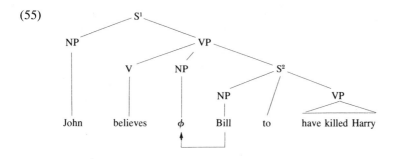

plement into the empty object position in S¹, as is indicated in diagram 55. The result is of course the correct surface form, diagram 56. More important, observe that if the subcategorization condition 53*b* is considered to be, in effect, a part of the semantic representation of the verb *believe,* we have also accounted correctly for the interpretation of the

(56)

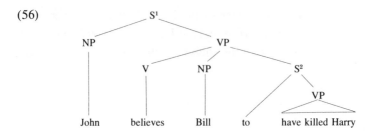

sentence *John believes Bill to have killed Harry*. The reason is that at the point where the verb *believe* is actually inserted in S^1, there is no object NP. Hence if it is the syntactic structure at the point where verbs are inserted that determines (in part) the semantic interpretation of sentences, this derivation will ensure that the NP *Bill* will not be interpreted as having a grammatical relation to the verb *believe*. We may summarize the derivation of this sentence as follows:

(57) S^2: 1. Lexical insertion: *kill*.
     S^1: 1. Lexical insertion: *believe*.
           2. Raising.

Consider next how we are to derive the sentence *John persuaded Bill to kill Harry*. Exactly the same syntactic structure, that in diagram 50, is involved as before. Furthermore, exactly the same lexical items may be inserted on the S^2 cycle, producing the intermediate stage of diagram 54. Suppose, however, that at this point we *apply first raising, then lexical insertion*. The result of applying raising to diagram 54 is a structure of the form shown in diagram 58. It is immediately

(58)

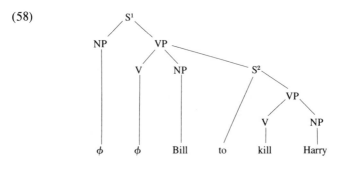

evident that at this point the conditions for insertion of the verb *per-suade* are met, whereas the conditions for insertion of *believe* are not. We may therefore insert *persuade* along with the subject NP *John*, producing finally the structure shown in diagram 59, identical to that of

(59)

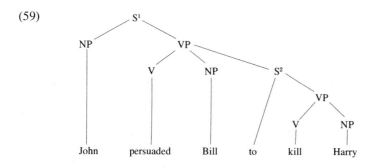

diagram 56. Once again, if it is the syntactic structure at the point where lexical items are inserted that is relevant to the semantic interpretation, we have also accounted correctly for the interpretation of this sentence. For at the point where *persuade* was inserted, the NP *Bill* was in fact in the object position in the matrix clause by virtue of the prior application of raising. We may thus summarize the derivation of the sentence *John persuaded Bill to kill Harry* in the following manner:

(60) S²: 1. Lexical insertion: *kill.*
　　　 S¹: 1. Raising.
　　　　　 2. Lexical insertion: *persuade.*

When we compare summaries 60 and 57, we see that the only difference between them is that in one case we have applied a lexical insertion rule first, followed by raising, whereas in the other case we have applied raising first, followed by lexical insertion. It follows immediately that there cannot be a level of deep structure in any empirically meaningful sense, since there is no fixed point in any arbitrary derivation that contains all of the information concerning grammatical relations necessary for semantic interpretation.[11]

I have argued, first, that there is no syntactic motivation for supposing that there are two separate and unrelated rules of equi-NP deletion and raising in the grammar of English. In fact, a grammar that contains these two rules is clearly inadequate, since it fails to express the obvious syntactic generalization that all infinitive complements in English are formed by placement of the subject of the infinitive complement in some lexically determined position in the matrix clause. Second, a grammar that assumes a level of deep structure cannot avoid splitting up the process of infinitive formation in this unmotivated way, since the only way it has of accounting for the difference in interpretation between sentences containing such verbs as *persuade* and *try*, on the one hand, and *believe* and *seem*, on the other, is to assume that they derive from different underlying structures. The only way to ensure that these underlying structures are mapped onto the correct surface forms, however, is to break up the unified syntactic process of infinitive formation into the two unrelated rules of equi and raising. It

11. It would be possible to avoid the conclusion that there is no level of deep structure by redefining the notion 'co-occurrence transformation' in an appropriate way. Suppose, for example, following a suggestion made by Noam Chomsky (personal communication), we define a CT as a rule that may replace one node by another node of the same category if the replaced node is either empty or identical to the replacing node (identity here includes identity of reference). Given this definition, it would be possible to retain the assumption that the lexical insertion rule for *persuade* precedes raising on the S^1 cycle in the derivation discussed in the text. Thus suppose that we insert *persuade* along with a pronominal object NP that is coreferential with the subject of the infinitive complement. Under the revised definition of CT, raising could then apply after lexical insertion, replacing the object NP in the matrix clause by the subject of the complement clause. Since all lexical insertion rules obviously could, by this artifice, be made to apply before raising on each syntactic cycle, the result would be a grammar equivalent to one containing a level of deep structure (see note 10). It is clear, however, that a proposal of this sort is merely a notational variant of the theory proposed here, since there is no motivation for redefining the notion 'co-occurrence transformation' in the manner suggested, aside from the fact that it allows one to avoid derivations in which lexical insertion rules follow such CTs as raising. Furthermore, such a theory would complicate the grammar, as it would require the reintroduction of a constraint (mentioned in connection with the discussion of equi in Section 4.3) requiring coreference between the object of *persuade* and the subject of the infinitive complement.

follows that a grammar containing a level of deep structure is inadequate to describe infinitive complementation in English. Finally, I
have shown that a grammar that does not assume a level of deep
structure, and in particular a grammar that (1) contains CTs, (2) permits cyclic lexical insertion, and (3) permits lexical insertion rules to
apply both before and after such syntactic rules as raising on the same
syntactic cycle can account correctly for the interpretation of sentences
containing infinitive complements without the need to break up the
single rule of raising into two unrelated parts. The obvious conclusion
is that an adequate grammar of English cannot contain a level of deep
structure.[12]

4.6. Raising into Subject Position

So far we have accounted for the contrasting interpretations of such
transitive verbs as *persuade* and *believe*, but we have not yet shown
how the analogous differences between such intransitive verbs as *try*
and *seem* can be accounted for in a theory without deep structure. The
classical theory, it will be recalled, accounts for the interpretation of
seem sentences by introducing a new rule into the grammar which
replaces a pronominal element in the subject position in the matrix
clause with the subject of the infinitive complement. Sentences with
try are derived by means of equi-NP deletion from underlying forms

---

12. Note that the form of this argument is precisely analogous to the one that Morris
Halle (1959) used to demonstrate the nonexistence of a taxonomic phonemic level in
phonology. Halle's point was that the assumption of an intermediate level between the
phonetic and lexical levels made it impossible to state certain phonological processes
in a unified way. In a precisely analogous fashion, the existence of an "intermediate"
level of deep structure that mediates between the lexicon and surface structure makes it
impossible to state the syntactic processes involved in infinitive formation in a unified
way. Similarly, just as the assumption of a taxonomic phonemic level in phonology
requires that phonological rules be divided arbitrarily into "phonemic" and
"morphophonemic" rules, so the existence of a level of deep structure requires an
arbitrary and unmotivated distinction between "lexical" rules and "purely syntactic"
rules, as I argued at length in the preceding chapters. The conclusion is the same in
both cases: get rid of the unnecessary intermediate level.

containing a subject NP that is coreferential with the subject of the infinitive complement. Furthermore, just as there is no relationship in the classical theory between raising into object position and equi, so there is no relationship between raising into subject position and equi.

Now I have already shown that splitting up the process of infinitive formation into the two unrelated rules of equi and raising is an unwarranted and syntactically unmotivated complication of the grammar of English. It is equally bad, however, to assume that the process of raising is split into two unrelated processes of raising into object position and raising into subject position.[13] Furthermore, although this

13. This point has been taken up recently by James McCawley (1970), who makes the interesting observation that raising can in fact be stated as a unitary process if English is assumed to have an underlying VSO word order. McCawley's argument is that if the subjects of both transitive and intransitive verbs originate in a position to the right of the main verb, then raising can be formulated as a single rule that raises the subject of the complement into postverbal position in the matrix clause. If the rule that places subject NPs in their surface position to the left of the main verb is ordered after raising, then the raised subject of such an intransitive verb as *seem* will automatically end up in subject position, whereas the object of such a verb as *believe* will of course remain in postverbal position.

There is surely no disputing McCawley's basic point that raising into subject and object positions should be statable as a unitary process (as has been realized for some time, e.g., by Rosenbaum [1967]). McCawley's point is further reinforced by the arguments in the preceding sections of this paper. For if raising and equi are the same rule, then raising into subject position and raising into object position must account not only for such verbs as *seem* and *believe*, but for such verbs as *try* and *persuade* as well. There are serious problems, however, with the solution he advocates. In the framework proposed here, no notion of deep structure can be appealed to. Consequently it is meaningless to assert that English has an "underlying" VSO word order, since English has no underlying structure at all, in the classical sense. We might still inquire, however, whether some variant of McCawley's VSO hypothesis might not be introduced into a theory without deep structure. In fact, such a possibility is perfectly feasible. The obvious analogue of the VSO hypothesis would be the assumption that both transitive and intransitive verbs are inserted into structures containing an empty subject NP. The rule of NP preposing would then automatically "move" the NP immediately to the right of the verb, into the subject position. In the case of transitive verbs the moved NP would of course be the agent, whereas in the case of intransitive verbs it would necessarily be the object.

But this possibility, too, must be rejected. The reason is simply that it is unnecessary, in the framework proposed here, to assume VSO word order at any point in syntactic derivations in order to state raising as a unitary process. Indeed, I have already shown in Section 4.2 that raising can be stated as a single CT. The most charitable view of McCawley's proposal is that it is an interesting *reductio ad absurdum* of the classical theory's approach to infinitive complements.

point does not seem to have been generally noticed, the classical theory is, in effect, forced to split the rule of equi into two unrelated parts as well, since it is necessary to specify for each verb a "controller." That is, it is necessary to specify whether it is the subject or the object of the matrix clause that is used to erase the pronominal subject of the infinitive complement. These two rules, which we might term "equi from subject position" and "equi from object position," are, as we have already seen, precisely parallel to the formally unrelated rules of raising into subject position and raising into object position.

All of these problems disappear at once if we combine the formulation of raising proposed in Section 4.2 with assumptions I and II of Section 4.5. Let us assume that among the PS rules of English are the following:

(61) *a.* S → NP   VP
    b. VP → V   (NP)   (S)

Since object NPs are optional, according to rule 61*a*, we can immediately generate such structures as that in diagram 62. Suppose

(62)

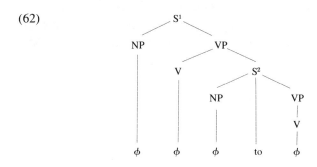

further that we subcategorize the verbs *seem* and *try* in the following manner:

(63) *a. seem*:   ____   S
    b. try: NP____   S

Lexical insertion rule 63*a* requires that *seem* be inserted (as is semantically correct) into a structure containing no NP arguments and an infinitive complement. The verb *try* requires not only an infinitive complement, but a subject NP as well, as is indicated in the subcategorization condition 63*b*.

Suppose now that on the S^2 cycle we insert the verb *leave*, along with a subject NP *John*. We now have an intermediate stage of the form shown in diagram 64. Going up to the S^1-cycle, recall that by

(64)

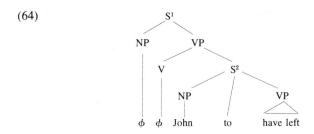

assumption II we may apply first either a lexical insertion rule or raising. Suppose that we attempt to apply a lexical insertion rule first. It is immediately evident that at this point the conditions for insertion of *seem* are met, since structure 64 contains an infinitive complement but no NP arguments. Hence we may insert *seem*, producing the structure shown in diagram 65. Now of course raising is applicable,

(65)

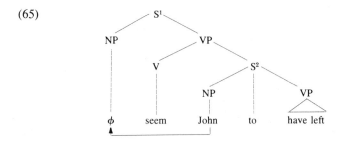

since we have an empty NP in the matrix clause that can be replaced by the subject of the infinitive complement. Hence raising will apply in the manner indicated in diagram 65, producing the final correct form,

(66)

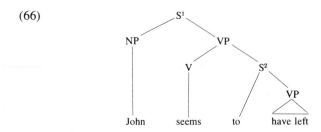

shown in diagram 66. Furthermore, if it is the structure at the point where a verb is actually inserted into a P-marker that is relevant to the interpretation of sentences, we have also accounted correctly for the interpretation of this sentence, since the NP *John* has a grammatical relation to the verb in the infinitive complement but not to the matrix verb *seem*.

Going back to the stage represented by diagram 64, before the application of any rules on the S^1 cycle, suppose we choose to apply raising first. We will then have a structure of the form shown in diagram 67. When we look at the subcategorization conditions in item 63, it is obvious that at this point the conditions for insertion of *try* are

(67)

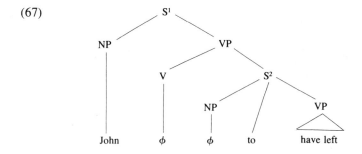

met, since we have a subject NP and an infinitive complement. Hence we may insert *try*, producing the final correct form, shown in diagram 68. Furthermore, since it is the structure at the point where the verb is inserted that determines the semantic interpretation of sentences, we have also accounted correctly for the interpretation of this sentence. For at the point where *try* was inserted, the NP *John* had already been

(68)

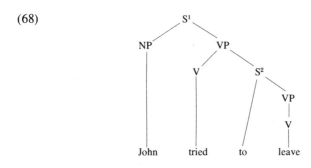

raised into the matrix clause. Hence *John,* in this case, is interpreted both as the subject of the matrix verb *try* and (on the previous cycle) as the subject of the verb *leave.*

These two derivations may therefore be summarized in the following form:

(69) S²: 1. Lexical insertion: *leave.*
  S¹: 1. Lexical insertion: *seem.*
    2. Raising.

(70) S²: 1. Lexical insertion: *leave.*
  S¹: 1. Raising.
    2. Lexical insertion: *try.*

Once again, the only difference between the two derivations is that in one case raising follows lexical insertion on the S¹ cycle, whereas in the other case it precedes. Furthermore, we have accounted correctly for the syntactic structure and semantic interpretation of both *try* and *seem* sentences, using only the single rule of raising as formulated earlier. This result is possible, however, only if we abandon the notion that there is a level of deep structure, in the classical sense.

Note that given the PS rules in 61 and the rule of raising, just three possible sentence types can be formed: (1) raising into subject position in intransitive structures, (2) raising into object position in transitive structures, and (3) raising into subject position in transitive structures. The interpretation of each of these sentence types may vary, depending on whether raising is applied before or after lexical insertion on the matrix cycle. We have just discussed derivations of the first type above, while derivations of the second type were discussed in Section 4.5. The question that now arises is whether there is a sentence type in English corresponding to the third possible type of derivation, raising into subject position in transitive structures.

In fact there is. Consider such a sentence as *John promised Mary to bring the book*. As is well known, in sentences containing such verbs as *promise*, it is the subject NP that controls the deletion of the complement subject, despite the fact that such verbs are transitive. In the theory proposed here, the special properties of such sentences are accounted for automatically if they are assigned to the third possible derivational class mentioned above. Thus suppose that we generate a structure of the form shown in diagram 71. It is immediately evident

(71)

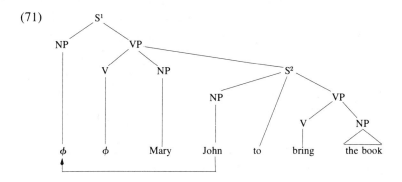

that in such a structure, raising, as we have formulated it, will replace the empty subject NP in S^1, producing a structure that is identical in form to that of such a sentence as *John persuaded Mary to bring the book*, but quite different in meaning. Furthermore, if we specify that raising must precede lexical insertion in this case, then the NP *John* will correctly be interpreted as the subject of the matrix verb *promise*, as is semantically correct.[14]

14. English has to my knowledge no transitive verbs that require lexical insertion to precede raising into subject position. In other words, there are no sentences of the form **John seemed Bill to have left*, where the subject of *seem* is also the understood subject of the infinitive complement. The nonexistence of such sentences is apparently an

We now have just five types of derivations for infinitive complements in English, depending on whether the matrix verb is transitive or intransitive, on whether raising precedes or follows lexical insertion, and on whether the subject of the complement is raised into subject or object position. Given the fact that the PS rules of English permit both transitive and intransitive structures and that the grammar of English contains a single rule of raising, these are (with one exception; see note 14) the only derivations that are logically possible. Notice, too, that these five derivational types correspond exactly to the observed class of complement types that actually occur in English (with the one exception already noted) in transitive and intransitive structures. Finally, since there is no simpler description of the data discussed so far, we may say that the theory proposed here, together with the language-specific PS rules, CTs, and lexical insertion rules of English, not only *describes* the data correctly, but also *explains* why it is that just these five complement types, and no others, occur in English.

There are, of course, further complement types that we have not yet discussed. They will be dealt with in Chapter 5. There are also some problems that I have simply ignored up to this point for the purposes of exposition. In particular, we have said nothing about the relationships *among* the various complement types, nor have we proposed a specific mechanism to determine which derivations are to be associated with which particular matrix verbs. The latter problem is best dealt with in Chapter 5, after discussion of the true *for-to* complements and WH-infinitive complements. For the moment, I shall assume that each verb is assigned a derivational class as a lexical property. I conclude this chapter by refining the analysis of raising just proposed so as to take account of the systematic relationships among complement types. In particular, it is essential that we relate the derivation of infinitive complements to the analysis of transitive and intransitive verbs proposed in Chapter 2.

---

accidental gap in the lexicon of English. Note that we do find such sentences as *John seems to Bill to have left*. Perhaps all of the verbs in this class happen to require dative objects for purely semantic reasons.

4.7 The Control Problem and the Problem of Transitivity

We have just seen that each of the possible derivations of infinitive complements that is permitted by our theory is in fact realized by some sentence type in English. A number of problems, however, still need to be discussed. Notice, first of all, that we have at present no way of predicting which transitive verbs behave like *persuade* and which like *promise*. The lexical insertion rule for both of these verbs must follow raising. Furthermore, both must have a subcategorization feature of the following form, since both are transitive:

(72) NP ＿＿ NP S

What, then, is to prevent a derivation of the sort shown in diagram 73 for such a sentence as *John promised Mary to leave?* We start out with

(73)

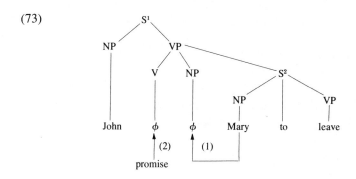

a structure containing a filled subject NP and an empty object NP in S^1, and apply first raising and then lexical insertion. Since the only empty NP that can be filled by the subject of the infinitive complement is in this case the object NP, raising will apply as indicated in diagram 73, after which the verb *promise* may be inserted, since condition 72 is met. The result is a sentence with the correct structure but the wrong interpretation. Similarly, there is apparently nothing to prevent a derivation of the sentence *John persuaded Mary to leave* in which the subject of the infinitive complement is incorrectly raised into the subject position in the matrix clause.

This problem (following Postal 1970) is now generally referred to in the literature as the "control problem." The difficulty is that there is apparently no general way to determine when equi is controlled by the subject and when it is controlled by the object. The analogous problem in the theory proposed here is how to determine which position in the matrix clause is to be filled by raising. Of course it would always be possible (in either theory) to mark the controller in some arbitrary way, making the application of equi or raising dependent on the presence of this mark. Alternatively, we could separate raising into two rules again (raising into subject position and raising into object position) and mark each verb for the particular rule it must undergo. All such "solutions" are equally ad hoc, however, and fail to shed any light on the problem. In any case, a more interesting approach is available, based on the discussion of transitivity in Chapter 2.

Notice, to begin with, that all verbs of the *promise* type, without exception, have an intransitive as well as a transitive form:

(74) *a*. John promised Mary to leave.
    b. John promised to leave.

(75) *a*. John begged Harry to be allowed to leave.
    b. John begged to be allowed to leave.

(76) *a*. John asked Bill what to do.
    b. John asked what to do.

When we recall the discussion of object transitivization in Chapter 2, this observation naturally suggests that the intransitive *b* sentences in examples 74–76 are the basic forms, while the transitive *a* sentences are derived. Such verbs as *persuade*, in contrast, are clearly basic transitives. How does this help us? Consider first the derivation of such a sentence as 74*b*. Obviously the verb *promise*, in its intransitive form, requires a derivation exactly like that of a verb of the *try* class (see diagram 77). But now we can simply apply the rule of object

(77)

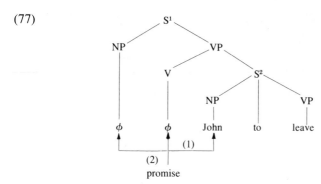

transitivization to the P-marker resulting from this derivation (see diagram 78). The result is a sentence that is identical in form to the sentence *John persuaded Mary to leave* but altogether different in its

(78)

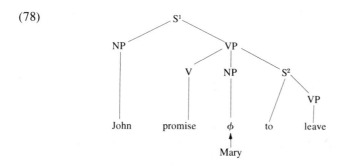

derivation, and therefore in its interpretation. In fact, what we have shown is that verbs of the *promise* type are a subclass of verbs of the *try* class. That is to say, *promise* is a basic intransitive of the same class as *try*. Unlike *try*, however, *promise* can undergo the further process of object transitivization.

Recall now that the verbs of the *promise* class constitute the only exceptions to Rosenbaum's distance principle, according to which the "controller" for equi is that NP which is nearest to the deleted subject of the infinitive complement. In the particular case of such a transitive verb as *persuade*, Rosenbaum's principle correctly predicts that the controller must be the object rather than the subject. Translated into the theory proposed here, Rosenbaum's principle says that raising must put the subject of an infinitive complement in the nearest available NP node in the matrix clause. This principle correctly predicts, for verbs of both the *believe* class and the *persuade* class, that the subject of the infinitive complement must be raised into the object position rather than the subject position.[15] Having removed the one exception to Rosenbaum's distance principle, we may invoke it to explain why the object is the controller for such transitive verbs as *persuade*. Quite unexpectedly, then, the solution to the control problem turns out to depend crucially on the proper formulation of such syntactic processes as transitivization, thus providing independent support, from a completely different part of the grammar, for the rules proposed in Chapter 2.

Not unexpectedly, there are other pairs of sentences with infinitive complements whose relationship can be accounted for in a similar manner. A clear instance of subject detransitivization, for example, is provided by the following pair:

(79) *a*. John proved Bill to be the culprit.
       b. Bill proved to be the culprit.

This example is of particular interest because the verb *prove* is one that requires raising *after* lexical insertion. Sentences 79*a* and 79*b* are therefore like sentences with *believe* and *seem*, respectively, as is shown by the fact that the raised NP can be an element such as existential *there*:

(80) *a*. John proved there to have been a riot.
       b. There proved to have been a riot.

15. Actually, as will become apparent in Chapter 5, it is necessary to invoke the distance principle only for verbs that require lexical insertion after raising. Furthermore, I strongly suspect that the concept of "nearest NP" is not nearly general enough. One might speculate that there is some universal hierarchy of availability based on grammatical relations of the type discussed by Keenan and Comrie (1972). A partial hierarchy of the form subject > direct object > indirect object is consistent with the data from English, for example.

The NP *Bill* in example 79 therefore has no grammatical relation to the verb *prove*, even though it is the grammatical object of sentence 79*a* and the grammatical subject of sentence 79*b*. Thus we see that such processes as detransitivization alter the grammatical relations in *sentences*, without regard to the way the NPs in question are related to the *verb*. This observation in turn demonstrates that such syntactic processes as detransitivization and causativization cannot be merely a matter of changing the "valence" of the verb or altering the relations between a verb and its arguments, as has been suggested by some theorists, because here we have a case where detransitivization operates on NPs that do not have *any* grammatical relation to the verb. It follows that surface structure grammatical relations are the fundamental notions in terms of which grammatical processes must be stated. The only way of escaping this conclusion is to deny a syntactic relationship between such pairs as those in examples 79 and 80, a conclusion that is clearly absurd.

Instances of subject transitivization are provided by the following examples:

(81) *a*. Bill got to take out the garbage.
     b. John got Bill to take out the garbage.

(82) *a*. Bill dared to do it.
     b. John dared Bill to do it.

Here the basic intransitive verbs *get* and *dare* are converted into transitives by addition of a new agent NP, with subsequent demotion of the subject into object position. There are relatively few pairs of this sort in English. Nonhomophonous but semantically related pairs of verbs, however, are quite common:

(83) *a*. John remembered to do it.
     b. I reminded John to do it.

(84) *a*. Bill went to buy some bread.
     b. I sent Bill to buy some bread.

(85) *a*. The dog learned to fetch.
     b. They taught the dog to fetch.

Consider finally the following pair of sentences:

(86) *a*. I want John to be examined by the doctor.
     b. I want to be examined by the doctor.

There is quite a large class of verbs in English, including *want, desire, expect,* and many others, which act on the one hand like verbs of the *believe* class (sentence 86*a*) and on the other hand like verbs of the *try* class (sentence 86*b*). Is there a principled explanation for this fact, or is it merely an accident that the lexicon of English happens to contain such a large number of verbs of this kind? In fact, it is probably not accidental, for notice that though they are derived differently, the subcategorization conditions associated with these two verb classes are the same, both of them being intransitive. The only difference between sentences 86*a* and 86*b* lies in the order in which the lexical insertion condition applies with respect to raising. Hence for such verbs as *want*, we do not need to specify the order of raising and lexical insertion. We can simply let the rules apply freely, thereby achieving a simplification in their lexical entries. Furthermore, these are the only two verb classes whose subcategorization conditions overlap in this way. It is therefore not surprising that homophonous pairs of verbs belonging to these two classes tend to be much more numerous than other pairs.

4.8 Concluding Remarks: Syntax without Deep Structure

If the arguments in this chapter are correct, there is no level of deep structure in the classical sense. In order for a syntactic level of deep structure to exist, it is essential that there be some class of "purely syntactic" transformations that are ordered in a block after all of the "lexical" transformations. We have just seen, however, that if the process of infinitive formation in English is to be described in the most general way (that is, in a way that captures the linguistically significant generalizations concerning infinitive formation), it is impossible to separate such purely syntactic rules as those of raising either from lexical insertion rules or from such other lexical rules as object transitivization. In the classical theory, raising would be considered a syntactic rule, object transitivization (or its equivalent) would be considered a "lexical redundancy rule," and the insertion rules for verbs would of course be lexical rules. We have just seen, however, that infinitive formation in English can be described adequately only if all three of these rules are allowed to apply in random sequential order to a representation of the surface form of a sentence. Obviously it is meaningless to speak of a "level" of deep structure in a grammar of this sort. On the contrary, it is the derivations themselves that determine both the form and the meaning of sentences. Corresponding to each possible derivational type that is permitted by the theory, given the particular rules of English, there is just one "construction" (to use a traditional term) with its own particular form and meaning. More generally, we might say that there is no sharp division, as there is in the classical theory, between the process of forming a sentence and the process of interpreting it semantically. Instead, at every point in a derivation, the application of a rule has both syntactic and semantic consequences. The rule of raising, for example, not only determines the syntactic form of infinitive constructions, but at the same time contributes to the semantic interpretation of those constructions. The *way* in which it contributes to the meaning of a sentence depends of course on the precise point in the derivation at which it is applied.

Finally, it is apparent that a theory of this type is possible only if transformational rules are permitted to take account of the grammatical relations of constituents. It seems likely that the necessity for a level of deep structure in the classical theory is simply an artifact of the particular definition of 'transformational rule' that was adopted in the earliest work on the theory of transformational-generative grammar. In particular, it is impossible to account for both the form and the meaning of infinitive complements in English within the classical theory of transformations unless an abstract level of deep structure is assumed. If the theory proposed in this work is correct, however, not only is a level of deep structure unnecessary, but it is in fact impossible, since the assumption of such a level not only would complicate the grammar unnecessarily but would also fail to capture proper generalizations concerning the process of infinitive formation in English.

5 Further Remarks on Infinitive Complements

5.1 Introduction

If the proposals in Chapter 4 are correct, the syntax of subjectless infinitive complements in English can be described by means of two simple and general rules, namely, raising and object transitivization. All of the special properties of the various types of infinitive constructions follow automatically once we have specified the ordering of these rules with respect to one another and with respect to the lexical insertion rules for specific verbs. A number of counterarguments could be brought forward against a theory of this kind. I shall not attempt to deal here with all of the objections that might be raised, but three problems in particular require discussion. The first has to do with what I shall term "true *for-to* complements," by which I mean certain infinitive complements that appear with an overt subject NP, usually marked by the so-called complementizer element *for*. The second has to do with infinitival indirect questions, or WH complements, and the third has to do with the rule of "tough movement," or object raising, as I shall term it. In the course of discussing these three constructions, I refine somewhat the analysis of infinitive complements suggested in Chapter 4 and at the same time clear up a number of problems that were alluded to there but never explicitly resolved.

5.2 True *For-To* Complements

The strongest syntactic argument that I am aware of for the existence of a rule of equi-NP deletion is based on the fact that there are certain verbs in English whose infinitive complement apparently allows an overt subject NP in surface structure, just in case this subject is not coreferential with the controller NP in the matrix clause. Consider the following pairs of sentences:

(1)   *a.* I would like for you to be examined by the doctor.
      b. I would like to be examined by the doctor.

(2)   *a.* It worries Bill for his friends to call him a liar.
      b. It worries Bill to be called a liar by his friends.

As has often been noted, such sentences as 1*a* and 2*a* are ungrammatical just in case the subject of the infinitive complement is coreferential with the relevant NP in the matrix clause:

(3)   *a.* *I would like for me to be examined by the doctor.
      b. *It worries Bill₁ for him₁ to be called a liar by his friends.

This gap in the paradigm of true *for-to* complements is of course filled by sentences 1*b* and 2*b*, which have just the interpretation that would be associated with such sentences as those in example 3 if they were not ungrammatical in English. Observations of this sort thus seem to provide a compelling argument for the existence of a rule that deletes the subject of an infinitive complement just in case it is coreferential with the controller NP in the matrix clause.

Straightforward as this analysis may seem, however, there are certain difficulties with it that have yet to receive adequate treatment. The first problem has to do with the status of the element *for*, which appears in true *for-to* complements but never in infinitives of the type discussed earlier, in which the subject NP is suppressed in surface structure. Emonds has noted (1976) that the *for* phrase that appears in such sentences must be a PP in surface structure. To see that this is so, it is sufficient to note that when the subject is a pronoun, it invariably occurs in the accusative case:

(4)   *a.* I would like for *him* to be examined by the doctor.
      b. *I would like for *he* to be examined by the doctor.

This fact is unexplainable if the element *for* is treated in just the same way as other complementizer morphemes, such as *that*. In fact, the element *that* behaves in just the opposite way from the complementizer *for*:

(5) *a*. I think that *he* should be examined by the doctor.
  b. *I think that *him* should be examined by the doctor.

If *for* + NP is a constituent in surface structure, and if, in particular, it is a PP constituent, the appearance of the accusative case is predictable, since in English the objects of prepositions require pronouns in the accusative case in surface structure.

The second problem is to explain the appearance of this PP node in sentence-initial position in infinitive complements. It would obviously be undesirable to extend the phrase-structure rules so as to allow PP nodes to appear in subject position, since PP nodes cannot in general appear in subject position in English. If such a solution were to be adopted, it would be necessary to account for the ungrammaticality of sentences of the form *with John went to the store, *about the war talked John,* and so forth. PPs can occur in English in topic position to the left of the subject NP, however, along with a number of other constituents such as NP, AP, and VP, as in the following examples:

(6) *a*. Bill I can't stand.
  b. In the garden they put a statue.
  c. Old and yellowed was the ancient manuscript.
  d. Speaking at today's luncheon is a well-known politician.
  e. That Bill is a Republican I can't believe.

In the framework proposed here, the phrase-structure rules characterize the surface form of sentences. We shall therefore extend the PS expansion rule for S in English in the following manner:

$$(7) \quad S \rightarrow \left(\left\{ \begin{array}{c} NP \\ PP \\ AP \\ VP \end{array} \right\} \right) \quad NP \quad \left(\left\{ \begin{array}{c} Tns \\ to \\ ing \end{array} \right\} \right) \quad VP$$

Given structures of this sort, we can define CTs of the appropriate sort to "move" various constituents into the empty nodes in presubject position provided by rule 7.[1] Of immediate interest here is the fact that rule 7 provides us with just the sort of structure we need for true *for-to* complements. Suppose we generate a structure of the sort shown in diagram 8 as a complement to such a verb as *like*. We shall now add a new rule to the grammar which operates in the manner indicated in diagram 8. This rule, which I shall refer to as *for*-subject formation

(8)

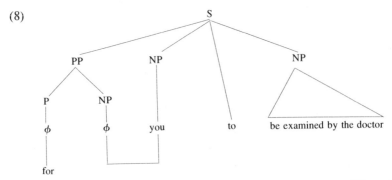

(FSF), moves the subject of the sentence into the empty PP node in topic position and simultaneously inserts the preposition *for*. We may state this rule formally in the following manner:

(9)   *For*-subject formation (FSF):

$X - [_S [_{PP} P{:}\phi \ NP{:}\phi] \ NP{:}x \ to \ \dots \ _S] - Y \Rightarrow$

$X - [_S [_{PP} P{:}for \ NP{:}x] \ NP{:}\phi \ to \dots \ _S] - Y$

1. See Bowers 1976 for independent arguments in support of this approach to certain types of topicalized sentences in English. Further arguments will be presented in Chapter 6. Note that it would be completely superfluous to assume that the nodes in presubject position in rule 7 are dominated by some such node as TOPIC, COMP, or Q, as has been suggested in much recent work. From the point of view adopted here, the introduction of such nodes in the PS rules for English is just as pointless as introducing a node SUBJECT to dominate the subject NP. Just as the relational notion 'subject of' can be defined in terms of the configuration provided by a set of PS rules, so the notion 'topic of' can also be defined in terms of a set of PS rules incorporating rule 7. Hence it is unnecessary to introduce some cover symbol that dominates all topicalized constituents in English. In fact, to do so is seriously to confuse categorial and relational notions. See Epée 1976 for further criticisms of the classical theory along these lines, based on data from Duala.

Note that since the application of FSF is explicitly restricted to infinitive complements, it will not produce *for* subjects in *that* clauses, gerundives, main clauses, and so forth.

Given the rule of FSF, along with PS rule 7, we immediately have a straightforward explanation for the seemingly rather peculiar structure of true *for-to* complements in English. The next problem is to prevent the occurrence of a *for* subject in infinitive complements of the type discussed in Chapter 4, for which raising is obligatory. The solution to this problem is apparent as soon as we observe that just three types of verbs take infinitive complements: (1) verbs that never take a *for* subject (all of the complements discussed earlier); (2) verbs for which a *for* subject is optional (such verbs as *like, worry,* and *bother* in the examples above); and (3) verbs that always require a *for* subject. Included in this third class are the verbs *scream, yell,* and a few others. The fact that these verbs always require a *for* subject is shown in the following examples:[2]

(10) *a*. I screamed for Mary to go.
     b. *I screamed to go.

(11) *a*. I yelled for Bill to put the cat out.
     b. *I yelled to put the cat out.

Verbs of this type have been discussed recently in the literature (see, for example, Postal 1970 and Jackendoff 1972), but their significance does not seem to have been properly appreciated. The fact that there are just three types of verbs in English, those that require a *for* subject, those for which it is optional, and those for which it is impossible, is precisely what we would expect under the assumption that the *for* phrase in presubject position is subcategorized by the matrix verb. If

---

2. Postal has noted (1970) that when these verbs take a *to* phrase, the object of the preposition *to* is the controller, as in *I screamed to Mary to go* and *I yelled at Bill to put the cat out.* In our terms the subject of the infinitive complement is raised into the matrix clause before lexical insertion just in case it contains a *to* phrase. The fact that the complements of these verbs undergo either FSF or raising, depending on the structure of the matrix clause, does not affect the analysis in the text.

this conclusion is correct, we may simply subcategorize the three verbs *try, like,* and *scream* in the following manner:

(12) *a.* *try:* NP _____ [s *to* VP . . .]
      b. *like:* NP _____ [s (*for* NP) *to* VP . . .]
      c. *scream:* NP _____ [s *for* NP *to* VP . . .]

As the lexical insertion rules for these verbs necessarily apply on the matrix cycle, the conditions for insertion of *scream,* for example, can be met only if the infinitive complement has undergone FSF on the previous cycle. Similarly, the conditions for insertion of *try* can be met only if FSF has failed to apply on the previous cycle. And finally such a verb as *like* will be insertable whether FSF has applied or not.

This analysis explains automatically the interesting fact noted by Emonds (1976) that no topicalization rule other than FSF is applicable in infinitive complements. None of the sentences in example 6, for instance, can be embedded as infinitive complements:

(13) *a.* *John believes me Bill not to be able to stand.
      b. *They tried in the garden to put the statue.
      c. *The ancient manuscript seems old and yellowed to be.
      d. *We found a well-known politician speaking at today's luncheon to be.
      e. *I screamed that Bill was a Republican for John not to believe.

though the nontopicalized variants are perfectly acceptable.

(14) *a.* John believes me not to be able to stand Bill.
      b. They tried to put the statue in the garden.
      c. The ancient manuscript seems to be old and yellowed.
      d. We found a well-known politician to be speaking at today's luncheon.
      e. I screamed for John not to believe that Bill was a Republican.

If these various topicalization rules were permitted to apply freely in infinitive complements, there would be no principled way of excluding such sentences as those in example 13. If, however, the constituent in topic position in infinitive complements is subcategorized by the matrix Verb, the fact that no topicalization rule other than FSF is permitted to apply is explained automatically by such subcategorization conditions as those in 12.[3]

Summarizing briefly, infinitive complements in English may be generated either with or without a *for* phrase preceding the subject NP. The distribution of these complement types is a property of particular verbs. In particular, the presence or absence of a *for* phrase in an infinitive complement is part of the information contained in the lexical insertion conditions for each matrix verb. If an infinitive contains a *for* phrase, then raising, as formulated in Chapter 4, will be inapplicable, as it does not allow for an intervening *for* phrase in its structural description. Nor can raising apply to the object of the *for* phrase itself, as raising applies only to subjects. (Note that this is yet another case in which it is crucial that transformations be able to refer to the grammatical relations).[4] If there is no *for* phrase in topic position in the infinitive complement, raising will necessarily apply, moving the sub-

---

3. The fact that other topicalized constituents may not co-occur with a *for* subject within the infinitive complement is of course an automatic consequence of the theory of CTs, combined with the fact that the PS rules for English permit only one topicalized constituent per clause. Notice that this restriction has already been built into rule 7 by making the list of topicalized constituents disjunctive. See Bowers 1976, Section 5.3 below, and also Chapter 6 for further discussion of this point.

4. Such a rule as FSF, incidentally, is very difficult to formulate coherently in a theory that assumes a level of deep structure. In order to account for the fact that the *for* phrase is a PP in surface structure, the classical theory must either introduce some new kind of rule that is capable of building structure—a strengthening of the theory for which there is little independent motivation—or generate the *for* phrase directly in the base. If the *for* phrase is generated in the subject position, difficulties of the sort referred to on p. 195 arise. If the PS rules generate both subject NPs and sentence-initial PPs, there is no natural way, under the classical theory of transformations, to prevent sentences containing NPs in both positions, thereby producing such ungrammatical sentences as * *John would like for Harry Bill to be examined by the doctor* and * *John screamed for Bill Harry to go.* The only way out of this dilemma would be to allow obligatorily empty nodes to be generated in deep structure, as would be possible, in a grammar that assumes some form of Emonds's structure-preserving constraint. As I have shown in Chapter 1, however, allowing obligatorily empty nodes in deep structure is tantamount to giving up a level of deep structure in any case. This point is further elaborated in connection with other topicalization phenomena in English in Bowers 1976.

ject NP into the matrix clause. Note that the effect of these rules is to ensure that the subjects of infinitive complements in English are always moved into some other position in the sentence.

Having determined the constituent structure of true *for-to* complements, we can now return to the problem with which we began this section, namely, the "gap in the paradigm" argument in support of a rule of equi. In particular, we must consider how to block such sentences as those in example 3, which contain a *for* phrase whose object is coreferential with the controller NP in the matrix clause. I shall argue that such sentences are not excluded by the rule of equi at all, but that they are instead excluded by the independently needed unlike-person constraint (see Postal 1969 and Chomsky 1973 for discussion). This constraint prevents such sentences as the following, containing noun-pronoun or pronoun-pronoun pairs that are the same in person and identical or overlapping in reference:

(15) *a*. *I like me.
      b. *We like us.
      c. *I like us.
      d. *We like me.
      e. *You$_1$ like you.
      f. *He$_1$ likes him.
      g. *John$_1$ likes him$_1$.

We note immediately that exactly the same restrictions hold for the *for* subjects of true *for-to* complements.

(16) *a*. *I would like for me to be examined by the doctor.
      b. *We would like for us to be examined by the doctor.
      c. *I would like for us to be examined by the doctor.
      d. *We would like for me to be examined by the doctor.
      e. *You$_1$ would like for you$_1$ to be examined by the doctor.
      f. *He$_1$ would like for him$_1$ to be examined by the doctor.
      g. *John$_1$ would like for him$_1$ to be examined by the doctor.

How can we justify the assumption that it is the unlike-person constraint that is responsible for the anomaly of the sentences in example

16 rather than the rule of equi? First of all, the unlike-person constraint applies in general to noun-pronoun and pronoun-pronoun pairs that are subcategorized by the main verb of the clause in which they appear. But we have just seen that there is good reason to suppose that the *for* phrase that occurs in true *for-to* complements is subcategorized by the verb in the matrix clause. That being the case, it is entirely natural to account for the sentences in examples 15 and 16 by means of the same rule.

One crucial fact, however, demonstrates conclusively that it cannot be equi that is responsible for the "gap in the paradigm" cases. Recall that among verbs that take true *for-to* complements, one class of verbs always requires the presence of a *for* subject. The infinitive complements of such verbs MUST have an overt subject NP and CANNOT undergo equi, as we can see in sentences 10*b* and 11*b*. But now observe that exactly the same constraints hold for the *for* subjects of these sentences as hold for all other *for* subjects:

(17) *a*. *I screamed for me to go.
      b. *I screamed for us to go.
      c. *We screamed for me to go.
      d. *We screamed for us to go.
      e. *You$_1$ screamed for you$_1$ to go.
      f. *He$_1$ screamed for him$_1$ to go.
      g. *John$_1$ screamed for him$_1$ to go.

Here, then, is a case in which equi cannot be responsible for the "gap in the paradigm," as equi is not applicable at all to the complements of such verbs as *scream* and *yell*. Yet exactly the same "gaps in the paradigm" are found in the complements of these verbs as in the complements of verbs that do permit equi. It follows that in order to account for the impossibility of the sentences in example 17, we must invoke some rule other than equi, such as the unlike-person constraint. But if the unlike-person constraint, or some principle similar to it, is needed in any case to account for the "gap in the paradigm" in the complements of such verbs as *scream* and *yell*, it is entirely superfluous to assume that a different rule (namely, equi) is responsible for exactly the same gaps in the paradigm in the complements of *like,* *worry,* and so on.

The "gap in the paradigm" argument, then, provides no support for the existence of a rule deleting the subjects of infinitive complements. On the contrary, when all of the relevant facts are taken into account, the evidence supports just the opposite conclusion. Taken in conjunction with the arguments against equi brought forward in Chapter 4, the evidence seems to point to the inescapable conclusion that there is no rule of equi. And if there is no rule of equi, there can be no level of deep structure of the kind that is assumed in the classical theory.

5.2.1 Extraposition

Before discussing WH complements, I must say a word about the rule of extraposition. It is well known that many complement sentences in English, including a number of true *for-to* complements, behave in certain respects like NP constituents. Such sentences as those in example 2 have alternate forms in which the *for-to* complement appears in subject position:

(18) *a*. For his friends to call him a liar worries Bill.
      b. To be called a liar by his friends worries Bill.

Rosenbaum (1967) accounts for such alternations by deriving both variants from an abstract underlying form containing an NP complement in the subject position whose head noun is the pronoun *it* (see diagram 19). The actual surface forms are then accounted for by means

(19)

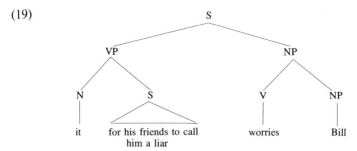

of two rules. The first rule, extraposition, optionally moves an S that is a complement to the head noun *it* to the end of the clause, producing surface forms such as those in example 2. The second rule, pronoun deletion, applies just in case extraposition does not, and obligatorily deletes the pronoun *it* when it occurs with a complement sentence, producing the sentences in example 18.

It is obvious that if the analysis of raising proposed here is correct, Rosenbaum's analysis of extraposition cannot be maintained without seriously complicating the grammar. Furthermore, from the point of view adopted here, Rosenbaum's analysis is unsatisfactory because it requires us to set up such abstract structures as diagram 19, which are never realized in surface structure in that form. In addition, a number of specific problems with Rosenbaum's treatment have been noted in the literature. Thus Lakoff and Ross (1966) have pointed out that Rosenbaum's rule of extraposition gives the wrong derived constituent structure, since the extraposed clause ends up under the domination of S rather than VP, incorrectly claiming the existence of a major constituent break between the object and the complement clause in such sentences as those in example 2. There are also problems with Rosenbaum's treatment of object-NP complements. As I have already pointed out in Chapter 4, Rosenbaum was forced to assume that extraposition applied to object-NP complements as well as subject-NP complements in order to state pronoun replacement (Rosenbaum's versions of raising) as a single rule. The evidence for extraposition from object position is extremely shaky, however, since the underlying pronoun *it* is almost always deleted obligatorily. In addition, in many cases Rosenbaum requires extraposition from object position to apply vacuously, an assumption for which there is no syntactic evidence. Finally, there is a theoretical argument against Rosenbaum's treatment of extraposition which has not been mentioned in the literature, but which seems to me to have some force. According to Rosenbaum, extraposition applies optionally, while the rule of pronoun deletion applies obligatorily, just in case extraposition has not been applied. We could equally well, however, let pronoun deletion be optional and extraposition obligatory, just in case pronoun deletion has not applied. The problem is to make a nonarbitrary choice between these two alternatives. Rosenbaum does offer one rather weak ordering argument in support of the first alternative, but it depends completely on the assumption that extraposition applies to object NPs, which, as we have just noted, is a dubious assumption in any case. In fact, there seems to be no principled way of choosing between the two alternatives. Thus the need to make an arbitrary choice between the two appears to be simply an artifact of an incorrect analysis.

All of these problems can be solved very simply if we assume, contra Rosenbaum, that the extraposed forms are basic, and that extraposition moves a sentential complement into the NP rather than out of it. Suppose that for such sentences as those in example 2 we assume the structure shown in diagram 20. As we noted in Chapter 4, the *it*

(20)

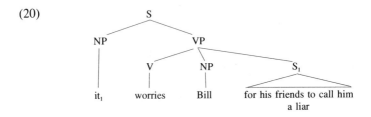

that appears in subject position in all cases of genuine extraposition is an anaphoric pronoun. Furthermore, it is clear that this *it* invariably refers to the complement sentence in the VP. Hence we may simply assume that the coreferentiality of the pronoun and the complement sentence (indicated by the identical indices in diagram 20) is a lexical property of the main verb. We now need a rule to carry out essentially the inverse of extraposition. Note first of all that sentences can occur as complements to such head nouns as *fact, idea, claim, notion, desire, wish,* and so forth. Hence the base rules for NP must allow for an S position to the right of the head noun. Let us assume that the rules for expanding NP are as follows:

(21) 1. NP → (NP) $\bar{\text{N}}$
      2. $\bar{\text{N}}$ → N (PP) (PP) ... (S)

Given these rules, we may immediately write the inverse of extraposition as a CT that replaces an empty S node that is a complement to the head noun *it* with a complement sentence, provided that the NP is the subject and that the complement S is immediately dominated by VP. At the same time, we require that the pronoun *it* and the complement S be marked with identical indices. The pronoun *it*, we shall assume, is deleted simultaneously with the movement of the complement S. Let us call this rule NP-complement formation (NPCF). It may be stated in the following manner:

(22) NP-complement formation (NPCF):

$$X-[_{\text{S}} [_{\text{NP}} [_{\bar{\text{N}}} \text{N}:it_1 \text{ S}:\phi \text{ }_{\bar{\text{N}}}] \text{ }_{\text{NP}}] \text{ } Tns \text{ } [_{\text{VP}} \text{V}:x \dots \text{ S}:y_1 \text{ }_{\text{VP}}] \text{ }_{\text{S}}]-Y \Rightarrow$$
$$X-[_{\text{S}} [_{\text{NP}} [_{\bar{\text{N}}} \text{N}:\phi \text{ S}:y_1 \text{ }_{\bar{\text{N}}}] \text{ }_{\text{NP}}] \text{ } Tns \text{ } [_{\text{VP}} \text{V}:x \dots \text{ S}:\phi \text{ }_{\text{VP}}] \text{ }_{\text{S}}]-Y$$

Given a structure of the form shown in diagram 23, NP-complement formation will operate in the manner indicated, replacing the empty S in the subject NP with the complement S and at the same time deleting the pronoun *it*.

(23)

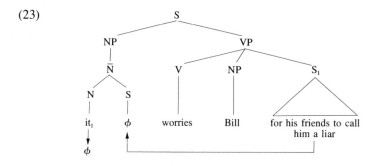

Under this reformulation of the process of extraposition, all of the problems mentioned earlier disappear. First of all, the rule of raising need not be complicated, since the infinitive complements of such verbs as *worry* will be to the right of the main verb at the point where raising is applicable. (In fact, raising is intrinsically ordered before

NPCF.) Second, we have related the extraposed and the nonextraposed forms of such sentences to one another directly without having to posit an underlying abstract NP complement. Third, there is no problem with the derived constituent structure of the extraposed sentences, since the complement sentence is generated directly in the proper position by the base rules and the lexical insertion rules for verbs. Fourth, we do not have to worry about the ordering of extraposition and pronoun deletion. Instead, the inverse of extraposition and the deletion of the pronoun apply simultaneously, expressing directly the co-occurrence relation between the presence of *it* and an extraposed clause. Finally, let us consider briefly the matter of object-NP complements. One possibility would be to extend NPCF so as to apply to object NPs as well as subject-NPs. If we did so, however, we would somehow have to make NPCF obligatory for object-NP complements, since the pronoun *it* never shows up in object position (except in a few cases, which I return to directly). In fact, the only real motivation for assuming that there are object-NP complements is the fact that we find such passive forms as the following:

(24) *a*. That the earth is round is believed by everyone.
 b. It is believed by everyone that the earth is round.

in which an object-NP complement has apparently been passivized (as in sentence 24*a*) and then extraposed (as in 24*b*). Pairs such as those in example 24, however, could equally well be accounted for by the rule of NPCF, as I have already formulated it, as long as we ensure that a pronoun that is coreferential with the complement sentence gets inserted in the subject position in passive forms. Let us assume, therefore, that such verbs as *believe* and *like,* which take object-NP complements, are subcategorized in the lexicon to take an object pronoun that is coreferential with the complement S. We shall then add a new rule to the grammar that deletes a pronominal object NP that is coreferential with the complement S:

(25) Object-pronoun deletion:
$$X - [_{VP} \text{ V}:x \text{ NP}:it_1 \ldots \text{ S}:y_1] - Y \Rightarrow$$
$$x - [_{VP} \text{ V}:x \text{ NP}:\phi \ldots \text{ S}:y_1] - Y$$

Since the transformational rules apply freely in any order they can, one of two things may happen to such an object pronoun. If it occurs in an active structure such as that in diagram 26, object-pronoun deletion

(26)

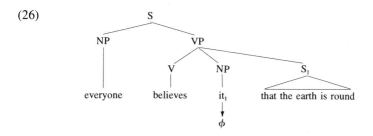

will apply, producing the sentence *everyone believes that the earth is round*. But suppose that an object pronoun of this sort occurs in a passive structure such as that in diagram 27. If object-pronoun deletion

(27)

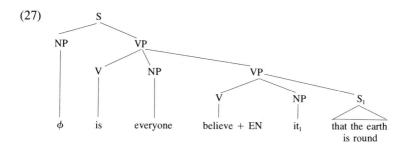

applies, the derivation will block, since there will be no way to fill in the empty subject NP after the application of the passive rules. Alternatively, we may apply agent postposing followed by object preposing, producing such sentences as 24b. Finally, we may apply NPCF, producing such sentences as 24a.

This analysis makes a rule of extraposition from object position or its inverse unnecessary, and at the same time accounts for such passive forms as those in example 24 by the regular rules of passivization and the rule of NPCF, which is needed in the grammar anyway. Furthermore, there is some indication that we may be correct in assuming the existence of a rule of object-pronoun deletion. Paul and Carol Kiparsky (1970) have observed that *resent, dislike*, and a few other verbs require the presence of a pronominal object:

(28) *a*. John resents it that people are always comparing him to Mozart.
    b. *John resents that people are always comparing him to Mozart.

(29) *a*. Bill dislikes it that Sally is so liberated.
    b. *Bill dislikes that Sally is so liberated.

Others, such as *believe* and *like*, seem to require the pronoun to be deleted in object position, though it can show up as the subject in passive sentences, as we have just seen. And there is still a third class of verbs for which the presence of a pronominal object is optional:

(30) *a*. I guarantee it that John is right.
    b. I guarantee that John is right.

These observations strongly suggest that the presence of a pronominal object that is coreferential with a complement sentence is simply a lexical property of particular verbs. If there is a rule of object-pronoun deletion in the grammar, we can account for it by classifying verbs in terms of whether they may, must, or cannot undergo the rule of object-pronoun deletion, leaving the rule of NP complement formation to apply perfectly generally to subject NPs. If NPCF were extended to apply to object NPs, it would have to be encumbered with ad hoc lexical restrictions, in order to account for the idiosyncratic restrictions on the appearance of an object pronoun discussed above.

If this analysis is correct, it is unnecessary to derive NP complements from underlying structures containing a sentential complement to a head noun *it*, as in the classical theory. Instead, we may assume that these sentential complements are generated in the same place as other sentential complements that we have discussed, namely, to the right of the main verb and directly dominated by the VP node. If, however, a verb also requires a pronominal NP that is coreferential with the sentential complement, the rule of NPCF will allow the sentential complement to occupy the empty S position in this NP, provided that it is in subject position, thus creating a true NP complement.[5] Apart from the advantages that have already been mentioned, this approach allows us to treat such verbs as *bother* and *worry* in exactly the same way as the other verbs that are optionally subcategorized to take an infinitive with a *for* subject. Thus we may subcategorize the verb *worry* in the following manner:

(31) *worry:* $[_{NP}$ *it*$_1]$ ——— NP $[_{S_1}$ *(for* NP) *to* VP]

5. There is undoubtedly more to be said on this subject. Ultimately, it seems to me, the notion of a CT must be generalized so as to permit operations reminiscent of the "generalized" or "double-based" transformation assumed in earlier versions of the classical theory. In particular, it is appropriate to represent such "global" processes as relative-clause formation and NP-complement formation, which apply in a given syntactic configuration independent of any particular lexical items, as operations that replace an empty node in some structure by an independently formed constituent of the same category. The rule of extraposition could then be regarded not as a "movement" transformation, but rather as a general condition of the formation of NP complements. Such a condition would say, in effect, that an NP complement can be formed in two alternative ways in English: (1) by inserting a sentential complement directly in the S position in the relevant NP, at the same time deleting the pronominal element *it*; and (2) by placing the sentential complement in postverbal position and marking the pronominal element coreferential with it. There are some indications that such an approach to extraposition is correct. Emonds has noted (1976) that extraposition is blocked for verbs that take an NP complement in both subject and object positions, for example, *that John has blood on his hands proves that he is the murderer*, but not **it proves that John is the murderer that he has blood on his hands*. This interesting fact can be explained in a principled way if it is assumed (1) that there is only a single S position in the VP and (2) that true NP complements can be formed only in subject position. Normally, an NP complement in subject position may be formed either by placing the sentential complement in the subject NP or by placing it in the S position in the VP, as was just suggested above. In the particular case in which the S position in VP is already taken by an object complement, however, the only place that a subject complement can go is in the subject NP itself. For further discussion of this matter, see Bowers 1979a and 1979b.

Then, whether the infinitive complement is formed by means of raising or FSF, the complement sentence will be able to undergo NPCF, thereby producing the nonextraposed sentences in example 18.

5.3   WH Complements

We must now consider briefly a number of problems that arise in connection with infinitive complements that are also indirect questions, or WH complements. Complements of this type occur after a small class of verbs including *tell, ask, wonder, know, learn, teach,* and a few others. Consider the following sentences:

(32) *a*. I wonder who to talk to.
       b. I told John who to talk to.
       c. I asked John who to talk to.

It is immediately apparent that the verbs *wonder, tell,* and *ask* correspond precisely to the verbs *try, persuade,* and *promise.* In sentence 32*a* the understood subject of the infinitive complement is the subject of the verb in the matrix clause; in 32*b* it is the object; and in 32*c* it is the subject again, despite the fact that *ask,* like *tell,* is a transitive verb.

These complements, however, have a number of peculiar properties that need to be explained. In particular, we must account for the placement of the *wh* words *who, what, where,* and so on at the beginning of the infinitive clause. It seems reasonable to assume that the *wh* word is moved by the same rule of *wh* movement that applies in the formation of *wh* questions in main clauses and in the formation of tensed indirect questions such as the following:[6]

(33) *a*. I wonder who I should talk to.
       b. I told John who he should talk to.
       c. I asked John who I should talk to.

---

6. I discuss the formation of questions in main clauses and in tensed indirect questions in more detail in Chapter 6.

At the same time it would be highly desirable to account for the fact (first noted, as far as I am aware, by Emonds [1976]) that the presence of a *wh* word in an infinitive complement is incompatible with the presence of a *for* subject. Thus the following sentences are uniformly impossible in English:

(34) *a.* *I wonder who for John to talk to.
     b. *I told Bill who for Mary to talk to.
     c. *I asked Mary who for Bill to talk to.

though the corresponding tensed WH complements are perfectly acceptable:

(35) *a.* I wonder who John should talk to.
     b. I told Bill who Mary should talk to.
     c. I asked Mary who Bill had talked to.

If we recall the analysis of *for* subjects proposed in Section 5.2, it is immediately evident that this odd restriction governing the formation of infinitival WH complements can be explained automatically if we assume that the "topic" position provided by rule 7 is not only the position to which the subjects of true *for-to* complements are moved, but also the position to which all *wh* phrases are moved.[7] Since an empty node may be filled, by definition, only by one constituent of the same type, it follows automatically that either FSF or *wh* movement may apply, but not both. Note that the constraint cannot be accounted for by a simple restriction on the occurrence of *wh* words in true *for-to* complements, since echo questions of the following sort are perfectly acceptable:

(36) *a.* You would like for John to talk to who(m)?
     b. It bothers you for John to be examined by which doctor?

---

7. Chapter 6 and Bowers 1976 present further arguments in support of this analysis. The incompatibility of *wh* movement and FSF is, it turns out, only one instance of a wide range of restrictions of this sort that can be explained automatically under an analysis of the kind proposed in the text.

In tensed WH complements no rule comparable to FSF raises the subject into topic position. On the contrary, the subjects of tensed clauses invariably remain in the subject position. Hence the topic position will always be available for *wh* movement, thus accounting for the sentences in example 35.

If this proposal is correct, such a sentence as 32*a* will be derived in the manner shown in diagram 37. On the S² cycle, the *wh* word ʼwho is

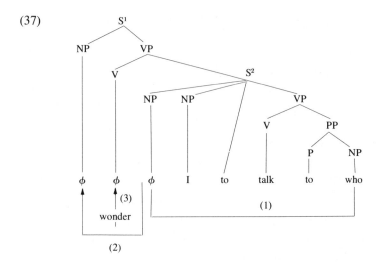

(37)

moved into the "topic" position to the left of the subject NP *I*. Then, on the S¹ cycle, raising applies, followed by the insertion of the main verb *wonder*. The result is the correct form: *I wonder who to talk to*.

One consequence of this analysis is that the subject of a WH infinitive complement MUST ALWAYS BE RAISED INTO THE MATRIX CLAUSE. Consider what happens if the subject of the WH infinitive complement is the only *wh* word in the complement. As it is the subject of the infinitive, it must be raised into the matrix clause. At the same time, as it is the only *wh* word in the infinitive complement, it must be moved into the topic position by *wh* movement. Obviously not both of these conditions can be met by a single NP. It follows that such sentences as the following should be ungrammatical, as indeed they are:[8]

(38) *a*. *Who wonders to talk to Bill?
     b. *Who did you tell to talk to Bill?
     c. *Who asked John to talk to Bill?

This observation, however, immediately raises a number of problems. First of all, if the *wh* word that is the subject of the infinitive complement is moved into the topic position on the lower cycle, and is thus prevented from undergoing raising, what is to prevent the relevant NP positions in the matrix clause from being filled lexically, thus fulfilling the requirements for the lexical insertion of a main verb and apparently predicting the grammaticality of such sentences as the following?

(39) *a*. *John wonders who to talk to Bill.
     b. *I told John who to talk to Bill.
     c. *I asked John who to talk to Bill.

This problem can be solved as soon as we note the interesting fact that subjects are structurally distinct from preposed *wh* words only when the *wh* word is derived from SOME POSITION OTHER THAN THE SUBJECT POSITION. In other words, the structural configuration of a sentence is unaltered by the application of *wh* movement to a subject NP. Thus the result of applying *wh* movement to a string of the form *who-to-talk-to-Bill* will be a string of exactly the same form. Furthermore, none of the structural relationships will be altered either, since the subject NP will still be immediately dominated by S.

---

8. Note that sentences 38*b* and 38*c* are unacceptable only when their complements are interpreted as WH complements. They are in fact grammatical sentences, but only under a rather different interpretation. The reason is that both *tell* and *ask* occur with non-WH-infinitive complements as well as with WH-infinitive complements. Thus sentences 38*b* and 38*c* are grammatical when they are understood as being the direct question forms of the sentences *you told someone to talk to Bill* and *someone asked John to talk to Bill,* respectively, but not when they are understood as being the direct question forms of 32*b* and 32*c*. I return to this point shortly.

This fact has a number of interesting consequences. Of immediate interest here is the fact that the structural description for raising will still be met, even though the subject NP has been moved by *wh* movement. This in turn means that if the relevant NP positions in the matrix clause are lexically filled, the derivation will block, since raising will be unable to apply. Hence the forms in example 39 will be impossible whether or not *wh* movement has (vacuously) applied to the *wh* word in subject position.

This explanation of the ungrammaticality of the sentences in example 39, however, apparently makes it impossible to explain the ungrammaticality of the sentences in example 38. For if raising applies to subject NPs whether or not they have been affected by *wh* movement, what is to prevent a *wh* word in subject position in the infinitive complement from being first preposed (vacuously, of course) by *wh* movement and then raised, thereby producing the ungrammatical forms in example 38? In order to resolve these difficulties satisfactorily, we must consider what sort of subcategorization conditions are to be associated with such verbs as *wonder, tell,* and *ask.*

Joan Bresnan (1970) has argued (correctly, I believe) that verbs must be subcategorized for complement types, and in particular that verbs must be subcategorized for whether or not they take WH complements. Now it has already been shown in Section 5.2 that the *for* phrase that appears in true *for-to* complements must be subcategorized by the matrix verb. Perhaps, then, the simplest way of ensuring that a verb occurs with a *wh* complement is simply to subcategorize it for a preposed *wh* constituent. We can then write subcategorization features of the following sort for the verbs *wonder, tell, ask,* and so forth:

(40) *a.* *wonder*: NP _____ [$_S$ [$_{NP}$ ... *wh*-PRO ...] *to* ... $_S$]
      b. *tell*: NP _____ NP [$_S$ [$_{NP}$ ... *wh*-PRO ...] *to* ... $_S$]

This device will immediately prevent the sentences in example 38 from being generated. For if the only *wh* word in the infinitive complement is in subject position, and this NP is raised, the conditions for insertion of a verb that takes a WH complement will no longer be met, since there will be no preposed *wh* word in the topic position in the infinitive complement. In fact, the only way that such subcategorization conditions as those above (40) can be satisfied is for some *wh* word that is *not* in subject position to be preposed into topic position.

One further peculiarity of these complements requires discussion. It is a fact that raising invariably applies before lexical insertion in WH infinitives. In other words, there are, as far as I am aware, no verbs like *seem* and *believe* that take WH-infinitive complements. Thus we find no sentences of the following sort in English:

(41) *a*. *John seems who to have talked to.
      b. *I believe John who to have talked to.
      c. *I wonder Bill who to have talked to.
      d. *I asked Bill who to have talked to.

Notice, however, that we have, in effect, already accounted for this fact in the subcategorization conditions just proposed for such verbs as *wonder, tell,* and *ask.* The reason is that in the subcategorization conditions for these verbs, no subject NP is specified between the preposed *wh* word and the infinitive marker *to.* This condition can be met only if the subject of the infinitive complement has already been removed by raising before lexical insertion on the matrix cycle. Hence the subcategorization conditions themselves ensure that raising can never take place after lexical insertion for these verbs.

Now recall that we have so far failed to provide any explicit mechanism to account for the order in which verbs require raising and lexical insertion to apply. The remarks just made concerning the application of raising in WH-infinitive complements suggest that the simplest way to impose correct ordering on the rules is to subcategorize verbs according to whether or not their infinitive complements contain a subject NP. We have already seen that it is necessary for the matrix verb to subcategorize such preposed constituents as the *wh* word that occurs in WH infinitives and the *for* subject of true *for-to* complements. Hence it is hardly surprising to find that it is also necessary for the matrix verb to subcategorize the subject of the infinitive complement. If a verb requires its infinitive complement to contain a subject NP, that simply means, in effect, that raising must apply *after* lexical insertion. If a verb requires that its infinitive complement contain no subject NP, then raising must already have applied at that point in the derivation.

The verbs *seem* and *believe* can now be subcategorized:

(42) *a. seem:* _____ [$_S$ NP *to* VP]
       b. believe: NP _____ [$_S$ NP *to* VP]

The verbs *try* and *persuade* will have subcategorization conditions of the following form:

(43) *a. try:* NP _____ [$_S$ *to* VP]
       b. persuade: NP _____ NP [$_S$ *to* VP]

Note that this proposal has the virtue of representing explicitly the difference between such a verb as *try* and such a verb as *believe*. Previously these verbs were assigned exactly the same subcategorization condition, namely, one of the form NP _____ S, but now they are represented quite differently, since the latter, but not the former, also requires its infinitive complement to have a subject NP. Furthermore, it is no longer necessary for verbs to be specifically marked for the ordering of raising and lexical insertion, as was assumed in Chapter 4. Instead, we may simply allow all of the rules, both the "purely syntactic" rules and the lexical insertion rules, to apply in random sequential order; that is, they may apply in any order whatsoever, whenever their structural description is met. All of the constraints on the class of possible derivations that are specific to English are provided by the intrinsic ordering constraints governing the application of the syntactic rules and the lexical insertion rules for specific verbs.

5.4   Object Raising

To complete this analysis of infinitive complements in English, it is necessary to discuss briefly the rule of "tough movement," as it is generally referred to in the literature. For reasons that will become obvious as we proceed, I prefer to rechristen this rule "object raising." This rule is meant to account for the relationship between pairs of sentences such as the following:

(44) *a.* John is easy to please.
      b. It is easy to please John.

As it is usually formulated, object raising applies to an underlying structure of roughly the form 44*b*, and replaces the pronoun *it* in subject position in the matrix clause with the object NP in the infinitive complement of various adjectives—*easy, tough, difficult, pleasant,* and a number of others. It should be apparent from our earlier discussion of raising into subject position that it is essential, if the classical theory is to be maintained, that such sentences as 44*a* have an underlying pronoun *it* in subject position in the matrix clause to serve as a place holder for the raised object NP in the infinitive complement. In this case, however, it is not so obvious that this assumption is wrong, since there are close paraphrases of the form 44*b* in which a pronoun *it* actually shows up in surface structure, together with an infinitive complement. A closer analysis, however, reveals that this formulation of object raising shares many of the defects that plague the classical analysis of raising.

Notice, first of all, that the classical analysis of object raising necessarily implies that such pairs as those in example 44 are synonymous. It is certainly true that the subject of sentence 44*a* is the understood object of the verb in the infinitive complement, but it is not so obvious that we want to consider sentences 44*a* and 44*b* to be synonymous. In particular, notice that 44*a* predicates something of John—being easy to please—whereas 44*b* predicates something—being easy—of the whole clause *to please John*. Note that the complement of 44*b* can be moved into the subject NP by the rule of NP-complement formation, to produce such a sentence as:

(45) To please John is easy.

thus demonstrating quite clearly that it is the whole clause in sentence 44*b* that is modified by the predicate *be easy*.

This difference does not, of course, show up clearly as long as we are focusing only on the fact that the subject of sentence 44*a* is the understood object of the verb in the complement sentence. It is easy to find cases, however, in which the two sentence types differ in meaning. Consider the following pairs, in which the raised object NP contains a quantifier:

(46) *a*. Three books were easy to read.
 b. It was easy to read three books.

(47) *a*. It is tough to read many books.
 b. Many books are tough to read.

Furthermore, there are pairs of sentences such as the following:

(48) *a*. Sonatas are easy to play on this violin.
 b. This violin is easy to play sonatas on.

The difference in meaning between sentences 48*a* and 48*b* is hard to explain if both are derived from an underlying structure of the form *it is easy to play sonatas on this violin*.

These observations strongly suggest that it is wrong to assume that such pairs as those in example 44 derive from the same underlying structure. At the same time, any theory must account for the fact that the subject of sentence 44*a* is understood as the object of the verb in the infinitive complement. In the framework proposed here, there is a straightforward way of describing these facts. Suppose that we derive such sentences as 44*b* from structures of the form shown in diagram 49, containing an anaphoric pronoun *it* in the subject position. When we recall the analysis of extraposition proposed in Section 5.2.1, it is evident that diagram 49 immediately accounts for the existence of such paraphrases as example 45, containing an NP complement in subject position. At the same time, the presence of the pronoun *it* in subject position in the matrix clause will prevent object raising from applying.

(49)

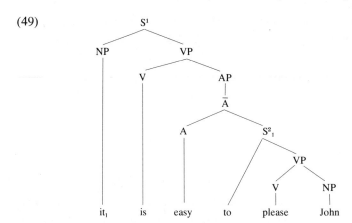

Consider next sentence 44*a*. In the framework proposed here, the simplest way of accounting for such sentences is to derive them from a structure like that shown in diagram 49 with an empty subject NP in the matrix clause, as in diagram 50. Given structures of this form, we can

(50)

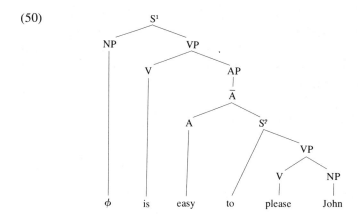

immediately formulate object raising as a CT that replaces an empty subject NP in the matrix clause with the object NP in the infinitive complement.[9]

9. Note that when the main verb is transitive, the raised object shows up in object position in the matrix clause: *I consider John easy to please, I found him easy to talk*

If this proposal is correct, we should expect to find sentences in English which are derived by means of object raising but which have no corresponding paraphrase of the *it is easy to please John* type. In fact, this prediction is correct, as Howard Lasnik and Robert Fiengo (1974) have noted. Thus we find such examples as the following:

(51) *a*. Mary is pretty to look at.
       b. *It is pretty to look at Mary.

Examples of this sort pose serious problems for the standard analysis of object raising. The point is that such adjectives as *pretty*, unlike such adjectives as *easy*, do not permit an NP complement, yet still undergo object raising. The classical theory has no reasonable source for such sentences. The only possibility is to add an ad hoc condition to the rule of tough movement making it obligatory for some adjectives but optional for others. At the same time, of course, the rule of extraposition will have to be made obligatory for these adjectives also, in order to prevent such sentences as *to look at Mary is pretty*. In fact, such sentences as 51*a* and 51*b* pose exactly the same problems for the classical theory as the *seem* sentences disucssed in Chapter 4 (Section 4.2). Just as in the case of *seem*, it is necessary to assume a nonexistent source of the form:

(52) [$_{NP}$ it [$_S$ to look at Mary]] is pretty

which is not only syntactically but semantically incorrect, and then add ad hoc conditions to the otherwise optional rules of extraposition and tough movement, making them obligatory for just this class of adjectives.

If such sentences as 44*a* and 44*b* are derived from different sources, in the manner just suggested, none of these problems arise. The only

---

to, and the like. Hence we have object raising into subject position and object raising into object position, just as in the case of subject raising. For other cases in which object raising raises the object of the infinitive into object position in the matrix clause, see Section 5.5.

thing that needs to be said about such an adjective as *pretty* is that it takes an infinitive complement but not a subject-NP complement, whereas such adjectives as *easy* take both types of complements. Thus sentence 51*a* will be derived automatically by means of object raising from a structure of the sort shown in diagram 53.

(53)

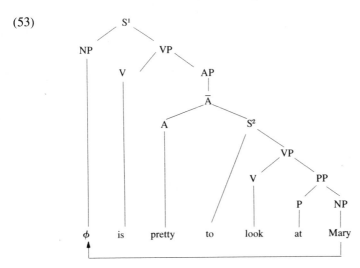

Yet, this analysis still fails to explain fully the difference between such sentences as *John is easy to please* and *Mary is pretty to look at*. In particular, note that such adjectives as *pretty* impose selectional restrictions on the subject, while such adjectives as *easy* do not. Thus we can have such sentences as *that situation is easy to deal with, that concept is easy to grasp, the house is easy to find.* But the corresponding sentences with *pretty* are impossible, since the subject nouns are not the type that are selected by the adjective *pretty: *that situation is pretty to deal with, *that concept is pretty to grasp, *the house is pretty to find,* and so on. If, as we have been assuming, the structure at the point where the adjectives *pretty* and *easy* are inserted in the matrix clause is the same in all of these cases:

(54) $[_{NP}\phi]-[_{V}\phi]-[_{AP}$ $\left\{ \begin{array}{c} \text{pretty} \\ \text{easy} \end{array} \right\}$ to look at Mary]

then the existence of selectional restrictions in the case of *pretty* is difficult to explain, though such a structure as 54 is perfectly consistent with the behavior of *easy*.

What we have here seems to be yet another case in which it is necessary to permit a syntactic rule (in this case, object raising) to apply both before and after the lexical insertion rules on the matrix cycle. If such adjectives as *pretty* are subcategorized to take a subject NP, object raising will apply first on the matrix cycle, followed by lexical insertion, as in diagram 55. The raised object NP will then be

(55)

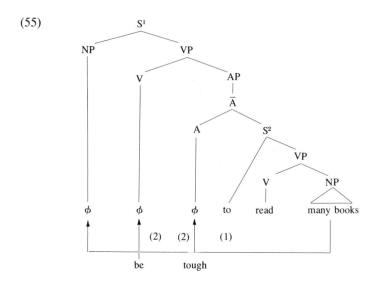

interpreted not only as the object of the verb in the infinitive complement, but also as the subject of the predicate in the matrix clause. Such an adjective as *easy*, which has to be subjectless at the point where it is inserted, will not permit raising to apply until after lexical insertion.

Notice that it might still be possible to preserve the appearance of a level of deep structure if we derived the *pretty to look at* examples from structures containing an NP in both the matrix clause and the infinitive complement. Such an analysis would then require a rule very similar to equi, deleting the object of the complement sentence under identity with the subject of the matrix clause. Just such an analysis has been suggested by Lasnik and Fiengo (1974), who propose to derive the sentence *Mary is pretty to look at* from a structure such as that in diagram 56. The indexed element PRO is of course not an actual NP,

(56)

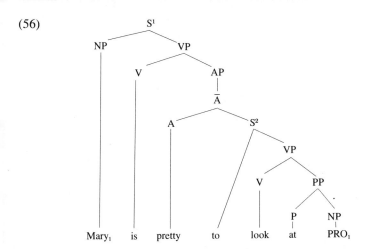

but rather a pro form with the special property of being coreferential with the subject of the matrix clause. This pro form must be present and must be deleted obligatorily, just as in the case of equi. In fact, it is evident that the only real reason for setting up this special pro form in the infinitive complement is to preserve the appearance of a level of deep structure at all costs. Hence the introduction of such devices into underlying representations is tantamount to giving up a level of deep structure in any case. Every time we come across a case in which lexical insertion must follow the application of some syntactic rule, we can always artificially preserve a level of deep structure by setting up a special pro form in underlying representations and replacing the syntactic rule in question with an obligatory deletion rule. But since the only motivation for setting up these pro forms is to preserve a level of deep structure in the face of counterexamples, their use is at best a notational variant of a theory without deep structure.

The real objection to object deletion, however, as in the case of equi, is that it requires the process of object raising to be split up arbitrarily into the two unrelated rules of object raising and object deletion, failing once again to express a syntactic generalization of English grammar. Furthermore, if subject raising and object raising are themselves distinct manifestations of a single, very general syntactic process of raising, a rule of object deletion is inconsistent with the analysis of subject raising proposed earlier.

5.5   Constructions with Both Subject Raising and Object Raising

To conclude this chapter I shall discuss briefly a class of sentences containing infinitive complements which have the interesting property of permitting both subject raising and object raising to apply. Consider, for example, the following sentences:

(57) *a*. I gave Mary a book to read.
     b. John bought a book for Mary to read.
     c. Mary handed Harry an apple to peel.
     d. John bought a book to read.
     e. I found a present to give to Mary.
     f. I have a painting for you to look at.
     g. John used the knife to cut the salami with.
     h. Bill left the article for us to read.

Before these constructions are analyzed in detail, two points must be made. First, the infinitives in these examples are not, as one might be tempted to think, reduced forms of *in order to* clauses. The two constructions are quite distinct in several respects. In particular, the object NP in a true *in order to* construction may never be absent in surface structure, as it is in the sentences in example 57. Instead, there must be a pronoun that is coreferential with the relevant NP in the matrix clause. In fact, the subject of an *in order to* clause may not be absent either, unless it happens to be coreferential with the subject of the matrix clause. Thus we find *in order to* constructions of the following sort corresponding to the sentences in example 57:

(58)   *a*. I gave Mary a book in order for *her* to read *it*.
       b. John bought a book for Mary in order for *her* to read *it*.
       c. Mary handed Harry an apple in order for *him* to peel *it*.
       d. John bought the book in order to read *it*.
       e. I found a present in order to give *it* to Mary.
       f. John used the knife in order to cut the salami with *it*.

There are, however, no sentences of the following form:

(59)   *a*. *I gave Mary a book in order to read.
       b. *John bought a book for Mary in order to read.
       c. *Mary handed Harry an apple in order to peel.

and so on. One might, of course, attempt to derive the forms in example 57 from underlying forms like those in example 58 by deleting the coreferential pronouns. Such a derivation, however, would have to ignore the obvious differences in meaning between the sentences of the two types. The sentence *I bought a book for Mary to read* is not equivalent in meaning to *I bought a book in order for Mary to read it,* nor does one even imply the other. Rather, the former implies a sentence of the form *the book is for Mary to read,* a point to which I shall return shortly.

The second point is that the sentences in example 57 cannot be derived from underlying relative clauses with a *for-to* relative. In other words, the sentence *I gave Mary a book to read* cannot derive from a structure of the form *I–gave–a book to read–to Mary.* To see that this is so, it is necessary only to try to passivize the putative complex object. The result either is ungrammatical or has a sense that is quite different from the one that we are interested in:

(60)   *a*. ?A book to read was given to Mary.
       b. ?A book for Mary to read was bought by John.
       c. ?An apple to peel was handed to Harry by Mary.
       d. ?A book to read was bought by John.
       e. ?The knife to cut the salami with was used by John.

The object NP by itself, however—unaccompanied, that is, by the infinitive clause—is perfectly amenable to passivization, and the resulting sentences are equivalent in meaning to the active forms in example 57:

(61) *a*. A book was given to Mary to read.
     b. An apple was handed to Harry to peel by Mary.
     c. The knife was used to cut the salami with by John.
     d. The article was left by Bill for us to read.

and so on. If these infinitive complements are neither reduced *in order to* clauses nor infinitival relatives, the only reasonable conclusion seems to be that they are infinitive complements of the usual sort. Let us consider, therefore, how we are to derive such sentences under the assumption that they are infinitive complements that are subcategorized by the main verb.

The most striking fact about these complements is that the object of the matrix clause is invariably understood as the object of the infinitive complement. This fact immediately suggests that the rule of object raising is responsible for raising the object of the infinitive complement into the matrix clause. Furthermore, since the object of the matrix clause obviously has a grammatical relation to the matrix verb, object raising must apply before lexical insertion.

Consider next what happens to the subject of the infinitive complement. In such sentences as 57*a* and 57*c*, the understood subject of an infinitive complement is the indirect object. In sentences 57*b*, 57*f*, and 57*h*, the understood subject of the infinitive is the NP in the benefactive *for* phrase.[10] In the remaining examples, the understood subject of

10. It is easy to show that the *for* phrases in these examples are benefactive phrases and not the *for* subjects of true *for-to* complements, because they can undergo the regular rule of dative movement. Thus corresponding to examples 57*b* and 57*h* we find the alternative forms: *John bought Mary a book to read* and *Bill left us an article to read*. (Dative movement does not apply in 57*f*, **I have you a painting to look at*, because *for* dative movement is generally impossible with the verb *have*: *I have a book for you*, but **I have you a book*.) Likewise, the examples with indirect objects have alternative forms containing *to* dative phrases: *I gave a book to Mary to read, Mary handed an apple to Harry to peel*. For a much more detailed analysis of the

the infinitive complement is the subject of the matrix clause. Notice, however, that since the object NP in all of these examples is filled in by object raising, we cannot raise the subjects of these infinitive complements into the object position, as we did in the case of the infinitive complements discussed in Chapter 4. These observations strongly suggest that subject raising must be extended so as to raise the subjects of infinitive complements into the indirect-object position as well as the direct-object position.

If these proposals are correct, then we may derive such a sentence as 57*a* in the manner shown in diagram 62. The subject NP *Mary* is

(62)

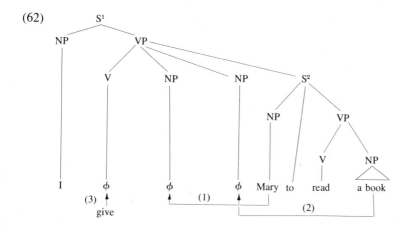

raised into the indirect-object position by the rule of subject raising. At the same time, the object of the infinitive complement *a book* is raised into the object position by the rule of object raising. Finally, we may insert the verb *give*. The result is a structure of the form shown in diagram 63, in which all of the arguments of the verb in the infinitive complement have been removed, leaving behind the infinitive form *to read:*

---

grammatical relations in these sentences than is presented here, see Bowers 1973: 530–38.

(63)

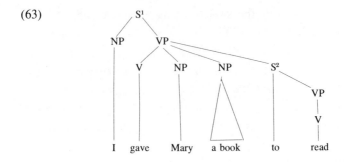

Notice that we now have two rules that raise constituents out of an infinitive complement. The first (subject raising) applies only to subjects; the second (object raising) applies to virtually any constituent that is a complement of the verb, that is, to nonsubjects. Together these two rules make it possible for any constituent that is subcategorized by the verb in an infinitive complement to be raised into the matrix clause. This fact strongly suggests that there is just a single, rather general syntactic process of raising, and that the particular constituent that is raised in any given sentence is determined by the matrix verb (or adjective).

6 Topicalization Processes

6.1 Introduction

I suggested in Chapter 5 that the phrase-structure rules for English must provide a "topic" position to the left of the subject NP, into which constituents of various kinds can be moved. We have seen that in a number of instances this assumption, together with the theory of CTs, allows us to provide a general explanation for the incompatibility of certain fronting rules. In particular, we can explain automatically why the presence of a *for* subject in an infinitive complement prevents the application of any other fronting rules within the complement clause. Similarly, if we assume that the topic position is also the position to which *wh* words are moved in WH infinitives, then we can immediately explain in a principled way an otherwise rather odd restriction preventing the occurrence of *for* subjects in WH infinitives. In fact, these particular restrictions are only representative of a wide range of similar constraints governing the co-occurrence of topicalized constituents in English, all of which can be explained automatically in the theory proposed here, given the correct set of PS rules. At the same time, however, a closer look at the variety of constructions involving topicalized constituents in English reveals that matters are considerably more complex than was indicated in our earlier discussion. We must therefore examine in some detail the system of topicalization processes in English. Among the phenomena in question are a number of well-known processes: *wh* movement, subject-auxiliary inversion, locative preposing, VP preposing, and others. I shall attempt to show that in every case the reformulation of rules that is required in the framework proposed here leads to a simplification of the statement of particular rules and in many cases to more general rules in place of the many ad hoc and unsystematic restrictions required in the classical theory.

6.2 Why Topicalized Sentences Can't Be Relativized or Questioned

Langendoen has noted (1973) that the subject in such sentences as the following, containing a preposed locative phrase:

(1) *a.* In the garden stands a fountain.
     b. Over that fence is the outside world.

can be neither questioned nor relativized:

(2) *a.* *What does in the garden stand?
     b. *What kind of world must over that fence be?

(3) *a.* *The fountain that in the garden stands is my favorite.
     b. *The kind of world that over the fence must be is
         unimaginable.

If the postposed NP in such sentences is a direct object, this fact is difficult to explain in the classical theory, since direct objects normally present no obstacle to either questioning or relativization:

(4) *a.* What boy does Mark know?
     b. The boy that Mark knows is tall.

Langendoen therefore proposes an analysis of locative inversion that results in a derived constituent structure of the sort shown in diagram 5

(5)

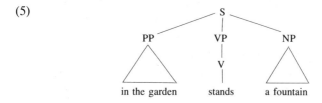

for such sentences as 1*a*. Citing research by Keenan (in particular, Keenan and Comrie 1972), which indicates that NPs are relativizable or not (and by extension subject to questioning or not), depending on their surface syntactic structure before relativization (or questioning), Langendoen argues that in English, at any rate, direct objects are subject to relativization or questioning, whereas the postposed NP in such a structure as that shown in diagram 5 is below the cut-off point for accessibility to relativization or questioning.[1] This explanation will not work, however, for such sentences as those in examples 2 and 3 not only show that locative-inversion sentences such as those in example 1 cannot be questioned or relativized, but also show that such sentences as the following, in which only the locative phrase has been preposed, cannot be questioned or relativized:

(6)   *a*. In the garden a fountain stands.
     b. On the fence an old man sat.

As the NP *a fountain* in sentence 6*a* is the subject, and as subjects are certainly "accessible" to questioning and relativization in English, it follows that it cannot be merely the position of the NP that is to be questioned or relativized that is responsible for the ungrammaticality of the sentences in examples 2 and 3. Furthermore, in transitive sentences with a preposed locative phrase:

(7)   *a*. In the closet the boy put the mop.
     b. Beside the window they put the chair.

1. Langendoen argues further that these facts refute the structure-preserving hypothesis proposed in Emonds 1976, since the only way to account for locative-inversion sentences in Emonds's framework is by means of a structure-preserving permutation rule, which would result in a structure containing the NP *a fountain* in the direct-object position, thus predicting, falsely, that the postposed NP in such examples should be subject to relativization and questioning. This attempted refutation of Emonds's theory is discussed in detail in Bowers 1976, where it is shown that an alternative analysis is possible in Emonds's framework which accounts for the fact that these sentences cannot be questioned or relativized in a much less ad hoc way than Langendoen's analysis does. This explanation will be discussed directly. The reader should note, however, that in this work I have accepted Langendoen's claim that locative-inversion sentences have a surface structure of the form shown in diagram 5, whereas in the paper referred to above I argued that the postposed NP was in the

neither the subject nor the direct object can be relativized or questioned:

(8) *a.* *Who in the closet put the mop?
     b. *Who beside the window put the chair?
     c. *What in the closet did the boy put?
     d. *What beside the window did they put?

(9) *a.* *The boy that in the closet put the mop was John.
     b. *The man who beside the window put the chair was Bill.
     c. *The mop that in the closet the boy put was wet.
     d. *The chair that beside the window they put is ugly.

Examples of this sort demonstrate that it is the presence of the preposed locative phrase that is responsible for the inability of such sentences to be questioned or relativized, and that the constituent structure of the postposed NP in such sentences as those in example 1 is simply irrelevant. It is also worth noting that the incompatibility of preposed locative phrases with relativization and questioning cannot be attributed simply to the presence of a *wh* word, since echo questions containing a preposed locative are perfectly acceptable:

(10) *a.* In the garden stands which fountain?
      b. Over that fence is what?

It seems, therefore, that the restriction has to do with the application of the rules themselves. The relevant generalization seems to be that locative preposing and *wh* movement cannot both apply within the same clause.

The next question, then, is how this generalization is to be captured in the grammar. The theory proposed here has a straightforward way of dealing with this problem. Let us suppose that the PS rules for English

---

direct-object position. My reasons for accepting this aspect of Langendoen's analysis have to do with some new facts that were not discussed in either Langendoen's paper or mine. I shall discuss this matter shortly.

contain (as a first approximation) the following expansion rule for the node S:

(11) $S \rightarrow \left(\left\{ \begin{array}{c} NP \\ PP \end{array} \right\} \right) \quad NP \quad \left(\left\{ \begin{array}{c} Tns \\ to \end{array} \right\} \right) \quad VP$

This rule will immediately allow us to construct P-markers of the sort shown in diagram 12. We can now define a CT that simply fills the

(12)

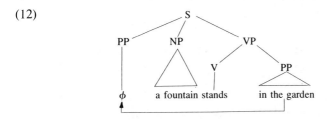

empty PP node in topic position with a locative phrase of the appropriate sort. This rule will operate in the manner shown in diagram 12. At the same time let us formulate the rule of *wh* movement as a CT that replaces an empty node of the appropriate category in the topic position. We can then derive such a sentence as *what did you see in the garden?* (ignoring for the moment the problem of the preposed auxiliary element) as in diagram 13. It is immediately evident that when the

(13)

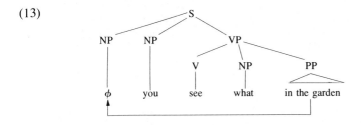

rules are formulated in this way, locative preposing and *wh* movement can never apply within the same clause. The reason is simply that PS rule 11 allows for either a PP or an NP in the topic position, but not both. Since a node can be filled, by definition, only by a single constituent, it follows at once that either locative preposing or *wh* movement may apply in a given clause, but not both.[2] At the same time, this analysis explains why locative preposing and *wh* movement are incompatible in transitive sentences, as well as in intransitive sentences. Thus the sentences in examples 8 and 9 are ungrammatical for exactly the same reason that the sentences in examples 2 and 3 are.

As further confirmation of the correctness of this approach, consider the well-known fact that no more than one *wh* word may be fronted in a single clause in English. This fact can be seen in the following sentences:

(14) *a.* Who saw what?
     b. *Who what saw?
     c. *What did who see?
     d. The man who saw what has come to dinner.
     e. *The man who what saw has come to dinner.
     f. *The man what who saw has come to dinner.

2. I explicitly reject the proposal in Emonds 1970 (which is also implicitly accepted in Chomsky 1970 and 1973 that the theory of grammar should permit nodes to be "doubly filled." Emonds's only real argument for the use of such a device rests on what seems to me a fundamentally wrong analysis of extraposition, which attempts to treat it as a root transformation rather than as a structure-preserving rule. This matter is discussed in Bowers 1973, pp. 638n–40n.

Chomsky's decision to permit "doubly filled" nodes (or, in his terminology, to allow "feature complexes" to be associated with nonlexical as well as lexical phrase categories) is dictated at least in part by (1) his desire to derive the subject of such nominals as *the enemy's destruction of the city* from the subject position in deep structure; (2) the fact that the element *there* which appears in such existential sentences as *there is a mouse in my room* must have the structure of an NP; and (3) the fact that the pronoun *it* which appears with the "pro-verb" *do* in pseudo-cleft sentences, and in other constructions as well, must have the structure of an NP. It has already been shown in earlier chapters that in the first two cases the necessity of feature complexes is simply a consequence of the classical theory of transformations, and that the problems that these examples pose simply disappear under the theory proposed here. The same is true in the third case as well. For discussion, see Bowers 1973, chap. 4. See also McCawley 1973 and 1975 for criticism of the use of doubly filled nodes.

With respect to the discussion in the text, note that the possibility of allowing doubly filled nodes would immediately turn my claim that there is only one constituent allowed in the topic position into an ad hoc and unexplained statement of fact, instead of an automatic consequence of the theory of co-occurrence transformations. The same would be true in innumerable other cases also. In short, to permit doubly filled nodes in the theory of grammar would be to add enormously to its power, without any gain in explanatory adequacy.

This fact has frequently been noted in the literature but has never been explained adequately. It is an automatic consequence of the theory proposed here, however, together with the language-specific PS rules for English, that no more than one *wh* word will be able to be fronted within a single clause. There is nothing to prevent *wh* movement from applying twice in the same sentence, though, as long as the *wh* words are in separate clauses. Thus if a sentence contains one or more verbs that require WH complements, *wh* movement can apply in each of the WH complements as well as in the main clause, producing such perfectly acceptable sentences as:

(15) *a.* When did you ask Bill who he had talked to?
      b. Why did you tell Bill who he should ask what to do?
      c. Why is he wondering what to do?
      d. When did he tell John who to ask what to do?

Furthermore, if *wh* movement is formulated in such a way that the *wh* word is attracted to the nearest topic position by which it is dominated, we can also explain automatically why *wh* words cannot cross over one another. Thus it is perfectly possible to move a *wh* word into a topic node several clauses up from it, as in the following examples:

(16) *a.* Who did you tell Bill to persuade Mary to talk to ϕ?
      b. I asked John who he had persuaded Mary to talk to ϕ.

but a *wh* word cannot cross over a *wh* word in an embedded indirect question to produce such sentences as:

(17) *a.* *Who did you ask John who he had persuaded Mary to talk to ϕ?
      b. *I asked John who he had told Mary what to talk about with ϕ.

What this amounts to is that a *wh* word must fall within the scope of the nearest direct or indirect question by which it is dominated. Notice, incidentally, that since the preposed *wh* word in an indirect question is, as I proposed in Chapter 5, subcategorized by the matrix verb, it will be impossible to place a *wh* word in the topic position unless the main verb in the clause above it is subcategorized to take indirect questions. One consequence of this fact is that in a complex sentence containing no verbs that take indirect questions, the only place to which a *wh* word can be moved is the topic position in the topmost clause. Thus from sentence 18*a* we may form only the direct question 18*b*:

(18) *a*. They persuaded Bill to force Mary to talk to John.
　　　 b. Who did they persuade Bill to force Mary to talk to?

since neither the verb *persuade* nor the verb *force* is subcategorized to take a WH complement. One immediate advantage of this analysis is that it makes it unnecessary to posit an underlying abstract "complementizer" element for WH complements that is never realized in surface structure. Since, in the theory proposed here, the lexical insertion transformations are applied cyclically, it is possible to subcategorize the preposed *wh* word directly. In the classical theory there is no way to subcategorize the *wh* word directly, since all lexical items have to be inserted before any of the purely syntactic transformations, such as *wh* movement, are applied. The classical theory is thus forced to set up an abstract complementizer element, such as WH, so that the lexical-insertion rule for verbs that take indirect questions can, in effect, "know" whether *wh* movement is going to apply in the syntactic derivation. From the point of view adopted here, the necessity of a WH complementizer is simply an artifact of a theory that assumes that there must be an underlying level of deep structure.

　　This discussion brings me directly to another major criticism of the classical theory of deep structure. It has been proposed at various times (the earliest such proposal was that of Katz and Postal in 1964) that the rule of *wh* movement should be triggered by an underlying abstract element of some sort that would be generated by the base rules in presubject position. At first this element was conceived of as a sort of abstract "grammatical morpheme" (e.g., Katz and Postal's element Q). More recently it has been argued (e.g., Bresnan 1970) that there should be an actual node, called variously COMP, TOPIC, and so forth, that would be generated in presubject position. It should be apparent, however, that the syntactic motivation for generating such a deep structure element is absolutely nil. The status of such deep-structure elements is exactly the same as the status of the *by*-Δ phrase that was supposed to trigger the passive rule. In both cases, these elements are necessary in order to cover up the basic inadequacy of the classical theory of transformations. Just as the *by* phrase was set up to act as a place holder for the rule of agent postposing, so the element Q is set up to act as a placeholder for the fronted *wh* word. Strictly speaking, however, there is no syntactic motivation for assuming abstract elements of this sort. It is frequently argued that the Q node, in particular, is necessary in order to account for the semantic interpretation of question sentences. This argument is completely circular, since a question sentence can be identified equally well on the basis of the surface form of sentences in English. Hence, the fact that the semantic interpretation of question sentences differs from that of declarative sentences, far from being an argument in support of a level of deep structure, is simply one more indication that the theory of deep structure (and the theory of transformations on which it is based) is basically incorrect, and that transformations are not, in fact, "meaning-preserving," as has generally been supposed.[3]

More recent proposals that there should be a node TOPIC or the like in presubject position are somewhat better than the original Katz and Postal suggestion to the extent that they are based on the recognition of a need for a syntactic position in topic position to which constituents of various kinds can be moved. In some respects, however, they are even

---

3. In fact, it is questionable, as Partee (1971) has noted, that the claim that transformations are meaning-preserving is even an empirical hypothesis in the case of such obligatory transformations as question formation. The point is that if a transformations applies obligatorily in the presence of some abstract element such as Q, then there is no surface form to which one can compare its meaning and hence no way to determine whether it changes meaning or not. This fact reflects, of course, the basically circular nature of the original arguments in support of underlying Q markers. More generally, I would claim that *only* in a theory (such as the one proposed here) in which surface forms are related to one another directly can one meaningfully ask to what extent transformations change meaning.

worse, since they lead to a serious confusion between categorial and relational notions. In fact, there is no more justification for setting up a node TOPIC in deep structure than there is for assuming that the subject NP is immediately dominated in deep structure by a node SUBJECT, or that direct objects are immediately dominated by a node OBJECT. The point is that 'topic' is a relational notion, just as 'subject' and 'object' are. One of the earliest arguments in support of phrase-structure grammars was that such relational notions as 'subject of' and 'object of' could be defined directly in terms of a given set of P-markers, without the need to assume them as primitives in the theory of grammar. Exactly the same is true of the relational notion 'topic of.' Given a PS expansion rule for S of form 11, we can define the notion 'topic of' configurationally in exactly the same way that we define other relational terms such as 'subject of' and 'object of.'

The need to introducing such spurious nodes as TOPIC and COMP into the base rules is attributable, once again, to the nature of the classical theory of deep structure, and to the theory of transformations on which it is based. In the theory proposed here, these problems are nonexistent. Since the PS rules characterize surface forms rather than abstract underlying structures, we can simply introduce the categories that can appear in topic position directly in the phrase-structure expansion rule for S. Such notions as 'topic of' (or whatever refinements of this notion are necessary) can then be defined directly in terms of the PS rules for English, or whatever language we happen to be concerned with, without the need to assume relational notions as primitives in the theory of grammar.[4] At the same time, since the co-occurrence transformations

---

4. This is not to imply that it is impossible to find universal definitions for such relational terms as subject and object. I venture to predict, however, that a great deal of empirical work will have to be done to set up grammars for particular languages and then compare them with one another before any useful generalizations will be forthcoming. Furthermore, it seems likely that universal generalizations concerning the basic grammatical functions will be of the implicational kind. Thus we may find that a language with certain feature will manifest grammatical relations in one way, whereas a language with other features will manifest grammatical relations in quite a different way. In general, it seems doubtful to me that there is any fixed set of base rules that is common to all natural languages. This fact, however, should not discourage the search for the formal features that are common to the grammars of all natural languages.

must be stated in terms of grammatical relations rather than in terms of linear strings of elements, we can state rules of the form "Move the direct object of the sentence into the topic position" directly, without having to appeal to such 'nodes' as TOPIC and COMP to act as place holders for the moved constituent.

As for the difference in semantic interpretation between questions and declaratives, I have already argued in earlier chapters that the process of forming a sentence cannot be strictly separated from the process of interpreting it semantically. In a theory of the sort proposed here, every rule is both syntactic and semantic, in the sense that it simultaneously plays a role in generating the set of syntactically well-formed sentences of the language and contributes something to the meaning of the sentence. The rules of topicalization and question formation are not exceptional in this regard. The interesting question is not *whether* transformations change meaning, but *how* they change meaning. Thus we may ask what aspects of meaning are preserved under a given transformation and which are changed; whether some subclass of rules changes meaning in a specific way, as compared with other subclasses; and so forth. In the case of topicalization rules such as locative preposing and *wh* movement, it is immediately apparent that the functional relationship between the main verb and its arguments is unaffected by the transformations, whereas the topic-comment relations and the modal structure, respectively, are radically altered. This fact is directly reflected in the rules, since preposing rules such as locative preposing and *wh* movement are intrinsically ordered after the lexical-insertion rules for specific verbs. Once again, the point is that the surface forms of English, plus a set of CTs of the type defined here, are sufficient to support explicit principles of semantic interpretation, without the need to assume an additional syntactic level of deep structure.

6.3   Topicalization, VP Preposing, and AP Preposing

If the analysis proposed in Section 6.2 is correct, we should expect to find that other topicalized constituents are incompatible with questioning and relativization as well. Let us consider first the rule of topicalization, which relates pairs of sentences such as the following:

(19) *a.* I can't stand that guy.
     b. That guy I can't stand.

(20) *a.* They are putting that fountain in the garden.
     b. That fountain they are putting in the garden.

If the sentences 19*b* and 20*b* are formed by moving an NP constituent in the VP into the NP in the topic position, they should not be subject to questioning or relativization. That this prediction is correct is shown by the unacceptability of the following examples:

(21) *a.* *Who that guy can't stand?
     b. *The man who that guy can't stand.

(22) *a.* *Who that fountain is putting in the garden?
     b. *The people who that fountain are putting in the garden.

Furthermore, notice that a topicalized NP is incompatible with locative preposing:[5]

(23) *a.* *That fountain in the garden they are putting.
     b. *In the garden that fountain they are putting.

(24) *a.* *That mop out of the window John threw.
     b. *Out of the window that mop John threw.

This result, too, is predictable under the analysis proposed here.

Consider next the rule of VP preposing, which relates pairs of sentences such as the following:

---

5. Note, however, that sentences containing a "dislocated" NP are, in general, compatible with preposed constituents of various kinds: *that mop, out of the window he threw it; that fountain, in the garden they are putting it.* We shall discuss this construction in Section 6.7.

(25) *a.* Speaking at today's luncheon is a well-known politician.
       b. A well-known politician is speaking at today's luncheon.

(26) *a.* Arrested by the police was an escaped convict.
       b. An escaped convict was arrested by the police.

If we ignore for the moment the problem of accounting for the post-posed subject NP, it is apparent that VP preposing must be formulated so as to move a progressive or passive VP complement into the topic position at the beginning of the sentence. We shall therefore extend the PS expansion rule for S in order to permit the constituent VP, as well as NP and PP, to be generated in the topic position:

$$(27) \quad S \rightarrow \left(\left\{ \begin{array}{c} NP \\ PP \\ VP \end{array} \right\} \right) \quad NP \quad \left(\left\{ \begin{array}{c} Tns \\ to \end{array} \right\} \right) \quad VP$$

We can then formulate VP preposing as a CT that will operate in the manner shown in diagram 28. This analysis predicts that sentences

(28)

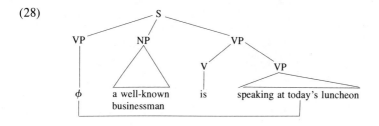

containing a preposed VP constituent should be immune to questioning and relativization. Once again, this prediction is correct:

(29) *a.* *Who speaking at today's luncheon is?
       b. *The man who speaking at today's luncheon is is a friend of mine.

(30) *a.* *Who arrested by the police was?
       b. *The convict who arrested by the police was is a friend of mine.

Furthermore, VP preposing is also incompatible with topicalization and locative preposing, as is shown by the ungrammaticality of the following examples:

(31) *a.* *That politician speaking at today's luncheon is.
      b. *That convict arrested by the police was.

(32) *a.* *At today's luncheon speaking is a well-known politician.
      b. *In the park arrested by the police was an escaped convict.

Consider, finally, the rule of AP preposing, which accounts for the relationship between such sentences as the following:[6]

(33) *a.* Bill was so tired that he could barely stand up.
      b. So tired was Bill that he could barely stand up.

The appearance of the AP *so tired* at the beginning of the sentence suggests immediately that we need to revise the expansion rule for S one more time to allow for AP constituents in the topic position:

(34)
$$S \rightarrow \left(\left\{ \begin{matrix} NP \\ PP \\ VP \\ AP \end{matrix} \right\} \right) NP \left(\left\{ \begin{matrix} Tns \\ to \end{matrix} \right\} \right) VP$$

Predictably, such sentences as 33*b* can be neither relativized nor questioned:

(35) *a.* *Who so tired was that he could barely stand up.
      b. *The boy who so tired was that he could barely stand up was Bill.

Furthermore, such sentences cannot undergo any of the other topicalization rules that we have discussed so far:

6. For a more detailed discussion of the derivation of these sentences than will be presented here, see Bowers 1975b.

(36) *a.* *Bill so tired was that he could barely stand up.
     b. *So obnoxious being was Bill that nobody wanted to talk to him.
     c. *In the garden so beautiful did the fountain look that nobody wanted to move it.

though the corresponding sentences with only a topicalized AP are perfectly acceptable:

(37) *a.* So tired was Bill that he could barely stand up.
     b. So obnoxious was Bill that nobody wanted to speak to him.
     c. So beautiful did the fountain look in the garden that nobody wanted to move it.

Still other rules of this sort in English prepose some constituent into the topic position. I leave it to the reader to verify that in these cases as well the presence of the preposed constituent makes it impossible to apply any other fronting rule.[7] Note that we have not yet accounted for the inversion of the subject and the main verb which characteristically accompanies a number of these rules. We shall deal with this matter shortly. First, however, it is necessary to discuss the rule of subject-auxiliary inversion.

6.4 Subject-Auxiliary Inversion

According to the classical analysis of the auxiliary proposed in the earliest work on transformational-generative grammer (e.g., Chomsky 1957), direct questions in English are formed by a rule that inverts the subject NP and the element Tense, along with the first verbal element of the auxiliary. If there is no verbal element in the auxiliary, the tense marker alone is inverted and a special rule of *do* support inserts the

7. See Emonds 1976 for further observations of this sort. The discussion in this section is based largely on Emonds's work, though the explanation proposed here differs from his in a number of respects.

verbal element *do* next to the tense marker, producing the question forms of sentences with the simple present or past tense. This analysis, while it accounts neatly for the distribution of the auxiliary elements in question sentences, suffers from a number of defects. First of all, this analysis requires a term of the following sort in the structural description of the rule of subject-auxiliary inversion:

$$(38) \quad \text{Tns} \quad \left(\left\{ \begin{array}{l} \text{M} \\ \text{have} \\ \text{be} \end{array} \right\} \right)$$

As John Ross (1969a) noted, this rather heterogenous collection of elements is not even a constituent. In this respect it stands in marked contrast to other familiar syntactic rules in English, which apply to constituents rather than to disjunctive sets of "grammatical morphemes," affixes, and such categories as Modal. Second, it is implicit in this analysis that there is no relationship whatsoever between the verbal elements *M, have,* and *be* that appear in the auxiliary and the same forms when they occur as main verbs. As I pointed out in Chapter 3, such an analysis is dubious even on morphological grounds, let alone on syntactic grounds.

Now if the reanalysis of the auxiliary elements proposed in Chapter 3 is correct, we can immediately remedy these defects by simply formulating the rule of subject-auxiliary inversion to apply to the first verb in the VP constituent. We shall assume in addition that the rule specifies the presence of the morpheme *Tns* to the right of the Verb. This condition will ensure that subject-auxiliary inversion is intrinsically ordered after the rule that attaches the tense morpheme to the main verb. At the same time, it will prevent subject-auxiliary inversion from applying in infinitives, gerundives, and other nontensed clauses. Note that just as in the classical analysis, we shall have to specify that subject-auxiliary inversion applies only to the specific lexical items *be* and *have,* in addition to the modal verbs *shall, will, can, could,* and so on. In addition, we shall have to assume that the auxiliary verb *do* is generated directly as a main verb, just like the other auxiliary elements, and that this element too is included in the restricted set of verbal elements to which subject-auxiliary inversion applies. This conclusion does not seem implausible, however, since, as is well known, the element *do* appears regularly in declarative sentences with contrastive stress:

(39) *a.* John *did* go to the store.
  b. Bill *does* like beans.

Hence the distribution of *do* can be accounted for quite simply if we incorporate into the grammar a rule that deletes *do* when it is immediately dominated by VP and is unstressed. This rule, combined with the rule of subject-auxiliary inversion, will ensure that *do* appears only when it either is stressed or has been preposed in question sentences.

The next question that arises is how to account for the position of the auxiliary verbs in question sentences. Obviously, the auxiliary elements can co-occur with constituents in the topic position, since subject-auxiliary inversion applies in *wh* questions as well as in simple yes/no questions:

(40) *a.* Who did you see?
  b. Where has he gone?
  c. Why is he doing that?

We must therefore revise the expansion rule for S to allow (as a first approximation) for an optimal element V between the topic position and the subject NP:

$$(41) \quad S \rightarrow \quad \left(\left\{ \begin{array}{c} NP \\ PP \\ VP \\ AP \end{array} \right\} \right) \quad (V) \quad NP \quad \left(\left\{ \begin{array}{c} Tns \\ to \end{array} \right\} \right) \quad VP$$

This revision will immediately allow us to formulate the rule of subject auxiliary inversion as a CT that moves the first verb in the VP into an empty V node in presubject position:

(42) Subject-auxiliary inversion:
$$[_S \ldots V{:}\phi{-}NP{:}x \; [_{VP} \; V{:}y \; + \; Tns \ldots _{VP}] \ldots _S] \Rightarrow$$
$$[_S \ldots V{:}y \; + \; Tns{-}NP{:}x \; [_{VP} \; V{:}\phi \ldots _{VP}] \ldots _S]$$

We may then derive such a sentence as *is John leaving?* in the manner shown in diagram 43. Similarly, we may derive a *wh* question such as *who is John talking to?* as in diagram 44.

(43)

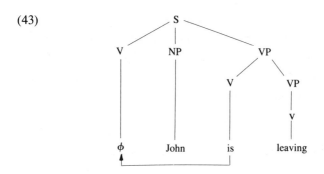

(44)

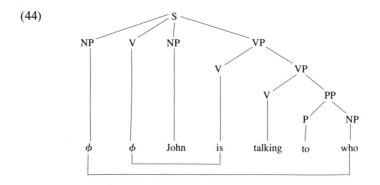

Consider next what happens when the *wh* word occurs in the subject position. As is well known, the word order in such cases remains unaltered in English. Thus the *wh* question forms of such sentences as the following:

(45) *a.* Someone was at the party.
       b. John left.

    c. Bill was standing on the corner.

    d. Harry was arrested.

are identical, except that a *wh* word is in subject position:

(46) *a.* Who was at the party?

      b. Who left?

      c. Who was standing on the corner?

      d. Who was arrested?

In the classical theory, this fact is usually accounted for by permitting the two rules of subject-auxiliary inversion and *wh* movement to apply in the order just given to underlying forms containing a *wh* word, whether that word is in subject or postverbal position. Thus a string of the form *who –was –at the party* would first be converted to one of the form *was –who –at the party,* after which *wh* movement would convert it to one with exactly the same linear order of elements as before. Obviously the same artifice could be used in the framework proposed here. Thus we might derive such a sentence as *who was at the party?* as in diagram 47. There are several indications, however, that such an

(47)

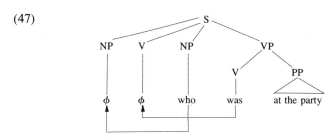

approach is incorrect. For one thing, this sort of derivation results in a derived constituent structure of the kind shown in diagram 48, and in

(48)

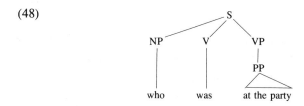

general any analysis of this kind predicts that a major constituent break should occur after the first verbal element in all questions containing a *wh* word in subject position. Unfortunately, there seems to be no evidence in support of derived constituent structures of this type. In fact, it seems intuitively obvious that the constituent structure of the *wh* question *who was at the party?* is identical to that of the corresponding declarative sentence, *John was at the party*. Second, notice that this proposal apparently predicts that the question form of a sentence in the simple present or past tense, such as *John left,* should be of the form **who did leave?* Since, as I mentioned above, subject-auxiliary inversion must be formulated so as to apply only to a restricted set of verbs, including *have, be, do,* and the modals, the only way that we can derive a question form of such sentences is by preposing the auxiliary verb *do.* Third, it does not seem to be an accident that preposing of the auxiliary fails to take place, just in case the *wh* word is in subject position. In fact, it seems apparent that the function of subject-auxiliary inversion in *wh* questions is precisely to break up the sequence of two NPs that would otherwise occur at the beginning of the clause when the *wh* word is not a subject.

These observations strongly suggest that it is incorrect to permit *wh* movement and subject-auxiliary inversion to apply in sentences in which the *wh* word is in subject position. Let us suppose, instead, that *wh* movement is restricted to NPs that are dominated by the VP constituent. We can then reformulate subject-auxiliary inversion so that it applies either when a *wh* word is in topic position or when there is no constituent at all in that position:

(49) Subject-auxiliary inversion:
$$[_S \, ([\ldots \, wh\text{–PRO}\ldots]) \, V{:}\phi \, NP{:}y \, [_{VP} \, V{:}x\text{–}X_{VP}] \, _S] \Rightarrow$$
$$[_S \, ([\ldots \, wh\text{–PRO}\ldots]) \, V{:}x \, NP{:}y \, [_{VP} \, V{:}\phi\text{–}X_{VP}] \, _S[$$

If there is no *wh* word in the topic position, subject-auxiliary inversion will apply, producing such yes/no questions as *did John leave?* and *is John leaving?* If a *wh* word is in topic position, subject-auxiliary inversion will again apply, producing such sentences as *when did you see John?* and *what have you told John?* When the *wh* word is in subject position, however, neither subject-auxiliary inversion nor *wh* movement will be applicable,[8] and we shall come out with a structure that is identical to that of the corresponding declarative sentence (see diagram 50).

(50)

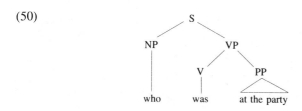

If this analysis is correct, we can say that the preposed auxiliary element in *wh* questions is essentially a device to mark questioned constituents that are *not* subjects. The existence of such a device is not unparalleled in other languages. In Duala, for example (Epée 1975), the verb is marked with one of two affixes in *wh* questions, depending on whether the questioned constituent is the subject of the clause or is dominated by the VP constituent. If the questioned constituent is not a subject, the verb is marked with the invariable affix -*no*. If the questioned constituent is the subject, the verb is marked with the same pronominal form that occurs in relative clauses. This latter fact may be significant, for notice that in English, as in Duala, the relativized constituent agrees with the verb in the embedded clause just in case it is

---

8. Except in echo questions, where it is possible (with a different intonation) to get sentences of the form *was who at the party?*, just as it is possible to get echo questions of the form *did I see who at the party?*, in which subject-auxiliary inversion but not *wh* movement has applied. Notice, incidentally, that the existence of echo questions of this kind is predicted by the analysis proposed here. Thus if we generate a structure containing a *wh* word and an empty V node in presubject position but no empty node of the appropriate category in the topic position, questions of this kind will be produced automatically by the application of subject-auxiliary inversion. Notice further that if we generate structures containing a *wh* word but neither an empty V node nor an empty topic node, we will get echo questions of the form *who has left?*, *you saw whom(m)?*, *you were doing what?*, and so forth, which are also possible in English. Thus every possible derivation that is permitted by the structures and CTs proposed thus far is realized by some sentence type in English.

the subject. Thus we have *the men who are here, the man who is here*, and so forth. These facts suggest, once again, that a *wh* form in the subject position is in fact a subject, and that *wh* movement applies only to constituents that are not subjects.

If this conclusion is correct, we have yet another clear case in which a transformation must be allowed to refer to the grammatical relation of a constituent. The point is that the most general way of formulating *wh* movement in English (and also in Duala) is to say that it applies to any *wh* marked constituent that is not a subject. If transformations are permitted to refer to grammatical relations, it is a simple matter to formulate *wh* movement correctly. We simply require in the structural description for *wh* movement that the *wh* word be dominated by the VP constituent in the clause in question. In a theory that does not permit transformations to refer to the grammatical relations, there is no natural way to formulate *wh* movement so as to express this generalization. To conclude, then, we shall write the rule of *wh* movement in the following manner:

(51) *Wh* movement:
$$[_S \ \alpha{:}\phi \ldots [_{VP} \ X{-}[_\alpha \ldots wh\text{-PRO} \ldots \ ]{-}Y]] \Rightarrow$$
$$[_S \ [_\alpha \ldots wh\text{-PRO} \ldots \ ] \ldots [_{VP} \ X{-}\alpha{:}\phi{-}Y]]$$

where α = NP, VP, PP, ...

This formulation of *wh* movement correctly predicts that a *wh* word that is the subject of an embedded clause can be preposed into topic position—for example, *who do you think is coming to the party?*—and consequently will be marked with a preposed auxiliary verb. Likewise in Duala, the verb is marked with the affix *-no* when the *wh* word is the subject of an embedded clause. Thus to require without qualification that the *wh* word not be a subject is to overstate the case: it must not be the subject of the questioned clause. That is precisely what is expressed in rule 51, which requires only that the *wh* word be dominated by the VP constituent in the questioned clause, thus permitting subjects of embedded clauses to be preposed.

6.5 Imperatives

If the analysis just proposed is correct, the PS rules for English must be able to generate an optional V node between the topic position and the subject position. We might therefore ask whether there is any independent motivation for generating such a node in that position. In fact, at least one construction in English requires a verbal element to the left of the subject NP which cannot be derived by means of subject-auxiliary inversion. I refer to non-second-person imperative sentences with the element *let*. Consider, for example, the following sentences:

(52)   *a.* Let us go then, you and I.
      b. Let me be careful.
      c. Let them eat cake.
      d. Let him be hung for his misdeeds.
      e. Let it be decided that he shall hang.

Sentences of this type, though identical in form to normal *you* imperatives with the main verb *let,* are nevertheless quite different in meaning. They are, in fact, true non-second-person imperative forms. As such, they have no understood second-person subject, as is the case with *you* imperatives with *let*. Furthermore, when the subject is the first-person-plural pronoun *us,* the difference actually shows up phonologically, since the pronoun may be contracted with the verb *let* in first-person imperatives but not in second-person imperatives with *let*. Thus the following examples can be interpreted only as first-person-imperative forms:[9]

(53)   *a.* Let's go.
      b. Let's be careful.

9. Note that in some dialects the form *let's* is no longer perceived as a contracted form. In such dialects the pronoun is repeated, giving such forms as *let's us go to the movies* and *let's you and me be careful.*

The facts can be explained if we allow the imperative element *let* to be generated under the V node in presubject position. Thus I propose to derive such a sentence as *let us go* from a structure of the sort shown in diagram 54. A normal *you* imperative of the same form will be derived

(54)

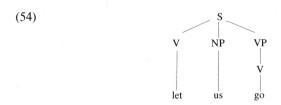

from an entirely different structure (see diagram 55). If the contraction rule for *let us* is formulated so as to apply only to subjects, the nonambiguity of the sentences in example 53 is accounted for automatically.

(55)

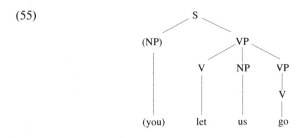

Notice that *let* imperatives and *you* imperatives are in complementary distribution. Just as there are no normal imperative forms with non-second-person subjects:

(56) *a.* *Me go!
      b. *Us go!
      c. *Them go!
      d. *Him go!

so there are no *let* imperatives with a second-person subject:

(57) *Let you go!

This observation suggests that there is a rule in English requiring that the element *let* be inserted in the V position before the subject NP just in case the subject is not a second-person pronoun. If such a rule is to work properly, we must somehow ensure that the main verb is in its bare-infinitive form, since we do not want *let* to be inserted in tensed sentences or in sentences with the complementizer *to* or *-ing:*

(58)   *a.* *Let us went.
       b. *Let him eats cake.
       c. *Let us to go.
       d. *Let us going.

Now it is generally assumed, following the analysis of imperatives first proposed by Katz and Postal (1964), that normal *you* imperatives are derived from underlying forms containing the modal *will.* Aside from the arguments that are usually brought forward in favor of such an analysis, which I shall deal with shortly, this proposal has the advantage of explaining why the main verb occurs in its infinitival form, since in English the modals generally require bare infinitives. While this proposal has at least some initial plausibility in the case of *you* imperatives, it fails in the case of *let* imperatives, since such forms as the following are impossible:

(59)   *a.* *Let us will go.
       b. *Let's will go.

It follows that if we wish to account for the obvious connection between *let* and *you* imperatives, and in particular for the complementary distribution between the pronominal forms that can occur as subjects in the two constructions, then we cannot derive imperatives from underlying sentences containing the modal *will.* It is therefore necessary to examine closely the arguments that are said to support a rule of *will* deletion.

There are two main arguments for deriving imperatives from underlying forms with *will,* one semantic and the other syntactic. The semantic argument is extremely weak. It is based simply on the fact that such sentences as *you will go away* can, under certain circumstances, have the illocutionary force of a command or request of some sort. This proves nothing, however, since, as is well known, a wide range of sentence types can have the illocutionary force of a command. In isolation from any syntactic considerations, there is just as strong an argument for deriving imperatives from *would you go away?, could you go away?,* and so forth, or from any of the innumerable other sentence types in English that can function in discourse as commands. It is sometimes suggested that sentences with *will* are particularly appropriate as sources of imperatives, since a command, if carried out, must necessarily take place at some point in time after the command is uttered. Again, this form of argument is extremely weak in the absence of syntactic arguments. It is well known, for example, that the present tense in English can also function as a sort of future, as in *I leave tomorrow* and *he arrives at noon day after tomorrow.* No one has seriously suggested, however, that present-tense forms of this sort should be derived from underlying forms containing the modal *will.* Similarly, present progressive forms can also have future reference, as in *I am leaving tomorrow,* yet it has never been suggested that this fact provides support for the derivation of progressive forms from underlying forms with an explicit modal *will.* Finally, notice that other modal forms besides *will* could serve equally well as underlying forms of imperatives, if semantic arguments of this sort are to be taken seriously. Thus we might argue that the underlying form of such an imperative sentence as *go away* is *you must go away.* Certainly an imperative sentence may have the same sense of obligation that is associated with the root modal *must.* Furthermore, *must* has an implied future reference, just as imperatives do. In short, semantic evidence of this sort is at best capable of ruling out sources of imperatives that are totally implausible. There is still such a wide range of possible sources of imperatives that are compatible with the semantic data that no argument based on semantic evidence alone is capable of deciding among the various alternatives. Let us turn therefore to the syntactic evidence and see whether it provides any support for the derivation of imperatives from underlying forms containing *will.*

The only real syntactic evidence in support of such derivations is the observation (Katz and Postal 1964) that imperatives can occur with negative tag questions containing the modal *will:*

(60) *a.* Go away, won't you?
      b. Be quiet, won't you?

Likewise, negative imperatives can occur with positive tags containing the modal *will:*

(61) *a.* Don't get upset, will you?
      b. Don't do anything rash, will you?

Katz and Postal assume that the tags in these imperative forms are the type that occurs in such sentences as the following:

(62) *a.* He left, didn't he?
      b. He didn't leave, did he?

(63) *a.* He will leave, won't he?
      b. He won't leave, will he?

As is well known, the tag in questions of this sort consists of the first element of the auxiliary, inverted with a pronominal copy of the subject NP. Furthermore, the polarity of the tag must be the opposite of that in the main clause. If we assume that the tags in examples 60 and 61 are formed in the same way as those in examples 62 and 63, it of course follows immediately that imperatives must have a deleted modal *will* in underlying structure.

This argument, however, is vitiated by the fact that positive as well as negative tags can occur with such imperatives as those in example 60:

(64) *a.* Go away, will you?
      b. Be quiet, will you?

Notice too that other modals besides *will* may occur as tags to imperatives:

(65) *a.* Go away, can't you?
     b. Be quiet, can you?
     c. Shut the door, could you?
     d. Leave me alone, couldn't you?
     e. Take me home, would you?
     f. Let me help, wouldn't you?

Finally, still other question forms can occur as tags to imperatives which do not fit into the standard format for the forming of tag questions at all:

(66) *a.* Shut the door, why don't you?
     b. Take them to the movies, why can't you?

In short, it appears that at least as much evidence supports the derivation of imperatives from underlying forms containing *can, could,* and *would* as supports their derivation from underlying forms containing the modal *will.* In addition, Katz and Postal's proposal fails completely to account for the fact that imperatives can occur with both negative and positive tags, as well as with such tags as *why don't you?* and *why can't you?*

Surveying the various tags that can occur with imperatives, one is immediately struck by the fact that in every case the so-called imperative form has a corresponding grammatical question form:

(67) *a.* Won't you go away?
     b. Will you go away?
     c. Can't you go away?
     d. Can you be quiet?
     e. Could you shut the door?
     f. Couldn't you leave me alone?
     g. Would you take me home?
     h. Wouldn't you let me help?
     i. Why don't you shut the door?
     j. Why can't you take them to the movies?

This observation strongly suggests that imperatives with tags are formed directly from such sentences as those in example 67 by a rule that takes the preposed auxiliary element, along with the subject NP, and forms a parenthetical element to the right of the VP.[10] Further confirmation of the essential correctness of this proposal can be found in the fact that the subject NP cannot be retained in the imperative form. Examples of the following sort sound anomalous to me:

(68) *a.* *You go away, won't you?
      b. *You be quiet, will you?
      c. *You shut the door, could you?
      d. *You leave me alone, couldn't you?
      e. *You shut the door, why don't you?

Imperative tags contrast in this respect with regular tags such as those in examples 62 and 63, suggesting that in the former the subject NP, along with the preposed auxiliary, is simply moved out of the clause entirely, whereas in the latter it is copied. If this analysis is correct, then the same rule that accounts for imperative tags could also be used to account for such imperative forms as the following, containing a postposed subject:

(69) *a.* Go away, you.
      b. Be quiet, you.
      c. Shut the door, you.
      d. Take me home, you.

10. Alternatively, we might suppose that the VP is moved to the left of the preposed auxiliary and subject NP. A discussion of the structure that should be assigned to parentheticals would go well beyond the limits of this book. Generally speaking, it seems to have been assumed that parenthetical elements and the clauses with which they are associated must be dominated by some common node. There are strong indications, however (e.g., the large intonation break that occurs on either or both sides of a parenthetical), that this assumption is incorrect. Nothing in principle prevents one from assuming that parenthetical elements are linearly ordered with respect to the elements in the clause with which they are associated but do not enter into any dominance relationships with the nodes in that clause. This hypothesis would of course require that linguistic theory permit not only trees but "forests" (Wall 1972). This is almost certainly necessary in any case if discourse is to be dealt with at all in linguistic theory.

The only difference between these forms and the imperative tags is that the latter derive from questions containing a preposed auxiliary, whereas the former derive from imperatives of the form *you must go away, you be quiet,* which do not have a preposed auxiliary. If the rule forming imperatives is formulated so as to postpose the subject and, optionally, a preposed auxiliary, both sentence types can be accounted for by means of the same rule.

Another serious difficulty facing the standard analysis of imperatives in English is to account for the appearance of the auxiliary element *do* in negative imperatives. According to the usual analysis of the auxiliary, the element *do* is introduced as the bearer of an unattached *Tns* element. Under Katz and Postal's analysis of the imperative, however, there is no *Tns* affix after the deletion of the auxiliary *will* to which the element *do* can be attached. Furthermore, even if the rule were formulated so as to leave a *Tns* element behind, we would get the wrong results anyway, since the auxiliary element *do* is untensed in imperative sentences, just as the main verb is in positive imperatives:

(70) *Didn't go away!

Finally, notice that if the subject *you* is not deleted, then the auxiliary *do,* along with the negative, must be preposed:

(71) *a.* *You don't go away!
     b. Don't you go away!

Worse yet, note that negative imperatives with *do* can occur with the imperative tag *will you,* as in the sentences in example 61. None of these facts has yet received an adequate explanation, nor is there much likelihood that they will under the standard analysis of the imperative.

To summarize, then, not only is there no evidence to support the derivation of imperatives from underlying forms containing the auxiliary *will,* but in fact there are a great many strong arguments against any such proposal. The fact is that imperative sentences in English are simply bare-infinitive forms. They are not tensed, they do not contain the auxiliary *will* or any other modal element, and they are infinitival in form. When we recall the arguments in Chapter 3 for generating bare-infinitive complements in the base rules, these observations strongly suggest that bare infinitives occur not only in complements, but in main clauses as well. In particular, it is the bare infinitive that occurs in imperative sentences. I propose, therefore, to generate an imperative form such as *You be quiet!* in the manner shown in diagram 72. This proposal, if correct, solves immediately most of the problems

(72)

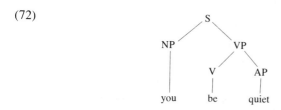

mentioned earlier. First of all, the relationship between *you* imperatives and *let* imperatives becomes transparent. We simply generate nouns and pronouns of any person and number in main clauses with the bare-infinitive form of the main verb. If the subject is second person (as in diagram 72), we may either leave it as it is or optionally delete the pronoun *you,* producing such imperative forms as *be quiet!* If the subject is not second person, the verb *let* must be inserted obligatorily in the V node in presubject position, producing the imperative forms discussed earlier: *let us go, let's go, let him be hung, let them eat cake,* and the like. The formation of imperative tags we have already described above. Contrary to Katz and Postal's analysis, these forms do not provide evidence of an underlying *will* in imperative sentences, but rather of the existence of a rule for forming imperatives from questions with a preposed modal.

Consider next negative imperatives with *do.* According to the analysis of the auxiliary elements proposed here, *do* is to be treated as a main verb that requires a VP complement, just like the other auxiliary elements. Such negative imperatives as sentence 71*b* can therefore be derived from a structure of the sort shown in diagram 73 by the regular

(73)

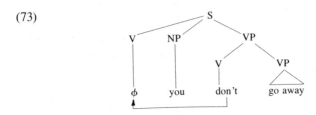

rule of subject-auxiliary inversion. If, in addition, the subject pronoun *you* is deleted, we shall then of course derive negative imperatives of the form *don't go away!*

Consider, finally, negative imperatives with the tag *will you?*, such as those in example 61. Let us suppose that the process of contracting the negative element *not* can take place either before or after subject-auxiliary inversion. If we generate a structure of the sort shown in diagram 74, one of two things can happen. If contraction takes place

(74)

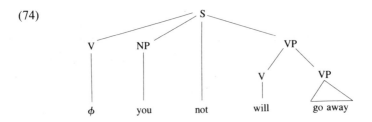

first, the contracted modal *won't* will be moved into presubject position, producing a question of the form *won't you go away?* We may then proceed to form the negative imperative, *go away, won't you?*, in the manner described above.[11] Suppose, however, that we apply subject-auxiliary inversion before contraction. The result will be a structure of the sort shown in diagram 75. We can, of course, stop at this point, deriving the sentence *will you not go away?* (though sentences of this type may be possible only with extra stress on the negative element *not,* a problem that I shall not attempt to deal with

---

11. Note that such forms are impossible if the modal + negative element is not contracted: **go away, will you not?* This fact shows that contraction is a necessary prerequisite for the formation of imperative tags.

(75)

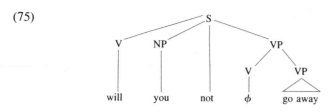

here). But suppose that we go on and form an imperative tag. The result will be a structure of the form:

(76) not–φ–go away, will you

At this point, we may simply require that the empty V node that is left behind by subject-auxiliary inversion be lexically filled by the verb *do*, as is always the case in imperative sentences, and the result (after contraction of *not* with *do*) will be the correct negative imperative tag *don't go away, will you?* Note that the subject *you* cannot co-occur with the tag *will you?*:

(77) *Don't you go away, will you?

showing once again that the rule for forming imperative tags must move the subject rather than copy it.

If these arguments are correct, it is impossible to derive imperative sentences in English from underlying declarative sentences containing the modal *will*. On the contrary, imperatives are simply bare infinitives that happen to occur in a main clause rather than as complements to some other verb. We might ask, however, whether there is any independent motivation for generating tenseless main clauses in English in the PS rules. In fact, a number of constructions require tenseless main clauses in English. Notice, first of all, that a number of modal verbs, including *must* and *ought*, do not distinguish present and past tense forms as do the modal pairs *will/would, shall/should, can/could,* and so on. There is clearly no motivation for distinguishing between the past- and present-tense forms of such verbs. If it is possible to generate tenseless main clauses, however, there is no need to assume that these verbs have past-tense forms that are phonologically the same as the present-tense forms. In fact, one might well ask whether there is any real motivation in present-day English for calling *would* the past-tense form of *will*. I shall not attempt to resolve this issue here, but merely point out that if, as I suspect, the answer to this question should be in the negative, then all of the modals can simply be generated as tenseless main clauses.

A somewhat more interesting construction that requires tenseless main clauses has been pointed out by Philip Cohen (1969), who discusses "incredulity" questions of the following sort:

(78) *a.* Me, go to Rome?
       b. Him, be careful?
       c. Us, live in a trailer?
       d. Her, buy a canary?

As Cohen observes, the nominal element in preverbal position cannot be the subject, since it is in the accusative case. Furthermore, the verb is in the unmarked, or bare-infinitive, form. Notice, incidentally, that topicalized sentences of this sort do not, as we would expect, permit other fronting rules to apply:

(79) *a.* *Me, Mary, talk to?
       b. *Him, in the garden put a fountain?
       c. *Her, who talk to?
       d. *Us, so tired were that we could hardly stand up?
       e. *John, speaking at today's luncheon is?

suggesting that the subject is moved into the topic position, as in the other cases we have discussed. But what about the bare-infinitive form of the main verb? Cohen suggests that the rule that fronts the subject should be formulated so as to convert the main verb into its infinitival form. It would be much simpler, however, to make the rule topicalizing the subject itself dependent on the presence of a bare-infinitive

form. We could then derive such a sentence as 78*a* as in diagram 80.[12]
If we assume that topicalized pronouns are automatically assigned to

(80)

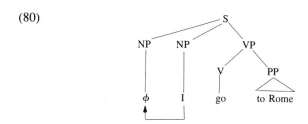

the accusative case, a derivation of this sort will suffice to account for
the form of incredulity questions in English.

Let us consider, finally, whether there are any examples in English
of a full sentential complement that requires a verb in the bare-
infinitive form. We have seen a number of examples of main clauses
that must be analyzed as bare infinitives; I have also discussed bare-
infinitive complements, which I argued were VPs. The question, then,
is whether there are complement sentences that require a bare infinitive. In fact, there are. A small class of verbs in English, including
order, demand, insist, require, and so on, takes complements of the
following sort:

(81) *a.* I demand that you be on time.
  b. We insist that the luggage be examined.
  c. They ordered that the men leave at once.
  d. I require that John hand his paper in on time.

It is immediately evident that the verb in these complement sentences
is in the unmarked infinitival form. In particular, there is no tense
marker, as there is in most *that* clauses. In many languages that distin-

12. Alternatively, one might argue that the topicalized NP is, in this case, taken out
from under the domination of the S node completely. This hypothesis might help to
explain the fact that in such sentences both the topicalized subject and the VP have a
rising question intonation, with a long intonation break in between. See note 10 above.

guish systematically between indicative and subjunctive forms, the complements to verbs of this type would of course be in the subjunctive mood. Insofar as such sentences as those in example 81 have been discussed at all in the literature, they seem to have been assumed to be subjunctive complements of some kind. If bare-infinitive complements can be generated in main clauses, however, there is no need to introduce into the grammar of English an ad hoc and unmotivated distinction between "subjunctive" and "indicative" complements.[13] Instead, we may simply subcategorize verbs for a tensed *that* clause or one with a bare infinitive.

If this analysis is correct, we may characterize directly the surface form of such a sentence as 81*a* in the manner shown in diagram 82. It

(82)

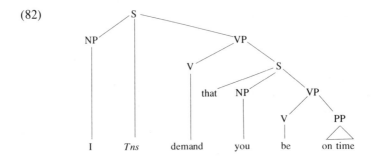

can hardly be an accident that the unmarked bare infinitive occurs both in imperative sentences and in the complements of such imperative verbs as *demand, insist, order, require*. One might be tempted to

13. It should be emphasized that this claim does not imply that there is no point in searching for universal definitions of such notions as 'subjunctive mood.' This point is, simply, that as far as the grammar of English is concerned, there is little motivation for introducing a formal distinction between subjunctive and indicative. Generally speaking, one expects to find that languages make use of the formal devices at their disposal in ways that reflect the principles of universal grammar. Hence it is perhaps not surprising that this particular use of the bare-infinitive complement in English parallels certain uses of the subjunctive mood in languages that have a formally marked distinction between subjunctive and indicative. It would be a mistake, however, to jump from this observation to the conclusion that English must have an underlying indicative/subjunctive distinction in every respect parallel to the formally marked distinction that is found in other languages.

"explain" this fact by assuming that imperatives are derived from an underlying structure containing an abstract imperative verb of some sort which is deleted obligatorily in surface structure. This proposal, however, is just as circular as the argument for setting up an abstract morpheme Q in deep structure in order to "explain" why sentences that have undergone subject-auxiliary inversion and/or *wh* movement are interpreted as questions. There is surely no doubt that there is a semantic explanation for the fact that both imperatives and the complements of imperative verbs require the "unmarked," and in particular the untensed, form of the verb in English. The setting up of an "underlying" imperative verb for imperative sentences which is deleted obligatorily, however, would not explain this correlation. Rather, it would merely restate the observed correlation in a roundabout and misleading fashion. It does not solve the real problem, which is why the unmarked form of the verb is appropriate in both cases.

I have argued in this section that the existence of the *let* imperative construction provides independent motivation for generating a V node in presubject position in the PS rules for English. Furthermore, a close examination of the regular *you* imperative leads to the conclusion that imperative forms in general cannot be derived from underlying forms with a modal *will*. Instead, it is simpler to analyze these constructions as bare-infinitive complements, thus providing further support for the analysis of bare-infinitive complements proposed in Chapter 3 and at the same time providing further support for the view that the surface forms of sentences are generated directly by the PS rules.

6.6   Subject-VP Inversion

We now return briefly to the topicalized sentences with which we began this chapter, for the careful reader will have noticed that we have so far failed to account for the inversion of subject and verb that accompanies many topicalization processes. Sometimes inversion is optional, as in the case of locative preposing, and sometimes it is obligatory, as in the case of VP preposing and AP preposing. In none of these instances, however, have we yet provided explicit rules to account for the change in word order that accompanies topicalization.

Let us consider first the rules of locative preposing and VP preposing. Recalling that we have available a V node in presubject position, we might be tempted to suppose that the word order in such sentences as those in example 83 could be accounted for by the rule of subject-auxiliary inversion:

(83) *a.* In the garden stands a fountain.
      b. Down the hill ran John.
      c. Sitting on the fence were three birds.
      d. Discovered in the garden was an old fountain.

Threre are a number of serious difficulties with this proposal, however. First of all, in order to account for such sentences as 83*a* and 83*b,* we would have to permit subject-auxiliary inversion to apply to other verbs besides the auxiliary verbs *be, have, do,* and the modals. It would thus be extremely difficult to explain why there are no questions in English of the form:

(84) *a.* Ran John?
      b. Who spoke John to?

Second, recall that subject-auxiliary inversion must be formulated so as to apply to the first auxiliary verb to the right of the subject. In general, only one verb may be fronted in question sentences in English. If this were not the case, then we would expect to find questions of the following form:

(85) *a.* *Who have been you talking to?
      b. *Who were arrested you by?
      c. *What did say he to you?
      d. *Who was being John examined by?

The rule that accounts for inversion in topicalized sentences behaves completely differently in this respect, however, as the following sentences show:

266

(86) *a.* On the fence were sitting three birds.
    b. In the garden was discovered an old fountain.
    c. On the third floor must have been the fuse box.
    d. In this restaurant have eaten many famous people

Examples of this sort show quite conclusively that the inversion rule for topicalized sentences applies not to the first verb in a complex VP, but rather to the whole VP. Finally, notice that whereas subject-auxiliary inversion applies in both transitive and intransitive sentences, the inversion rule for topicalized sentences applies only to intransitive sentences. Thus examples of the following sort are uniformly ungrammatical in English:

(87) *a.* *In the corner was putting John the mop.
    b. *In the garden discovered the men an old fountain.
    c. *Sitting on the fence saw I three birds.
    d. *In this restaurant have eaten many famous people roast beef.

It is apparent, therefore, that the two inversion processes cannot be accounted for by a single rule.

At the same time, I have already pointed out that topicalization and inversion are incompatible with questioning in English, a fact that suggests that although the inversion rule for topicalized sentences may not be the same as subject-auxiliary inversion, it must nevertheless be formulated in a way that makes it possible to account for the incompatibility of the two processes. This observation immediately suggests a way of accounting for both inversion processes without the need to complicate the PS rules at all. Instead of providing a node V between the topic position and the subject position, let us generate a VP node. Thus the expansion rule for S will now look as follows:

$$(88) \quad S \rightarrow \left(\left\{ \begin{array}{c} NP \\ PP \\ VP \\ AP \end{array} \right\} \right) \quad (VP) \quad NP \quad \left(\left\{ \begin{array}{c} Tns \\ to \end{array} \right\} \right) \quad VP$$

If VPs can appear between the topic position and the subject position, we can immediately write a CT that will move the VP into this position, thereby producing the desired inversion of the subject and the VP. To be more concrete, let us consider how we may derive such a sentence as 86*a*. The first rule to apply is locative preposing, which moves the PP *on the fence* into the topic position in the manner indicated in diagram 89. We could of course stop at this point, producing

(89)

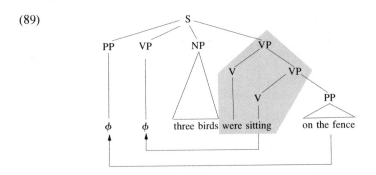

the grammatical sentence *on the fence three birds were sitting*. Alternatively, we can apply subject-VP inversion to the VP *were sitting*, producing a sentence of the form shown in diagram 90. Obviously, a

(90)

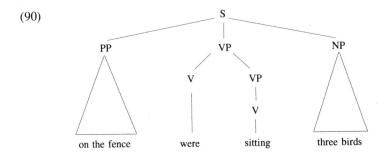

derivation of exactly the same sort can be used to account for the other sentences in example 86 as well.

Let us consider next sentence 83*c*. In order to produce sentences of this kind, we must apply two rules, both of which apply to VPs. The first rule, VP preposing, moves a passive or progressive VP into the topic position. Note that this rule applies not only in intransitive sentences, but in transitive sentences also. Thus we have such sentences as the following:

(91) *a*. Sitting on the fence I saw three birds.
      b. Hiding in my room I found an escaped convict.

The second rule, subject-VP inversion, applies only in intransitive sentences:

(92) *a*. *Sitting on the fence three birds were.
      b. Sitting on the fence were three birds.
      c. *Sitting on the fence saw I three birds.
      d. *Hiding in my room found I an escaped convict.

Thus example sentence 83*c* would be derived as in diagram 93. First, VP preposing applies, producing an intermediate structure of the form

(93)

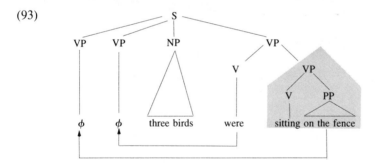

shown in diagram 94. Then subject-VP inversion applies, moving the VP (which now contains only the single verb *be*) into the VP position

(94)

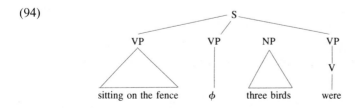

269

after the topic. The result is the correct surface form shown in diagram 95. The passive sentence 83*d* would of course be derived in exactly the same fashion.

(95)

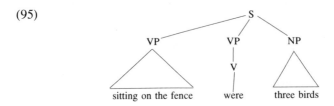

Notice that we do not have to reformulate the rule of subject-auxiliary inversion at all. The reason is that the VP node between the topic and the subject may either be left empty or be expanded into an empty V. Thus such a question sentence as *has John left?* would be derived from a structure of the sort shown in diagram 96. To form a

(96)

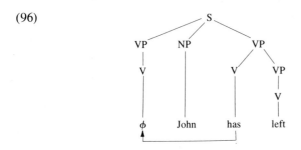

question sentence in English, the rule of subject-auxiliary inversion moves only the single V node to the VP position to the left of the subject NP. Although subject-auxiliary inversion and subject-VP inversion are entirely different rules, they are still incompatible with one another, since the constituent that is moved must in both cases occupy the same position in a surface P-marker.

Consider, finally, the rule of AP preposing. Is the obligatory inversion that takes place in sentences with a preposed AP produced by subject-auxiliary inversion or by subject-VP inversion? It is easy to show that in this case the former is the relevant rule, since only the first element of the auxiliary may be preposed in such sentences:

(97)   *a.* So tired must John have been that he went straight to bed.
      b. *So tired must have been John that he went straight to bed.

Thus topicalization rules may trigger either subject-auxiliary inversion or subject-VP inversion, but not both.[14] In the theory proposed here, this fact is an automatic consequence of the PS rules and CTs for English presented in this chapter.

6.7   Some Apparent Counterexamples

To conclude this chapter I shall discuss a number of sentence types in English which appear to be counterexamples to the rules presented in the preceding sections. I shall show that these examples are not in fact counterexamples at all, but merely show that there are still other levels of topicalization in English that have to be accounted for.

The chief example of this sort is the rule of right and left dislocation (first discussed in Ross, 1967), which produces such sentences as:

(98)   *a.* That guy, I can't stand him.
      b. That woman over there, she is a good friend of mine.
      c. Nobody likes him, the postman.
      d. She is their favorite teacher, Mrs. Jones.

Not only are dislocated constituents compatible with questions, but they can in fact co-occur with all of the topicalized constituents that we have discussed so far, though in some cases the resulting sentences sound a bit awkward (particularly in the case of topicalization):

---

14. In general, rules that front an "affective" element, such as the element *so* that appears in APs, various negative expressions, *wh* words, and so on, require subject-auxiliary inversion, whereas such purely "stylistic" transformations as locative preposing and VP preposing require subject-NP inversion.

(99) *a.* That guy, how can you stand him?
  b. What did you say to him, the salesman?
  c. In the garden we decided to put it, our Rodin.
  d. My friend, so tired was he that he could barely stand up.
  e. That friend of mine that you met yesterday, Bill he can't stand.
  f. Standing in the garden it is, our new Brancusi.

Notice, however, that dislocation differs crucially from all of the other topicalization rules discussed so far, in that it requires a pronominal copy of the dislocated constituent somewhere in the sentence with which it is associated. Furthermore, as Emonds (1976) has noted, dislocated sentences cannot be embedded. These observations strongly suggest that dislocated sentences are not "moved," but rather are generated directly in some higher topic position, and that there is a rule that requires coreference between the dislocated constituent and some pronoun in the sentence it is associated with. Where could this higher topic position be located? One plausible suggestion is that there is a higher S constituent, which can be expanded into a dislocated constituent, plus the usual sentence node. Thus suppose that the initial symbol in the PS rules is S′ rather than S, and that there is a rule in the grammar of the following sort:

(100) S′ → (NP) S

Such a sentence as 99*a* would then have roughly the structure shown in diagram 101. In order to account for right-dislocated sentences, how-

(101)

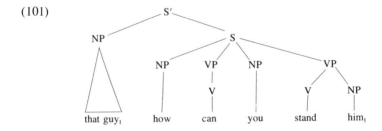

ever, we must also allow for an optional NP constituent on the right of S in the PS expansion rule (100), apparently predicting that sentences with both a left- and a right-dislocated constituent should be acceptable in English:

(102) Cats$_1$, he$_2$ can't stand them$_1$, Bill$_2$.

Although such sentences as 102 do not seem totally impossible, they do not seem particularly felicitous either, suggesting that we are dealing here with something other than a rule of grammar.

A second difficulty with such structures as that in diagram 101 is that there seems to be no compelling evidence in support of the constituent structures that they assign to dislocated sentences. In simple sentences there is abundant syntactic motivation for hierarchical structures of various kinds, in order to account for the grammatical relations among constituents. In dislocated sentences, however, the only relevant consideration seems to be whether the dislocated constituent is to the left or to the right of the sentence with which it is associated. The grammatical function of the dislocated constituent is accounted for completely by the coreference relation between it and the relevant pronoun in the main clause. This fact immediately leads one to wonder why dislocated constituents should be part of the sentences with which they are associated at all. Coreference relationships extend, in any case, over whole stretches of discourse, so that in principle nothing prevents us from simply treating a dislocated constituent as an element in a chain of discourse. Furthermore, there is some phonological support for this view, since dislocated constituents have the falling intonation contour that is typically assigned to whole sentences. Note in particular the difference in intonation between a dislocated sentence and a sentence with a topicalized constituent. We might represent the two contours roughly as follows:

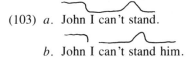

(103) *a.* John I can't stand.

　　 b. John I can't stand him.

In short, it appears to me that there is simply no compelling reason to assume that a dislocated constituent is part of the sentence that contains its antecedent. Accordingly, I suggest that the structure assigned to dislocated sentences should indicate the linear order of the dislocated constituent and the sentence it is associated with but not the dominance of one constituent over the other. If this assumption is correct, we may represent a left-dislocated sentence as in diagram 104 and a right-dislocated constituent as in diagram 105. Unless evidence

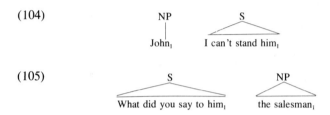

(104)

NP — John$_i$

S — I can't stand him$_i$

(105)

S — What did you say to him$_i$

NP — the salesman$_i$

to the contrary is forthcoming, it appears to me that representations of this sort are sufficient to account for the structure of dislocated sentences.

Other topicalized sentences in English, however, suggest that a second level of topicalization within the boundaries of a single sentence must be provided by the PS rules. In particular, it appears that adverbs of time and place, as well as various other adverbials that are not subcategorized by the verb, can appear in questions if an intonation break of some kind occurs between the adverbial and the preposed *wh* word. Consider, for example, the following sentences:

(106) *a.* At 3:00, who do you think appeared at the door?
    b. By 10:00 P.M., how many people were left in the park?
    c. Yesterday, what were you talking about with Mary?
    d. In your country, how many drug addicts are there?
    e. Over the by rock wall, did you see that chipmunk?
    f. In England, how many people really live?

In some cases, it is even possible to find minimal pairs. Thus the locative phrase *in England* in sentence 106*f* can occur in topic posi-

274

tion, because it is not closely linked with the verb *live,* in this sense. It cannot, however, be topicalized in such a sentence as *how many people live in England?.*:

(107) In England how many people live?

presumably because the locative phrase is in this case subcategorized by the verb.[15] In any case, it is important to observe that the normal intonation contour for such sentences as those in example 106 (not, that is, in rapid speech) requires an intonation break between the topicalized adverbial and the rest of the sentence, and thus suggests a major constituent break between the two.

Similar observations hold for sentences containing other topicalized constituents. Consider the following sentences:

(108) *a.* By the side of the road, sitting on a fence were three crows.
     b. By 10:00, down the hill rolled John.
     c. In our garden, near the big oak tree is standing a fountain.
     d. In all my years, never have I seen such confusion.
     e. After the party, so drunk was Harry that he could barely stand up.

Once again, it appears that there must be an intonation break between the topicalized place or time adverbial and the rest of the sentence. An even clearer example of this sort is provided by the *of* or *out of phrase* that is associated with superlative APs, which is regularly placed at the front of the sentence, set off by an intonation break (see Ross 1964 and Bowers 1968 for discussion of superlatives):

(109) *a.* Out of the whole senior class, which girl did John like best?
     b. Of the three sprinters, John was definitely the fastest.
     c. Of all his paintings, he is proudest of that one.

---

15. Doubtless this observation is related to the fact, noted in Chomsky 1965, that *England* can be pseudo-passivized when the locative phrase is subcategorized by the verb, though not when it functions as a place adverbial.

All of these observations suggest that the PS rules for English must provide another position for topicalized constituents to the left of the one proposed earlier, and that this topic position should in all likelihood be followed by a major constituent break. Accordingly, I propose to introduce such a position under a higher node, S', by means of the following rule:

(110) S'→ (PP)   S

(111)

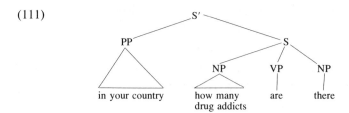

We can then assign such a sentence as example 106*d* a structure of the sort shown in diagram 111. Note that if Emonds (1976) is correct in treating such adverbial clauses as the following:

(112) *a.* Before he went to the party, John put on a tie.
      b. After he came back, he took it off.
      c. While he was brushing his teeth, he heard a noise.
      d. When he looked, he could see nothing.
      e. Because there was nobody in the house, he went to bed.

as PPs that require sentential complements, then the PP node in rule 110 also provides a natural place for preposed adverbial clauses, which also require an intonation break before the main clause.

If the analysis of dislocated sentences proposed earlier is correct, we should expect to find dislocated constituents co-occurring with topicalized constituents of every type. In fact, this prediction appears to be correct. Thus consider sentences of the following sort, which, for me at least, approach the limit of complexity that is permitted in topicalized sentences in English:

276

(113) *a.* That guy we were talking to, in his country, how many drug addicts did he say there were?
 b. Your friend, out of the whole senior class, which girl does he like the best?
 c. John, before he went to the party, he put on a tie.
 d. In our garden, near the big oak tree it is standing, our Rodin.
 e. My artist friend, of all his paintings, he is proudest of that one.

With this observation, I must conclude this discussion of topicalization processes in English. It is obvious that the whole matter is considerably more complicated than has generally been supposed. Further speculation at this point would be premature, however, especially in view of the fact that topicalization processes are intertwined with discourse phenomena that are barely beginning to be understood. It seems safe to conclude that there is at least a subset of topicalized sentences in English that are fairly tightly linked with the main clause. Within this restricted domain, there are strong constraints on the number of preposed constituents that may occur within a single clause, and these constraints can be explained in a systematic way in the framework proposed here. In addition, as least one other "level" of topicalization appears to be available for constituents that are not subcategorized by the main verb. Beyond that, as I have tried to indicate in the brief discussion of dislocated constituents, topicalization processes begin to merge with discourse phenomena in ways that are not yet very well understood.

Bibliography

Aissen, Judith 1974. Verb raising. *Linguistic Inquiry* 5.3:325–366.

Anderson, Steven R., and Kiparsky, Paul, eds. 1973. *A Festschrift for Morris Halle*. New York: Holt, Rinehart & Winston.

Babby, Leonard H. 1975. A transformational analysis of transitive -SJA verbs in Russian. *Lingua* 35:297–332.

_____ and Brecht, Richard D. 1975. The syntax of voice in Russian. *Language* 51:342–367.

Bach, Emmon, and Harms, Robert. 1968. *Universals in Linguistic Theory*. New York: Holt, Rinehart & Winston.

Binnick, R. A.; Davison, A.; Green, G.; and Morgan, J., eds. 1969. *Papers from the Fifth Regional Meeting of the Chicago Linguistic Society*. Linguistics Department, University of Chicago.

Bowers, John S. 1968. Surface structure interpretation in English superlatives. Unpublished paper.

_____. 1973. Grammatical relations. Doctoral dissertation, M.I.T.

_____. 1975a. Some adjectival nominalizations in English. *Lingua* 37:341–361.

_____. 1975b. Adjectives and adverbs in English. *Foundations of Language* 13:529–562.

_____. 1976. On surface structure grammatical relations and the structure-preserving hypothesis. *Linguistic Analysis* 2.3:225–242.

_____. 1979a. On negative transportation. In Waugh and van Coetsem 1979.

_____. 1979b. On restrictive and non-restrictive relative clauses. Unpublished paper, Cornell University.

_____ and Reichenbach, Uwe K. H. 1979. Montague grammar and transformational grammar: A review of *Formal Philosophy: Selected Papers of Richard Montague*. *Linguistic Analysis* 5.2:195–246.

Bresnan, Joan 1970. On complementizers: Toward a syntactic theory of complement types. *Foundations of Language* 6:297–321.

Chomsky, Noam. 1955. The logical structure of linguistic theory. Microfilm, M.I.T. library.

Bibliography

————. 1957. *Syntactic Structures.* The Hague: Mouton.

————. 1961. On the notion of "Rule of Grammar." In *Structure of Language and Its Mathematical Aspects.* Proceedings of the Twelfth Symposium in Applied Mathematics, 12:6–24. Also in Fodor and Katz 1964.

————. 1965. *Aspects of the Theory of Syntax.* Cambridge, Mass.: M.I.T. Press.

————. 1970. Remarks on nominalization. In Jacobs and Rosenbaum 1970; also in Chomsky 1972b.

————. 1971. Deep structure, surface structure, and semantic interpretation. In Steinberg and Jakobovits 1971; also in Chomsky 1972b.

————. 1972a. Some empirical issues in the theory of transformational grammar. In Chomsky 1972b; also in Peters 1972.

————. 1972b. *Studies on Semantics in Generative Grammar.* The Hague: Mouton.

————. 1973. Conditions on transformations. In Anderson and Kiparsky 1973.

Cohen, Philip. 1969. Incredulity questions. Unpublished paper, Cornell University.

Dougherty, Roy. C. 1970. Review of Bach and Harms 1968. *Foundations of Language* 1970:505–561.

Emonds, Joseph E. 1970. Root and structure-preserving transformations. Doctoral dissertation, M.I.T. Distributed in mimeo by Indiana University Linguistics Club.

————. 1972a. Evidence that indirect object movement is a structure-preserving rule. *Foundations of Language* 8:546–561.

————. 1972b. A reformulation of certain syntactic transformations. In Peters 1972.

————. 1976. *A Transformational Approach to English Syntax: Root, Structure-Preserving, and Local Transformations.* New York: Academic Press.

Epée, Roger. 1975. The case for a focus position in Duala. *Proceedings of the Sixth Conference on African Linguistics.*

————. 1976. Generative syntactic studies in Duala. Doctoral dissertation, Cornell University.

Fillmore, Charles J. 1968. The case for case. In Bach and Harms 1968.

———— and Langendoen, D. Terence, eds. 1971. *Studies in Linguistic Semantics.* New York: Holt, Rinehart & Winston.

Fodor, Jerry A. 1970. Three reasons for not deriving *kill* from *cause to die. Linguistic Inquiry* 1.4:429–438.

———— and Katz, Jerrold J. 1964. *The Structure of Language: Readings in the Philosophy of Language.* Englewood Cliffs, N. J.: Prentice-Hall.

Hall, Barbara. 1965. Subject and object in modern English. Doctoral dissertation, M.I.T.

Halle, Morris. 1959. *The Sound Pattern of Russian*. The Hague: Mouton.

Hasegawa, Kinsuke. 1968. The passive construction in English. *Language* 44:230–243.

Herschensohn, Julia. 1979. French causatives: Traces, filters, conditioning and the cycle. Unpublished paper, Cornell University.

Jackendoff, Ray S. 1972. *Semantic Interpretation in Generative Grammar*. Cambridge, Mass.: M.I.T. Press.

––––––. 1975. Morphological and semantic regularities in the lexicon. *Language* 51:639–671.

Jacobs, Roderick A., and Rosenbaum, Peter S., eds. 1970. *Readings in English Transformational Grammar*. New York: John Wiley.

Jankowsky, Kurt R., ed. 1973. *Georgetown University Round Table on Languages and Linguistics: Language and International Studies*. Washington, D.C.: Georgetown University Press.

Katz, Jerrold J. 1971. Generative semantics is interpretive semantics. *Linguistic Inquiry* 2:313–331.

––––––. 1973. Compositionality, idiomaticity, and lexical substitution. In Anderson and Kiparsky 1973.

–––––– and Postal, Paul M. 1964. *An Integrated Theory of Linguistic Descriptions*. Cambridge, Mass.: M.I.T. Press.

Kayne, Richard S. 1975. *French Syntax: The Transformational Cycle*. Cambridge, Mass.: M.I.T. Press.

Keenan, Edward L., and Comrie, Bernard. 1972. Noun phrase accessibility and universal grammar. Paper delivered at the winter meeting of the LSA, Atlanta.

Kiparsky, Paul, and Kiparsky, Carol. 1970. Fact. In *Progress in Linguistics,* ed. M. Bierwisch and K. E. Heidolph. The Hague: Mouton.

Lakoff, George 1965. On the nature of syntactic irregularity. Doctoral dissertation, Indiana University. Reprinted as *Irregularity in Syntax*. New York: Holt, Rinehart & Winston, 1970.

–––––– and Ross, J. R. 1966. A criterion for verb phrase constituency. NSF Report no. 17. Harvard Computation Laboratory, Harvard University.

Langendoen, D. Terence. 1973. The problem of grammatical relations in surface structure. In Jankowsky 1973.

Lasnik, Howard, and Fiengo, Robert. 1974. Complement object deletion. *Linguistic Inquiry* 5:535–571.

Lees, Robert B. 1960. *The Grammar of English Nominalizations*. Bloomington: Indiana University Press.

Bibliography

Lyons, John. 1968. *Introduction to Theoretical Linguistics*. Cambridge, England: Cambridge University Press.

McCawley, James D. 1970. English as a VSO language. *Language* 46:286–299.

———. 1973. External NPs versus annotated deep structures. *Linguistic Inquiry* 4:221–240.

———. 1975. Review of Chomsky 1972b. *Studies in English Linguistics* 3:209–311.

Partee, Barbara H. 1971. On the requirement that transformations preserve meaning. In Fillmore and Langendoen 1971.

Peters, Stanley. 1971. On restricting deletion transformations. NSF Report no. GS-2468. Austin, Tex.

———. 1972. *Goals of Linguistic Theory*. Englewood Cliffs, N.J.: Prentice-Hall.

——— and Ritchie, R. W. 1971. On restricting the base component of transformational grammars. *Information and Control* 18:483–501.

———. 1973. On the generative power of transformational grammars. *Information Sciences* 6:49–83.

Postal, Paul M. 1969. Review of A. McIntosh and M. A. K. Halliday, *Papers in General: Descriptive and Applied Linguistics*. *Foundations of Language* 5:409–439.

———. 1970. On coreferential complement subject deletion. *Linguistic Inquiry* 1.4:439–500.

——— 1974. *On Raising*. Cambridge, Mass.: M.I.T. Press.

Putnam, Hilary. 1961. Some issues in the theory of grammar. In *Structure of Language and Its Mathematical Aspects*. Proceedings of the Twelfth Symposium on Applied Mathematics, 12:25–42.

Reichenbach, Uwe K. H. 1976. On the compatibility of Montague grammar and transformational grammar. Unpublished paper, Cornell University.

Rosenbaum, Peter S. 1967. *The Grammar of English Predicate Complement Constructions*. Cambridge, Mass.: M.I.T. Press.

Ross, John R. 1964. A partial grammar of English superlatives. M.A. thesis, University of Pennsylvania.

———. 1967. Constraints on variables in syntax. Doctoral dissertation, M.I.T.

———. 1969a. Auxiliaries as main verbs. *Journal of Philosophical Linguistics* 1.1:77–102.

———. 1969b. Guess who? In Binnick et al. 1969.

———. 1972. Act. In *Semantics of Natural Languages,* ed. D. Davidson and G. Harman. Dordrecht: Reidel.

282

Ruwet, Nicholas. 1972. *Théorie syntaxique et syntaxe du français*. Paris: Seuil.

Sag, Ivan A. 1977. Deletion and logical form. Doctoral dissertation, M.I.T. Reproduced by Indiana University Linguistics Club.

Steinberg, Danny D., and Jakobovits, L. A. 1971. *Semantics: An Interdisciplinary Reader*. Cambridge, Eng.: Cambridge University.

Wall, Robert. 1972. *Introduction to Mathematical Linguistics*. Englewood Cliffs, N.J.: Prentice-Hall.

Waugh, Linda R., and van Coetsem, Franz. 1979. *Contributions to Grammatical Studies*. Leiden: E. J. Brill.

Index